# HILDEGARD OF BINGEN

GARLAND MEDIEVAL CASEBOOKS
VOLUME 20
GARLAND REFERENCE LIBRARY OF THE HUMANITIES
VOLUME 2037

# GARLAND MEDIEVAL CASEBOOKS

## JOYCE E. SALISBURY AND CHRISTOPHER KLEINHENZ, *Series Editors*

# Hildegard of Bingen
## A Book of Essays

Edited by
Maud Burnett McInerney

Garland Publishing, Inc.
A member of the Taylor & Francis Group
New York and London
1998

**Library of Congress Cataloging-in-Publication Data**

Hildegard of Bingen : a book of essays / [edited] by Maud Burnett McInerney.
      p.    cm. — (Garland reference library of the humanities ; v. 2037.
Garland medieval casebooks ; v. 20)
    Includes bibliographical references.
    ISBN 0-8153-2588-6 (hardcover : alk. paper)
    1. Hildegard, Saint, 1098–1179.   I. McInerney, Maud Burnett.
II. Series: Garland reference library of the humanities ; vol. 2037.
III. Series: Garland reference library of the humanities. Garland medieval
casebooks ; vol. 20.
    BV4700.H5H55   1998
    282'.092—dc21                        98-10288
                                                      CIP

Cover illustration: Ecclesia, from Hildegard of Bingen's *Scivias* II, 4.
Used with permission of Brepols Publishing, Turnhout, Belgium.

Printed on acid-free, 250-year-life paper
Manufactured in the United States of America

For
Annie Gerbenne
who will never believe how much she helped

# Contents

# Acknowledgments

I am particularly grateful to all the contributors to this volume, both those who have been involved from the very beginning and have demonstrated such marvelous patience as the book has slowly come together and those who leapt into the breach at the last moment. Many others have contributed as well in all sorts of ways. Joyce Salisbury read drafts, made invaluable comments, and soothed attacks of editorial anxiety; the people at Garland Publishing were both patient and efficient. There would be no illustrations without Margaret Schaus of Magill Library, no musical transcriptions without Robert F. Judd. The Academic Computing Center at Haverford College answered technical questions from the idiotic to the arcane, my colleagues kept my spirits up, and Carol Henry helped me to understand my new software. My thanks are also due to a great many of the students at Haverford, especially John Tracy and John Armour, as well as those members of my English 301 class whose enthusiasm for Hildegard confirmed my conviction that this is a necessary book. Finally, my husband, Jeremy McInerney, and my children have encouraged and supported me in ways without number.

Editor and publisher also gratefully acknowledge permission given by Brepols Publishing, Turnhout, Belgium to reproduce the images from the *Scivias* which appear in this volume, as well as the Staatsbibliothek of Munich and the Basel Kunstmuseum for other illustrations.

# List of Abbreviations

CSE     Corpus scriptorum ecclesiasticorum (Vienna 1866-1957).

CCCM  Corpus christianorum: continuatio medievalis (Turnhout, Belgium,1966-  ).

PG       *Patrologiae cursus completus: series graeca*, ed. J.P. Migne (Paris 1857-66)

PL       *Patrilogiae cursus completus: series latina*, ed. J.P. Migne (Paris 1841-64)

# Preface

*Sabina Flanagan*

The publication of this important collection of essays in 1998, the nine-hundredth anniversary of Hildegard's birth, is significant in several respects. That it is one of a number of books commemorating the birth of Hildegard rather than her death is noteworthy. Previously, as befitted Hildegard's status as a saint, the 800th, 850th, and 900th anniversaries of her death in 1879, 1929, and 1979, respectively, saw a flurry of celebratory publications, mostly in German. By contrast, the anniversaries of her birth in 1898 and 1948 seem to have passed almost without recognition. The fact that many new volumes will greet the anniversary of her birth this year, and that perhaps as many of these will be written in English as in German, is some measure of the extent to which Hildegard has now been incorporated into mainstream historical and academic studies.

Also remarkable is the fact that this significant shift, representing both a secularization and an internationalization of Hildegard studies, has been achieved in less than two decades. Why should the work of this Benedictine nun attract such intense attention nine centuries after her birth and at the turn of the new millennium? Part of the answer lies, no doubt, in the broad sweep of her interests, from music, theology, ethics and cosmology to zoology and medicine. Nor were those interests merely theoretical. The subjects over which she let her visionary imagination and understanding play also informed her own activities in the world and her practical engagement with it.

The ten essays collected here are a testimony to Hildegard's unusual accomplishments and wide-ranging preoccupations, usefully sketched in the Editor's Introduction. They deal, for example, with her interactions with contemporaries, as presented in her voluminous correspondence, her investigations into the natural world, particularly her manner of classification of animals, and the problematic relationship of her medical practice to cooking. Three essays are concerned to explore some of Hildegard's theological ideas (though the distinction between "theological" and "scientific" or even "practical" is a difficult one to draw here, since the entirety of Hildgard's life work was informed by her theological understanding). However, the relation of soul to body, the representation of Eve and Mary, and the concept of virginity as applied to male saints, would be generally recognized as "theological." One piece considers the mutually reinforcing relationship of text and music in one of Hildegard's responsories, while others relate aspects of Hildegard's thought to subsequent developments. Her influence on the Dominicans is traced through Tauler, who not only refers to her writings, but to illustrations from the *Scivias*, while Hildegard's understanding of the role of the allegorical figure of Synagoga in salvation history is used as a background for a reading of one of the *Canterbury Tales*. Finally, vaulting over several centuries, suggestive comparisons in terms of feminist theology are found by relating Hildegard to the nineteenth-century writer, Christina Rossetti.

Overall, the collection represents what could be termed the second wave or second generation of Hildegard scholarship in English. Such work takes as its foundation and starting point the general outlines of her life and thought established by such scholars as Peter Dronke and Barbara Newman. This second generation of Hildegard scholars includes some who are at the start of their academic careers and others already established in the fields of classics, religion, modern languages, medieval studies or music. All, however, share the possibility of considering certain aspects of Hildegard's work in more detail, or of interpreting it from different theoretical standpoints, or again, of going forward in time and space, using Hildegard's thought to illuminate that of later writers.

It is particularly gratifying to me, as someone who might be considered to belong to the first wave of Hildegard scholars, to have the opportunity of introducing such a varied, lively and stimulating collection of essays. Perhaps my reaction is best summed up by Godfrey's description of Jutta, Hildegard's mentor at Disibodenberg, *que iam ex discipula magistram ac preuiam semitarum excellentium eam fieri cum admiratione cernebat* (who recognized with admiration that the pupil had gone beyond the teacher and was forging ahead in ways of excellence).

Sabina Flanagan
University of Melbourne

# Introduction
## Hildegard of Bingen, Prophet and Polymath
*Maud Burnett McInerney*

In about 1163, in the great city of Cologne, an old woman wearing the simple, dark habit of a Benedictine addressed what was probably a huge crowd in the Cathedral.[1] She was over sixty years old and in chronic ill-health, but in spite of this she had come almost a hundred miles down the Rhine from her convent on the Rupertsberg mountain in order to preach against the Cathar heresy. Her name was Hildegard of Bingen, and old and ill though she was, she denounced the clergymen of Cologne with apocalyptic fervor for abandoning their flock to the heretics:

> The luminaries are missing from the firmament of God's justice in your utterances, as when the stars do not shine, for you are the night exhaling darkness, and you are like people who do not work, nor even walk in the light because of your indolence. But just as a snake hides in a cave after it has shed its skin, you walk in filth like disgusting beasts. . . . The power of God will crush and destroy your necks which have become stiff with iniquity, for they have been puffed up as with the breath of the wind, since you neither know God nor fear men. (Letter 15r)[2]

Her audience, composed largely of the very clergymen she called snakes, beasts and windbags, appears to have responded not with anger or outrage but with deep and heartfelt gratitude and admiration, judging from the reaction of Philip of Heinsberg, Dean of the Cathedral. Philip wrote to Hildegard on behalf of his chapter sometime after she delivered this sermon, asking for a copy, "since, given over as we are to carnal lusts, we all too readily ignore spiritual matters, neither seeing nor hearing them"(Letter 15). During the last ten years of her life, Hildegard undertook four preaching trips, travelling throughout southern Germany, covering hundreds of miles. According to her *vita*, she did so in order to instruct both the clergy and lay people "on matters pertaining to the preservation of their souls, along with those matters that God revealed to her" (*Vita* III.44).[3] She attacked the Cathars but also the indolence and weakness of the clergy, the venality of secular leaders and what she saw as the moral laxity of the whole era.

For us, reading any of Hildegard's sermons in the late twentieth century, it is the reaction of men like Philip which astonishes, along with the extraordinary rhetorical flourishes of the speeches themselves. In the twelfth century, however, that a woman should speak out in public at all was so remarkable that nothing she actually said can have seemed more astonishing than the simple fact of her speaking. Preaching by women was not just uncommon, it was forbidden on the authority of St. Paul (I Corinthians 14,34: "Women should keep silent in the churches, for they are not allowed to speak . . ."). Philip, in fact, acknowledges just how unusual Hildegard's appearance at Cologne was in his letter. "We were greatly astonished," he writes in the letter cited above, "that God works through such a fragile vessel, such a fragile sex, to display the great marvels of his secrets." This contrast, between her fragile, feminine self and the divine voice which spoke through it, was one which Hildegard amplified, developed and indeed exploited throughout her life. It became the foundation of an authority which was not subject to the laws of church or state, and which freed Hildegard to devote her extraordinary, erratic and eclectic intellect to an improbable range of subjects. Abbess, virgin, prophet, poet, theologian, scientist, musician, natural historian, exorcist, excommunicate and saint—no other single figure of the Middle Ages embodies quite so many contradictions. This collection of essays may serve to illuminate—but never to resolve—at least a few of these.

Hildegard's biography has been treated extensively elsewhere, notably in *Sister of Wisdom: St. Hildegard's Theology of the Feminine* by Barbara Newman and in *Hildegard of Bingen: A Visionary Life* by Sabina Flanagan. Nevertheless, it may be worth rehearsing a few of the most salient points here before moving on to consider the question of

Hildegard's access to formal education, and the related issue of the reception of her works in modern times.

Hildegard was born in 1098, the youngest child of an aristocratic family. According to the *vita*, she showed signs of extraordinary piety and visionary ability almost as soon as she could speak (I.2). At the age of eight, she was sent to live with a holy woman named Jutta at the monastery of St. Disibod. Other women joined them, and in time formed a community under the direction of the abbot of St. Disibod, with Jutta as abbess. When Jutta died, Hildegard took her place and apparently administered the small convent without much event until she was forty-two years old, when she was commanded by a divine voice to write down an account of the visions she had been seeing ever since her youth (I. 4). Hildegard obeyed the divine command and began, with the approval of her Abbot, to compose what would eventually become the *Scivias*, although not without misgivings. In 1147, she wrote to St. Bernard of Clairvaux, describing her visionary experience and asking for advice: should she speak out or be silent? Bernard's reply was encouraging: ". . . we most earnestly urge and beseech you to recognize this gift as grace and to respond eagerly to it with all humility and devotion. . . . But, on the other hand, when the learning and the anointing (which reveals all things to you) are within, what advice could we possibly give?" (Letter 1r). During the synod of Trier, held in the winter of 1147-48, when some supporters of Hildegard addressed Pope Eugenius III on her behalf, Bernard also spoke in her favor. As a result, Hildegard was granted apostolic license for her writings and also became an instant celebrity, entering into correspondence with a great many religious and secular figures across Europe.

Papal approval was evidently a great relief to Hildegard. The *Scivias* took her ten years to write, during which time she was also composing the songs of the *Symphonia*.[4] After the completion of her first book, however, her rate of literary output increased dramatically. Newman provides the following chronology for Hildegard's works: between 1151 and 1158, she wrote the *Physica*, an encyclopedia of what we would now call natural history, and the *Causae et Curae*, a medical text. Beginning in 1158, she expanded the visionary scope of the *Scivias* in the *Liber vitae meritorum* and the *De Operatione Dei*, which was completed in 1173 (*Sister* 10-11).

Receiving the approval of the Pope liberated more than Hildegard's literary genius; it also liberated her from the direct control of Kuno, abbot of St. Disibod. Hildegard decided to found a community of her own not far from St. Disibod on the site of an abandoned abbey which had, acccording to tradition, been founded over a century earlier by a holy and aristocratic young man known as Rupert or Robert. Godfrey's *vita* connects her decision to leave Disibodenberg both to her newfound celebrity—she was overwhelmed by the number of noble young women who wished to embrace the religious life—and to her prophetic gifts—the Holy Spirit revealed an appropriate site—thus establishing an overlap between the pragmatic and the prophetic which characterizes much of Hildegard's life. Abbot Kuno was less than enthusiastic about this project, and as a result Hildegard found herself embroiled in a struggle against authority which was to prove equally typical and which was finally only resolved by divine intervention in the form of an illness which threatened the seer's life. When Kuno granted her his permission to leave, Hildegard recovered instantly (*Vita* I.6). Her relationship with her former spiritual father was less resilient; several years later, in response to a conciliatory letter from Kuno, Hildegard accused him of "unabashed lasciviousness" (Letter 74r), although she did grant his request for an account of any visions she had had concerning St. Disibod.

Despite difficult beginnings, the foundation on the Rupertsberg was eventually a great success. Hildegard's life, however, never remained uneventful for long. Her favorite nun, Richardis von Stade, left her to become abbess in her own right, a defection which Hildegard seems to have taken very personally and which is documented in her correspondence.[5] In 1173, her amanuensis Volmar, who had been with her since the early days at Disibodenberg, died. He was replaced first by Godfrey, who began the composition of the *vita* but died in 1176, and then by Guibert of Gembloux, a passionate admirer of the abbess, who was nonetheless all too eager, in Hildegard's opinion, to interfere with the expression of the divine voice that spoke through her by "improving" her style (Newman, *Sister* 23). Finally, Hildegard became embroiled in a controversy concerning the burial of a young nobleman in the cemetery on the Rupertsberg. The young man in question had at one point been excommunicated, but Hildegard insisted (perfectly correctly) that he had been reconciled with the church before death and therefore was entitled to Christian burial. Her community was nonetheless placed under interdict by the prelates of Mainz; the ban was finally lifted in March of 1179 by the archbishop Christian of Mainz, who had been away in Rome during the dispute.[6] In the following September, at the age of eighty-one, Hildegard died. Revered as the sybil of the Rhine and the "feather on the breath of God" during her lifetime, she was never formally canonized.

The sheer volume of Hildegard's literary production is overwhelming; her letters alone occupy over two hundred pages of the edition of her works in the *Patrologia Latina*, a volume which runs to some 1,350 pages. This considerable output is all the more remarkable if we take into account that she did not begin to write until after age forty and that she claimed to have had little or no formal education. In one of the autobiographical passages in the *Vita*, Hildegard describes the way in which she was instructed directly by the Holy Spirit rather than a human teacher:

> In that vision I understood the writings of the prophets, evangelists and other holy ones, and some of the philosophers, without any human instruction, and I explained certain things according to these, although I had scarcely any understanding of texts, since I had been taught by an uneducated woman. (104)

This does not mean that Hildegard was illiterate by modern standards, nor is she slighting her teacher. Jutta, according to another passage in the *Vita* (1.1), had taught her young pupil the "songs of David"; the psaltery, as Flanagan points out, was the "universal primer of the Middle Ages" (32). Both women probably had at least enough Latin to get the sense of a text if not the subtleties, which is to say as much as many modern college students with a few semesters of Latin under their belts. This still left them uneducated in the medieval sense, since they had made no study of formal grammar, of rhetoric or dialectic, the trivium upon which the curriculum was based.

However weak she felt her Latin to be, the passage from the *Vita* makes it quite clear that Hildegard, in spite of her lack of formal education, was familiar with at least a part of the medieval canon of established authorities. Her statement concerning the types of authors she came to understand suggests a knowledge not only of Scripture (prophets and evangelists) but also of patristic writers (other holy ones) and even some classical authors.[7] Nonetheless, she was powerfully and perhaps painfully aware of the limitations and peculiarities of her own Latin. At the same time, she seems to have felt her erratic grammar and syntax to be "a mark that her inspiration must be divine because she herself scarcely knew how to write" (Newman, *Sister* 23).

Hildegard's contemporaries were not rendered unduly anxious by the idiosyncracies of her style, convinced as they were of the reality of her inspiration.[8] In 1148 or 49, Odo of Soissons described Hildegard as "bringing forth the melody of a new song" (*modos novi carminis*, Letter 40), a remark which suggests that he saw her compositions in the *Symphonia* as admirable in their originality. Hildegard was also much admired by certain French writers of the nineteenth century; Rémy de Gourmont, like his contemporary Huysmans, declared medieval Latin poetry and the mysticism it inspired the only palliative for the decadence of the *fin-de-siècle*. Although his appraisal will sound patronizing and even sexist to modern ears, de Gourmont was until the late twentieth century one of the very few scholars to admire Hildegard and her poetry whole heartedly, and I suspect that she herself would have appreciated the terms of his praise:

> Femme de supérieure essence, prophétesse, illuminée, visionnaire, poète, girovague, conseillère du peuple, des margraves et des empereurs, Hildegarde est un des esprits représentatifs du XIIe siècle allemand;—et comme elle reste bien de son sexe, franchement, comme son latin est bien féminin, comme, à travers les symboles, elle va droit vers l'homme, comme elle crie du fond de son coeur et de tous ses organes, la vierge contemplatrice: *"O quam magnum est in viribus suis latus viri!"* (125)

A woman of superior spirit, prophetess, illuminata, visionary, poet, wanderer, counselor to the common people, to counts and emperors, Hildegard represents the spirit of the twelfth century in Germany. And since she is in every respect a member of the female sex, just as her Latin is truly feminine, this contemplative virgin uses symbolism to direct her energies directly towards man, crying from the bottom of her heart and all her organs: "O how great in its forces is the flank of man!"

What de Gourmont does not note is that Hildegard goes on to identify the greatness of Man as Woman—the crown of creation in the poem he quotes, *O virga ac diadema*, is Eve, who is brought forth from the flank of Adam, and indeed several of the essays in this collection will argue that Hildegard's primary concern is with the female and the feminine, in her scientific works as well as her poems and visionary writings. Hildegard does, however, remain "bien de son sexe," in that she wrote in a decidedly feminine voice, according to her understanding of the term; her Latin was weak, and therefore, by her own definition, both feminine and powerful, a paradox de Gourmont seems to have understood. Twentieth-century scholarly attitudes to Hildegard's various works have been less than unanimous. The negative assessments of some modern hymnologists, in fact, seem to be reactions to precisely those qualities which de Gourmont labels as "feminine," mystical, and therefore admirable. In his *Concise History of Medieval Latin Hymnody*, Joseph Szövérffy disposes of Hildegard in a couple of lines, as "the voice of mysticism in twelfth-century hymnody. Her strange songs set to music are often thought to be first drafts" (86).[9] F.J.E. Raby is even more offhand in his treatment of "Hildegarde [sic], the famous mystic, whose sequences are in prose"(294). Both of these scholars appear to link their critical judgement of Hildegard with their distrust of her "mysticism."[10] Charles Singer, looking at Hildegard from the point of view of a historian of science, wrote that "we can perceive in Hildegard something of the nature of a complete and coherent philosophy, which separates her from the ages that went before her. Hildegard's works are heralds of the dawn of a new movement"(239). Like Raby and Szövérffy, however, Singer is uncomfortable with Hildegard's visions, which he attributes to "a functional nervous disorder"(231), perhaps "hystero-epilepsy"(238) or migraine. In fact, like many other women mystics, Hildegard has been the subject of as much medical diagnosis as critical interpretation, becoming one of Oliver Sacks' most famous case studies in *Migraine.*

Fortunately, the thrust of feminist medieval scholarship over the past decade or so, with its emphasis on depathologizing and recontextualizing the experience of medieval women, encourages us to read Hildegard's life and her works in increasingly complex and nuanced ways. The rehabilitation of Hildegard's reputation, in English at any rate, begins with the work of Peter Dronke in his 1970 book *Poetic Individuality in the Middle Ages* and has been carried on by the work of scholars such as Barbara Newman and Joan Cadden in the United States and Sabina Flanagan in Australia, to name only a few. This collection hopes to contribute to this current by providing a variety of perspectives on Hildegard, her work and her influence.

The first three essays in the collection concern themselves with Hildegard's relationship with the external world, both social and natural. Beverlee Rapp studies Hildegard's correspondence in order to demonstrate the accomplished and varied ways in which the abbess manipulates her own image. Rapp demonstrates that Hildegard's self-representation is affected by many variables, not least the gender of her correspondent. Kenneth J. Kitchell and Irven Resnick argue that Hildegard's *Physica* occupies an important and unrecognized position in the medieval bestiary tradition, while Marcia Chamberlain reads her medical treatise, the *Causae et Curae*, from a feminist perspective, revealing the ways Hildegard breaks down the traditional distinctions between doctors and cooks, between masculine and feminine modes of healing.

From the outside world of human affairs and scientific observation, we move to the interior and transcendent world of Hildegard's visionary and poetic works, although for Hildegard no such distinctions are ever absolute, a point which Jan Emerson's essay makes very strongly. Emerson invites us to see in the *Scivias* a disciplined, observational and systematic vision of the cosmos and reminds us that the oppositional distinction between the mystical and the scientific is modern, not medieval. Rebecca Garber's article focuses on the illuminations of the *Scivias*, made according to Hildegard's directions as illustrations of her visions. Garber notes that, while abstract forces are regularly personified as feminine figures in the *Scivias* and drawn accordingly, Eve and Mary, the only two actual women to appear, are consistently represented by the artist in non-human form. Garber argues that this allows the two women who, between them, encompass Christian history, to escape the limitations of corporeality.

Both essays on the *Symphonia* address the issue of virginity, which was of paramount importance to Hildegard. Kathryn Bumpass' reading of the "Spiritui Sancto" hymn, part of the cycle of songs to St. Ursula, demonstrates the way that Hildegard's meaning is conveyed through music as much as through words. My own essay considers the problem of male virginity. For Hildegard, virginity was an intensely corporeal phenomenon, rooted in the female body's physical capacity for intactness. Male bodies such as those of Rupert and John must therefore undergo an almost alchemical process of feminization in order to be called virgin.

The final part of the collection takes Hildegard beyond the twelfth century. Leonard Hindsley traces her influence upon the German Dominican mystics of the fourteenth century. Christine Rose and Frederick Roden both argue less for influence than for congruence. Rose uses Hildegard's image of Synagoga as a place from which to read the figures of the monstrous mothers-in-law in Chaucer's *Man of Law's Tale*, while Roden sees Hildegard and Christina Rossetti as two feminist theologians who share an "essentially feminine" impulse towards sapiential cosmology.

This book goes to press in the year that marks the nine hundredth anniversary of Hildegard's birth, after a quarter century which has seen an extraordinary movement towards the recovery of medieval women's history and medieval women's voices. It is time for Hildegard to be appreciated in the fullest context of medieval history. She is not simply a phenomenon, a sort of female Nostradamus of the Middle Ages, and it is the hope of all of us who have collaborated in this collection to help to re-establish her as a complex, original and important contributor to the intellectual currents of the twelfth century, as a part of the mainstream rather than the margin.

## NOTES

1. According to Flanagan, "the cases where Hildegard appeared 'before the clergy and people' suggest that she sometimes preached in the cathedral, while the other occasions would have been internal addresses, delivered most probably in the chapter house of the monastery, or possibly in the monastic church"(172).

2. References to the letters are to the translation by Baird and Ehrman.

3. Hildegard's *Vita* was begun by Godfrey of St. Disibod, her second secretary, and completed after his death by Theodoric of Echternach. It incorporates what Flanagan has called "autobiographical passages from an otherwise unknown work by Hildegard"(Flanagan 1-2; see also Newman, *Sister* 5). There is also a fragmentary life by Guibert de Gembloux, Hildegard's last secretary (Pitra 407-15; see also Dronke, *Women Writers* 144-65; Dronke prints the text of the autobiographical fragments, 231-41). All translations from the *Vita* are mine.

4. See Newman, *Symphonia* 6-12 on the dating and composition of the *Symphonia*.

5. See Epistle. 10, PL 197; the relationship between Richardis and Hildegard is discussed at some length by Newman (*Sister* 222-23), Dronke (*Women Writers* 154-59) and Flanagan (180-84).

6. Hildegard's correspondence on this subject with the prelates of Mainz and with the archbishop, Christian, have been preserved. See Letters 23, 24, and 24r.

7. Peter Dronke argues in "Problemata Hildegardiana" that Hildegard was actually familiar with at least some of the works of Lucan, Seneca and Cicero as well as various mystical and medical texts.

8. Hildegard has been acclaimed as a prophetess in the twentieth century as well as the twelfth. To the anonymous author of a French translation of the vita which appeared in 1907, she was not only a prophetess but also an apostle and martyr and an important weapon in the fight against Protestantism (*Vie de Ste. Hildegarde, thaumaturge et prophetesse du XIIème siècle*, Paris, 1907). More recently she has become an icon of New Age Catholicism, and an increasingly visible presence on the World Wide Web.

9. Szövérffy's assessment of Hildegard may be contrasted with his comments on her contemporary, Gottschalk of Aachen, whom he describes as the author of "strange and original sequences" (60), or Ohlo of St. Emmeram who may on Szövérffy's own testimony have composed fewer than 6 hymns but who rates several pages of coverage in the *Concise History* (62-65).

10. A notable exception, following in the tradition of de Gourmont, is Alain Michel; writing in 1976, he compares Hildegard to Baudelaire: ". . . cette virtuosité symboliste (qui s'exprime d'ailleurs dans l'oeuvre d'Hildegarde par des réfléxions sur l'ordre du cosmos ou sur le canon du corps humain) naît de l'extase méme: c'est une des plus puissantes apparitions de l'Esprit dans la poesie médiévale. Tous les commentateurs ne s'en sont pas aperçus parce que, souvent, ils avaient le goût trop classique; le romantisme, dont nous décélons ici une des sources les plus pures, leur faisait un peu defaut" (148).

## WORKS CITED

### Primary Texts

Godfrey and Theodoric. *Vita Sanctae Hildegardis*. PL 197: 91-150.

———. *Vie de Ste. Hildegarde, thaumaturge et prophetesse du XIème siècle*. Trans. anonymous. Paris: Chamonal, 1907.

Guibert de Gembloux. *Vita Sanctae Hildegardis*. Pitra 407-15.

Hildegard of Bingen. *The Letters of Hildegard of Bingen*. Ed. and trans. Joseph L. Baird and Radd K. Ehrman. Vol 1. New York: Oxford University Press, 1994.

———. *Symphonia: A Critical Edition of the Symphonia armonie celestium revelationum*. Trans. Barbara Newman. Ithaca: Cornell University Press, 1988.

## Secondary Texts

de Gourmont, Rémy. *Le latin mystique: les poètes de l'antiphonaire et la symbolique au moyen age.* Paris: Editions d'aujourd'hui, 1979.

Dronke, Peter. Poetic *Individuality in the Middle Ages: New Departures in Poetry 1000-1150.* Oxford: Oxford University Press, 1970.

————. "Problemata Hildegardiana." *Mitellateinisches Jahrbuch* 16 (1981): 97-113.

————. *Women Writers of the Middle Ages: A Critical Study of Texts from Perpetua (†203) to Marguerite Porete (†1310).* Cambridge: Cambridge University Press, 1984.

Flanagan, Sabina. *Hildegard of Bingen: A Visionary Life.* London: Routledge, 1989.

Michel, Alain. *In hymnis et canticis. Culture et beauté dans l'hymnique Chrétienne latine.* Louvain: Publications Universitaires, 1976.

Newman, Barbara. *Sister of Wisdom: St. Hildegard's Theology of the Feminine.* Berkeley: University of California Press, 1987.

Raby, F.J.E. *A History of Christian Latin Poetry From the Beginnings to the Close of the Middle Ages.* Oxford: Clarendon Press, 1927, rpt. 1953.

Sacks, Oliver. *Migraine.* Berkeley: University of California Press, 1992.

Singer, Charles. *From Magic to Science. Essays on the Scientific Twilight.* New York: Boni and Liveright, 1928.

Szövérffy, Joseph. *A Concise History of Medieval Latin Hymnody: Religious Lyrics Between Antiquity and Humanism.* Leyden: E.J. Brill, 1985.

# The Social World and
the Natural World

# A Woman Speaks
## Language and Self-Representation in Hildegard's Letters
*Beverlee Sian Rapp*

Language and rhetoric have always been as important in the history of ideas as have been the ideas themselves, for an inarticulately expressed idea, or one left untold, is doomed to be at most a historical curiosity, at worst without power or effect.[1] Hildegard of Bingen understood this. She was aware of her world and her times, not only in terms of their political and cultural aspects but also of how her use of language and self-representation could affect her ability to influence those events which concerned her. Keenly cognizant of her status as a "mere" woman in a man's world, she nevertheless used language to exploit her unique visionary gifts to procure for herself the power and influence she could not otherwise hope to have.[2] The manner in which Hildegard used language to further her own ends can be examined through her letters in terms of rhetoric and self-representation.

In these letters, almost 300 of which survive, Hildegard's interest in the political and cultural affairs of her times is apparent. Most of these letters are to, or are in response to, members of the religious community, monks, priests, bishops and popes. While dealing primarily with religious and theological matters, some of these letters display Hildegard's opinions about the political dealings within the church. Hildegard also corresponded with laity, mainly the aristocracy. These letters include correspondences with such important figures as Henry II of England (1133-1189; reigned from 1154), his wife Eleanor of Aquitaine (1122-1204; married Henry in 1152) and the Emperor Frederick Barbarossa (1123-1190; reigned from 1152), as well as other

princes and potentates. A substantial number of her letters are to
women, mostly but not exclusively nuns, and these letters provide an
interesting foil to the main corpus, for in these letters we can see
Hildegard dealing with these women on a basis of equality, and not as a
woman having to deal with her femininity in a very male world.

As a woman trying to assert herself in this man's world, Hildegard
needed to provide for herself the authority that women, by and large,
lacked.[3] In general, she resolved this problem in three ways. She called
upon her special status as a virgin, she manipulated language and image
to invert the roles of feminine and masculine, and through her visions
she assumed the voice of God. The first claim, that of virginity, was
natural for a woman who had been a nun since childhood. In Classical
Antiquity, and through the Middle Ages, it was believed that woman
represented the senses and the created world, with all its attendant evil,
whereas man represented reason and rationality. It was only by giving
up the created, the corporeal, which was her feminine sexuality, that a
woman could hope to attain the rationality of men. In the words of
Saint Jerome's *Commentary on Ephesians*,

> when a woman serves birth and children, she is as different from a
> man as the body is from the soul. But if she should wish to serve
> Christ more than the world, she ceases to be a woman and will be
> called man [*vir*]. (PL 26: 533)[4]

Christ's mother, Mary, was a virgin and had herself been born of
immaculate conception; thus Mary was able to attain her semi-divine
stature in the Christian theology of the twelfth century. This emphasis
on virginity was also important in practice. Hillinus, Archbishop of
Trier, declares to Hildegard that the wisdom of God has chosen "a
pleasant habitation for himself in your virginity" (26), and Bernard of
Clairvaux wrote that virginity was a sign of moral strength, and
especially so in a woman, to the extent that a virgin placed herself on a
"different existential plane from other human beings" (quoted in Shahar
27). For these, and other similar reasons, Hildegard's virginity gained
for her an acceptance of rationality and intellect not normally accorded
to women.

Virginity, however, was not enough to provide the degree of
authority Hildegard needed, so she had to create some for herself. She
did this by inverting language and meaning, that is, by calling her age
womanish and by assigning to women the strength needed to carry the

Church into the future.[5] In a letter to Hillinus dated around 1152, she writes "now the time is squalid and womanish . . . woman is a font of wisdom and a font of full joy, through which man achieves perfection" (26r). In a similar vein, she describes in a letter to Henry, Bishop of Beauvais, a vision in which she saw a woman as the personification of Pure Knowledge. "Her face was full bright," writes Hildegard, "her eyes as jacinth, and her clothing like a silk cloak. And on her shoulders she had a bishop's pallium like carnelian"(32r). Although it was common to personify virtues as women, it was highly unusual to describe them as bishops, for then, as now, women could hold no priestly office in the Catholic church. By inverting gender roles in this way, Hildegard presented women as viragos, strong, virile warriors in a world in which men had become lax and weak, thus paradoxically giving herself, as a woman, more authority.

Hildegard had one more claim to authority, for just as male authors declared themselves to be basing their works on previous, more worthy authors, so Hildegard too claimed a more worthy basis for her writings. But no deceased Father of the Church or ancient philosopher would do; rather, Hildegard claimed as her authority God Himself. The endorsement of her *Scivias* at the Synod of Trier, in 1147, before Pope Eugenius III and his assembled bishops, authenticated her visions; therefore, nobody could declare, when presented with a letter from the abbess quoting God in a vision, that she was going beyond her bounds in assuming His authority. For if God can communicate with a woman for the purpose of sending her religious visions, why should He not deign to express His political views through her as well? Further, the papal endorsement of the *Scivias* at the Synod also procured for Hildegard the authority of the Pope and all the attendant bishops. These men recognized the legitimacy of Hildegard's claims to divine inspiration, and subsequently a great many of her letters explicitly contain the words and admonitions of the Lord. This was the final means of gaining authority that Hildegard needed for her writings to be taken as seriously as if she were a man.

Once her authority was established, Hildegard was able to engage some of the most prominent minds of the twelfth century in correspondence, but although the extent of her fame is undoubted, some questions remain: how was her reputation so widely known? how did her fame spread? who initiated correspondence? The first two questions can be answered, in part, by the great impact of her *Scivias*. The large audience of bishops who heard this work read at Trier took their acquaintance with her work and consequently with her divine gift, back to their sees. Thus, knowledge of the existence of this unusual abbess quickly spread throughout much of Europe.

Consequently, Hildegard became known through Europe as a holy woman, and her aid was increasingly sought on various matters. As many letters to her demonstrate, she was called upon to provide prophecies as well as to perform other, more mystical, duties. One letter, from five abbots, written sometime before 1157, requested that Hildegard cure the bearer of the letter, a young woman, of her infertility, through her prayers and ministrations. They write:

> . . . this woman, the bearer of this letter, is a noble woman and the wife of a very loving husband. She comes to you with great devotion, humble and on foot, although she could have come on horseback and with a great entourage. The reason for her journey is thus: for a long time now she has remained sterile, although in her youth she bore children; but they have died, and unable to bear others, she and her husband have been afflicted with great sorrow. Therefore she has fled to you, handmaid and friend of Christ, having faith that you, through your worthiness and prayers, may ask God to let her conceive, and to present the blessed fruit of her womb to Christ, when the child is born. And so, because we were asked by her and her husband, we ask you, in this petition, to stand before God on her account, and be worthy to obtain what they desire. (70)

Another series of letters chronicles the attempts of the Abbot Gedolphus to exorcize a woman of a demon, with Hildegard's help. "But the clergy and the people too know how great are the miracles that the Fountain of Living Light makes apparent in you, and events prove the matter." He then proceeds to present her with the problem and requests her advice, "For that demon, when he was conjured up one day, told us that this possessed women could be freed through the virtue of your contemplation and the magnitude of divine revelation" (Migne 60). Hildegard responds by supplying a detailed description of the rites needed to free the woman, but the monk writes back that the exorcism was only partially successful, for the demon, although expelled, has returned and has informed them that Hildegard's personal presence is required for the exorcism to be a success. Therefore, says Gedolphus, "we send this same woman to Your Sanctity, so that the Lord may complete through you what we were unworthy to do because of our great sins, and when that ancient enemy is cast out, He who is powerful over all things will be glorified in you" (Migne 61) . From this, it is seen not only how Hildegard's fame had spread but also just how highly her divine gifts were regarded by members of the clergy and laity alike.

Another means by which Hildegard was able to make herself known to a large number of people was by engaging in preaching tours of her region of the Empire. While her reputation must already have been well established to undertake these tours, they nevertheless can only have helped to further spread the news of her talents. Starting at age 60, with papal sanction, she undertook four of these tours, all in her efforts to effect clerical and monastic reform. She preached mainly to monastic audiences, but it was not unknown for her to occasionally speak to mixed lay and clerical audiences in town churches and in public squares (Newman 9). She also, on occasion, undertook journeys to the courts of noblemen, for as Frederick Barbarossa writes,

> We make note to your sanctity, seeing that we now hold in our hands what you preached to us before, when, while staying in Ingelheim, we asked you to come to our presence. (Migne 27)

This clearly indicates that the abbess had indeed been at Frederick's court at Ingelheim sometime previously and that she delivered a speech or a sermon to him there, a copy of which he now possesses in the form of a letter. Such requests for copies of sermons delivered to monastic or lay audiences are found relatively frequently throughout the volumes of Hildegard's correspondence.

The third question, "who wrote to whom?" can be answered, in part at least, in the letters themselves. From passages found in various letters addressed to Hildegard, it seems that once her reputation and fame were known, people began writing to her to avail themselves of her unusual abilities. The Holy Roman Emperor Conrad III (1093-1152; reigned from 1138) expressed as much to the abbess in his letter to her when he wrote:

> For, as we have heard, the confession of the greatest praise abounds in you through the sanctity of your unstained life, and through the magnificence of the Spirit miraculously coming to you from above. Whence, although we may lead a secular life, we hasten towards you, we flee towards you, and we humbly seek the suffrage of your

prayers and exhortations, since we have lived for a long time in a manner other than we ought. (Migne XXVI)

Likewise, Count Philip of Flanders writes that "your holy existence and way of life have sounded in my ears very often, of all most agreeable reputations" (Migne XXVIII).

Many letters from clerics also express a desire to take advantage of Hildegard's famous talents. Philip, Archbishop of Cologne writes that

> ... many people know that you are gifted with a wealth of divine charisma, for which the faithful of the church rejoice ... thus gifted, therefore, like a woman who has discovered a beautiful pearl from among God's mysteries, may you ask what we seek, and transmit what admonitions God may give to you to us. ... (XVI)

Evidence that Hildegard's fame had reached far and wide is clear in this passage from a letter from Amalricus, Bishop of Jerusalem:

> From those many people who come to our parts from wide reaches of the world, and who kneel at the tomb of the Lord, we have heard many times that there is a divine virtue in you, that works through you, whence we offer our untiring thanks as humbly as we can.

His letter, too, ends with a plea that Hildegard send to him

> any consolation shown to you by heaven and we commend ourselves to your prayers, and to those of your sisters, because we are foundering in the turmoil of worldly cares; may you intercede to him whose chamber you hope to enter after this life's end. (XXXIV)

Such requests for consolation are far from unusual in the available corpus of letters. Further illustrating this is a letter from Hildegard to the Queen of England, Eleanor of Aquitaine,[6] imprisoned by her husband consequent to her involvement in a plot against the king. Although Eleanor's letter has been lost, Hildegard's reply makes it clear that she is indeed responding to a request for guidance:[7]

> Your mind is like unto a wall, which is in the vicissitude of a cloud, and you look all around you, but you do not have peace. Flee that, and remain in stability with God and men, and God will help you in

all your troubles. May God give his blessing and aid to you in all your affairs. (Pitra, Letter CXII).

Clearly, Hildegard's fame was sufficient to incite letters and comments concerning her abilities from important figures from all of Christendom. Nevertheless, Hildegard did, when she deemed it necessary, write unsolicited letters in reaction to events which she felt concerned her. In a letter to Pope Eugenius III from between 1148 and 1153, she warns him about the desires of the Emperor to seize ecclesiastical power and admonishes him to be on his guard so that the Emperor might not succeed:

> A gem lies on the road, but a bear coming along and seeing that it is very lovely, stretches out his paw and wishes to pick it up for himself. But, suddenly, an eagle comes and snatches the gem, covers it with its wings, and carries it to the chambers of the king. And this gem shines radiantly before the king's face when he sees it. And the king, on account of his love for the gem, gives the eagle golden sandals, and praises it highly for its rightousness. (III)

This letter is also striking in that it presents the situation in allegorical terms, for as Joseph Baird and Radd Ehrman suggest, the brutish and earthly bear is the Emperor, while the heaven-sent eagle is the pope; the jewel is ecclesiastical power, and the slippers are the approval of God (33n1). These images, although unfamiliar today, would have been as clearly understood to a twelfth-century pope as a maple leaf and stars and stripes are to a politician of the present. While such political allegory is something expected in visions, it is quite unusual in a personal letter.

In a similar vein, Hildegard also feels it necessary to admonish Conrad for the increasing tensions between the Empire and the Papacy which culminated in the hostilities under Frederick I (Conrad's nephew and successor as Emperor). While technically in response to a letter from Conrad, this reply does not answer the Emperor's requests for her prayers but rather sets before him a stern lecture about the impending evils of his times. She commands him to examine his position before God:

He who gives life to everybody says: Blessed are they who worthily
raise up the candlestick of the highest King, and whom God protects
in his great wisdom, so that he does not tear them from his heart.
Abide in him, o you king, and cast the squalour from your mind,
because God preserves all who seek him devotedly and purely. But
both hold your kingdom thus, and provide a single justice for your
people, so that you do not become alienated from the higher
kingdom. Hear in what manner you turn yourself from God; for the
times in which you live are inconstant, just as in a womanish person,[8]
and even incline themselves in a contrary justice, which intends to
destroy the justice in the vineyard of the Lord. But afterwards, worse
times will come, in which the true Israelites will be whipped, and in
which the Catholic throne will be moved in error; and therefore, their
newest things will be blasphemies, just as a cadaver in death. From
far and wide sorrow will burn in the vineyard of the Lord. (Migne
XXVIr)

While there is no doubt as to the sincerity of Hildegard's belief in
her gifts and in her perceived duty to inform the world of her visions,
there is, nevertheless, the possibility that the abbess was also engaged
in some form of self-promotion, of using her gifts—in very legitimate
ways—to increase her own personal power and further her influence.
The most striking case in point is her move from the abbey of St.
Disibod to Rupertsberg. This move, which was conducted against the
strenuous opposition of the monks of the abbey, as well as some of the
nuns, occurred in 1151, which happens to be the same year that the
*Scivias* was completed. It is known that Hildegard desired financial and
spiritual independence from the monks at St. Disibod, and in her
attempts to secure the consecration of the new abbey, she suffered what
Barbara Newman calls a "charismatic illness" (13) in order to convince
the abbot of St. Disibod that the move was indeed the will of God. Such
a tactic, be it genuine or contrived, could not have succeeded had
Hildegard not already been known to experience direct physical effects
with her visions, such as blinding headaches, along with geometric
shapes and many forms of light. These symptoms have led many
modern medical specialists to speculate that she may have suffered
from migraine headaches (Flanagan 200-06).[9]

These and other divinely inflicted illnesses can be seen as an
extension of Hildegard's bid for authority. While it is clear from her
writings that her illnesses were genuine, that is, not contrived to make

her point, they seem to have occurred only when all other avenues of appeal have been exhausted. This manipulation of body is similar to Hildegard's manipulation of words, as, for instance, when she alters her self-image in her letters to achieve her aims. In effect, when God's very words are not enough to convince Hildegard's adversaries to reverse their decisions, He makes His will manifest in Hildegard's body through these illnesses.

In order to have the influence she desired over people and events and to achieve her aims, Hildegard carefully sculpted her letters to carry the greatest possible influence by means of her use of language and self-representation. She was clearly aware of the effects of language and of the different responses that could be elicited by various forms of address and used these effects to her advantage. Instead of the lengthy passages of niceties which are expected in twelfth-century correspondence or the explicit sermonizing often found in such public letters, Hildegard begins her letters with uncompromising vehemence and allegory, often starting the body of her letters with dire admonitions from God. This must in itself have made a very unusual impression on the recipients of her letters, indicating that Hildegard was a law unto herself and a woman who expected to be taken seriously. From the very first words of her letters, therefore, it is clear that Hildegard was conscious of manipulating language to put herself at an advantage, even in her letters to other women, which are, in their other aspects, so comforting and tender. Never does Hildegard let people forget who she is.

This careful use of language is maintained throughout the letters. By changing and adjusting her tone and the severity or complacency of her words, Hildegard was able to manipulate the effect of her letters. As will be seen later, there is a definite difference in her tone when writing to men and to women, but this understanding and control over the power of the pen is never diminished. In her writings to men, Hildegard tended to use three approaches in her letters: a supplicatory, self-effacing tone; a humble, yet confident tone; and the tone of a woman afraid of nobody but God himself—confident, strident, and uninhibited. In contrast to this, her letters to other women are more akin to those of a patient mother guiding her children through a troubled time.

In the letters to men, the first approach, supplication, is characterized by a claim to humility and worthlessness. Such an approach is not unique to Hildegard but is, to all intents and purposes, the accepted, standard approach to letter-writing in the Middle Ages, the *topos* of false humility. This is not surprising in an age when authority is paramount, and people feel they cannot present material unless it has already been proven by earlier, more worthy, masters. Constantly under the shadow of the Great Ancients and Fathers, even such self-important luminaries as Bernard of Clairvaux proclaim themselves—as a matter of course—with expressions of their worthlessness. To this end, in his letter to Hildegard of 1146 or 47, Bernard writes:

> Brother Bernard, called Abbot of Clairvaux, offers to Hildegard, beloved daughter in Christ, whatever the prayer of a sinner is able. If you feel that our abilities are greater than our conscience maintains, it is perhaps due to your own humility. (1r)

Likewise, Eberhard calls himself "servant and Archbishop of the church of Salzburg, by the grace of God, although unworthy" (25), and Hermann writes that he is "Bishop of the church of Constance by the grace of God, although useless and worthless" (35). These are characteristic of the sorts of self-effacing remarks which are found in letters addressed to Hildegard; thus it comes as no surprise when she, too, uses such techniques in her letters.

A prime example of such an approach can be found in the short response to a request from Arnold, archbishop of Cologne, for a copy of her *Scivias*. The letter reads:

> Now, O shepherd of your people, I, a poor little woman, have sent my writings of truthful visions to you, as you asked. There is nothing of human origin or from my own will in its contents, but only what the Unfailing Light wished to show through his own words. Nor is what I write to you now of my own mind, or of any human thought, but it is composed of divine revelation. (14r)

The epithet "poor little woman," or a similar appellation, is found frequently in Hildegard's letters. In her first letter to Bernard of Clairvaux she calls herself "wretched, and indeed more than wretched in my womanly form," and claims that

> I have no formal training at all, for I can only read at a simple level, and not in an analytical manner . . . for I am untaught by any teacher

in external matters, but I am taught internally, in my soul. Hence my
uncertain speech. (1)

While this claim to no education is, perhaps, somewhat exaggerated, it
nevertheless implies that Hildegard is at her most humble.[10] Similarly
she introduces herself to Pope Eugenius with the words "I, formed as a
poor little woman" (2). In this case, as in the letter above, Hildegard is
semingly unsure of herself, seeking confirmation for her gifts and
beseeching the recipients of the letters to guide and support her. Her
tone is supplicatory, filled with the humility expected of a mere abbess
daring to approach the Pope or the great Abbot of Clairvaux. And, in
response to these humble, searching letters, Hildegard gets her wish
and her visions are given sanction. Hildegard uses a similar tactic
following the death, in 1173, of Volmar, her friend and secretary, who
had also served as the provost of the abbey on the Rupertsberg. Her
entreaties to the monks at her former community of St. Disibod failed
to secure a replacement for him, and Hildegard felt herself moved to
appeal to the Pope. Her words must have elicited the desired response
on the part of Alexander III because he granted her request, and
appointed a new provost to the abbey. She writes, "Now O most gentle
father, my sisters and I bend our knees in the presence of your paternal
piety, praying that you may deign to notice the poverty of this poor
little woman" (10). It is difficult to imagine so strong a woman as
Hildegard of Bingen using any more humble and supplicatory
language.

A further example of this means of self-presentation is found in
one of Hildegard's last letters. In 1179, Christian, Archbishop of
Mainz, had placed an interdict on the convent at Bingen after Hildegard
had refused to exhume the body of a young nobleman, once
excommunicated. Hildegard claimed, and rightly at that, that the young
man had been welcomed back to the Church before his death and was
therefore entitled to burial in the abbey's sacred ground. As a response
to the interdiction, Hildegard suffered one of her charismatic illnesses,
to which she alludes in her letter to the archbiship. The letter is filled
with humble, self-effacing language and attempts to impress upon
Christian the hardships and sorrows that Hildegard and her sisters had
been forced to endure for what she felt to be, with confirmation through
her visions, a just cause. The letter, which is long, contains several
examples of such language, but these can be summed up in Hildegard's
description of her visit to Mainz during Christian's absence in Italy:

> . . . although greatly ill,[11] I went to our superiors in Mainz, and I
> presented the words I had seen in the True Light, just as He ordered
> me. . . . Humbly, and with tears, I asked for mercy before them . . .
> but their eyes were so clouded that they could show me no sign of
> mercy, and I left them, full of tears. (24)

Here, too, Hildegard's humble and beseeching tone has the desired
effect, for shortly thereafter, she and her sisters received the lifting of
the interdict for which they had wished for so long.

Hildegard's second rhetorical approach in her letters is with a tone
conveying humility but confidence. This is perhaps the rarest means of
self-presentation, but when it does appear, it tends to suggest approval
or acceptance. This tone is used in Hildegard's letter to Hartwig,
Archbishop of Bremen, in response to his letter informing her of the
death of his sister Richardis, who had been one of Hildegard's favorite
nuns. Richardis had been one of the nuns who disapproved of the move
to the Rupertsberg and instead chose to become abbess of another
monastery, despite all attempts by Hildegard to prevent this. Hildegard
had appealed as far as the Pope to keep her beloved Richardis with her
and at times accused various Church officials of simony, saying that
Richardis used her family's considerable social prestige to secure the
position of abbess. All previous acrimony has been forgotten now;
Hildegard's tone has changed. There is no abject humility here nor any
raging but rather a quiet sense of acceptance. After a touching eulogy,
she concludes her letter by writing:

> Now you, dear Hartwig, sitting as Christ's representative, fulfill the
> wishes of your sister's soul, which need obliges you to do. And as
> she was always mindful of you, so now you must be of her, and do
> good works as she wished. Now I cast out of my heart that sorrow
> which you caused me over this, my daughter. May God give you,
> through the prayers of the saints, the dew of his grace and a blessed
> reward in the world to be. (13r)

This is similar to the tone used by Hildegard in her first letter to
Pope Eugenius (II), telling him of her visions and of her command from
God to set them to writing. Her tone is humble but confident, and while
she does not use harsh or unmoving language, neither does she shrink
from the task at hand. She claims that these visions are what "God
wished to teach me in a true vision" and continues that "now I send you

this letter in the true desire of God." She is aware that as a woman, she is at an immediate disadvantage, for "many people, wise in worldly matters, disparage these writings in the instability of their minds, because of my poor form, built from a rib, and untaught in matters philosophical" but then presents herself as the feather on the breath of God in a short allegorical passage couched in the words of "Him Who Is [*illum qui est*]." She concludes the letter by admonishing Eugenius that he should "take care not to spurn these mysteries of God, because they are a necessity which lies hidden and has not yet been uncovered." Hildegard is clearly displaying the confidence that will mark her most outrageous letters, but still with the deference expected of a provincial abbess addressing the Pope.

Hildegard's third approach is by far the most interesting, for it is here that she sheds all pretense of humility and supplication and cries out as the mouthpiece of God. This tone is most frequently used when Hildegard is angry or upset at the events which prompted her to pen her words or when her previous letters, using humbler, more supplicatory language, have not procured the desired results. This approach is frequently found in conjunction with visions and highly allegorical passages, similar to the one discussed above concerning the bear and the eagle. Hildegard's image of herself as a feather, touched by God, suspended in the air by His breath (II), suggests that she speaks only through the strength and will of God and not by her own volition; indeed many of her letters do begin with references to the words of the Lord. This means of introducing her subject is exemplified in the opening of the letter to Cardinals Bernard and Gregory when she writes, "The Fountain of Waters cries out to you, his followers: For my living and knowing sake, restrain and correct those dark traitors . . ." (7), or when she says to Frederick Barbarossa, "From the Highest Judge these words are directed at you" (Migne 27). In this vein Hildegard uses many epithets for God which are strongly reminiscent of the language of the Old Testament, such as the above "Fountain of Waters," the "Unfailing Light" (the burning bush on Mount Horeb) and "Him Who Is" ("I am that I am," Exodus 4:14). These phrases are not just linguistically powerful but also rhetorically profound, for the God of the Old Testament is usually portrayed as stern and vengeful, pouring out his anger on those who displease Him. Hildegard's visionary passages are equally forceful and equally suggestive of divine influence and retribution. At times, she prefaces the visions in her letters with some indication that they are indeed that, as in the

beginning of this letter to Odo of Soissons: "I write in a true vision of
the mysteries of God, seeing and hearing and knowing, as I do, in a
single manner" (41r) or when she writes to Prior Dimo, "I saw and
heard these words in a true vision"(58). One of the most powerful of
these passages is found in the first letter to the prelates of Mainz,
written soon after Hildegard had been placed under the interdict for
refusing to exhume the young nobleman:

> From a vision ingrained in my soul by God the Craftsman before I
> was born, I am compelled to write it because of the interdict with
> which we are bound by our superiors, for the sake of a certain dead
> man, buried by his priest in our monastery, without any objection.
> Then, a few days after his burial, he was ordered expelled from our
> cemetery by our superiors. Seized by no small terror at this, I looked
> to the True Light, as I am accustomed, and, with wakeful eyes, I saw
> in my soul that if the body of this dead man were carried off,
> according to their commands, that ejection would carry threats of
> great darkness, bringing danger to our parts, and like the dark clouds
> which appear before a thunderous storm, it would surround us. (23)

From this passage, it appears as though Hildegard could call upon her
visions almost at will, looking to God for the answers she needed to
immediate questions.

More often, however, Hildegard does away with the preliminaries,
and begins almost immediately with her vision or with such allegorical
language that could only have been inspired from above. In a punishing
letter to Gunther, Bishop of Speyer, Hildegard begins with a warning
from God but then continues with no further qualifications:

> Now you, O human [*homo*], who are enveloped in great darkness,
> rise up quickly after your ruin and build [an edifice] in heaven, so
> that the dark and sordid ones may be ashamed through your
> exaltation, when you arise from that darkness where you now lie,
> because you are scarcely alive on account of your deeds. . . . (41r)

To use allegorical language in a letter is one thing, but to imply that a
bishop was once one of the "dark and sordid ones" is another
altogether.

And yet Hildegard was not afraid to voice her opinions, and tact
often took a back seat to emotion. In the dispute over Richardis,

Hildegard writes to the nun's brother Hartwig, Archbishop of Bremen, that

> . . . if a person, in the disquiet of his mind, willingly seeks to become a Church Superior, seeking more the luxury of power than the wish of God, there is a rapacious wolf in him, and his soul will never seek the spiritual with faith. But there is simony. (12)

Likewise, in part of her dispute about Richardis with Heinrich, the Archbishop of Mainz, she sends him the following vitriolic letter:

> He Who Is says: I say to you, who are lacking in so many things: Heaven has been opened by the vengeance of the Lord, and ropes have been lowered against His enemies. But you, rise up, for your days are short, and remember that Nebuchadnezzar fell and that his crown perished. And many others have fallen who dared to exalt themselves to heaven. Ach! You speck of dust, why are you not ashamed to cast yourself to the heights, when you ought to be in the filth? Now, therefore, let mad men blush. But as for you, rise up, and give up your evil ways by fleeing them. (19)

It may only be coincidental that Heinrich had but a few months to live after receiving this letter.

Hildegard did not feel that only the community of the Church afforded her the freedom to write such words, for she took a similar tone in her dealings with laity. In the letter to Emperor Conrad III which is discussed above, she expresses her concerns with the political tensions between the Empire and the Papacy, warning Conrad of the dangers she sees if the present course of action is continued. In this letter, Hildegard uses the same symbolic, allegorical tone as with her clerical associates, and as in her letters to other members of the Church, she prefaces her letter with an admonition from God. Her intent is the same as in those letters—to warn, berate and threaten—and her tone, likewise, does not change. Further, that Hildegard predicts the impending schism in the church under Barbarossa ("the Catholic throne will be moved in error") speaks highly of her political astuteness, for she could see clearly where the ongoing tensions were leading; this may have provided some discomfort to Conrad and Frederick, for to have so influential a woman as Hildegard painfully aware of the consequences of every political move and not afraid to announce her conclusions to the world must have weighed upon their minds. Frederick tries to deal with Hildegard's influence (real or assumed) when he writes to her that:

> ... you should know for certain that concerning all your business, directed at us through you, we await neither the friendship nor hatred of any person, but, with respect to justice alone, we propose to judge equitably. (Migne 27)

Hildegard replies to this in yet another letter filled with symbolism and allegory. She warns Frederick in a vision, portraying him as a man who will not see, causing his land to be turned from greenness and fertility (*viriditas*, one of Hildegard's favorite images) to darkness and despair. She concludes:

> Therefore beware lest the highest king throw you down on account of the blindness of your eyes, which do not see rightly, how you ought to hold the staff of ruling justly in your hand. See so that you may be such a man, lest the grace of God be deficient in you. (Migne 27r)

Nor did Hildegard limit herself to the politics of her native land, however, as this following letter to the young Henry II of England shows.

> The Lord says to a certain man holding a certain office: yours are the gifts of gifts, even as you hold heaven by reigning, defending, protecting, and providing; but a very black bird from the north comes to you and says: You have the possibility to do whatsoever you desire; therefore do this and that, and this cause and that, because it is not useful for you that you look upon justice, since if you always look at it, you are not a lord but a servant. But you must not hear this thief advising you, who was denuding you in your first age of great glory, when you were made a beautiful shape from ashes, and later when you accepted the breath of life. Whence, even look diligently to your Father, who created you, because your mind is well-wishing, so that you may have done a good deed freely, except that the squalid habits of men are in you, and you have been enfolded with them for a certain time. Flee this bravely, dear son of God, and call upon your Father, since he extends his hand freely to your aid. Now live in eternity, and remain in eternal happiness. (Pitra 112)

Henry was also the Count of Anjou, and, thanks to his wife Eleanor, Duke of Aquitaine, so that his political power did not stop at the English Channel; nonetheless, he was still in no position directly to threaten Hildegard. Her concern for his moral well-being, once again, is well founded, for he was known as a rash young man, whose rashness was partly responsible for the murder of Archbishop Thomas à Becket in Canterbury Cathedral in 1170.

Hildegard also made the nature of her wisdom apparent to the laity as in this introduction to a letter to Count Philip of Flanders in response to his plea for intercession and guidance:

> O son of God, who himself created you in the first man, hear the words which I have seen and heard in my soul, with a wakeful mind and body, when I looked to the True Light on account of your anxious questioning. (Migne 28r)

There is no doubt in this letter that Hildegard saw her inspiration as coming directly from the Deity.

Hildegard's letters to other women show us yet another facet of her character, for they are quite different in many respects from her letters to men. Now, rather than being supplicatory or thundering, depending on the situation, she is supportive and encouraging, and while many of the outward characteristics of her letters remain—the visionary episodes, the voice of God, and the intricate allegory and symbolism—the tone of these letters is quite different. The letter to Queen Eleanor is but one example of this more encouraging style, and the final line, "may God give his blessing and aid to you in all your affairs" (Pitra 111), especially so. Further illustrating this is Hildegard's response to the concerns of a fellow nun, the Abbess of Glodens. In a letter concerning her ability to preside over her own abbey, the Abbess of Glodens asks Hildegard "what we ought to do, whether to stand in our joint obedience, or to cede, so that another may succeed and do better" (Migne 42). Hildegard's response is long and highly symbolic, culminating in a brief treatise on the seven plagues. Hildegard likens the Church to Mount Zion, and tells the abbess that the daughters of Zion are the foundation of the church. She continues:

> For, just as there are many mountains for the defense of lesser ones, through teaching and obedience, which are furnished for them in

God, so too there is a defense of many who stand in leadership from
the plots of their enemies. (Migne 42r)

She then encourages the abbess to hold firmly to her position and
to her ideals and to defeat her adversaries by winning them over to her
cause rather than by destroying them, a course of action which is more
"womanly" than the alternative.

In response to the many letters from her sister abbesses requesting
a reply and prayers for salvation, Hildegard takes the tone of a patient,
understanding mother, whose children are confused but well
intentioned. Now Hildegard assumes the voice not of the fierce, jealous
God of the Old Testament but of the gentle, loving Virgin Mary, when
she writes to one beseeching abbess:

Take care that you do not have a mind filled with uncertainty, in
which a cloud the colour of sapphire can not appear, and which often
obscures even the light of the sun. Rather, have great zeal, so that you
may stand firmly in certainty. (Migne 97r)

Another abbess requested that Hildegard

receive us in this place of sisters, and deign to favour us with the
protection of your holy prayers, so that, your most holy assistance
being merited, we may merit at last to reach the stadium of the
approaching life. (Migne 98)

Hildegard replies as follows:

The Living Light says: Dry sand is useless, and the earth which is
broken by too much plowing does not give good fruit, since it does
not have the just measure of its turning over. And the dry earth which
is rocky gives forth thorns and other useless plants; thus a
disagreeable abstinence, which does not have a just measure and
good state, destroys the flesh of man, since the greenness of just
renewal is not given to it. (Migne 98r)

Now God's voice does not chastise, but it advises and seeks to comfort,
and her mental landscape is filled with her own greenness, *viriditas*,
resplendent with allusions to prosperity and fertility. This could be seen
as the voice of the God of the New Testament.

Another letter concerns an abbess in a situation very similar to Hildegard's yet very different. The mystic Elizabeth of Schönau (1128/9-1164/5), slandered by members of her community because of her visions, writes to Hildegard for guidance. She recognizes Hildegard's matronly concern from previous correspondence, for she calls Hildegard "highly compassionate to my cause." She complains that

> a certain cloud of confusion has seized me recently in my soul, on account of the improper speeches of the people who say many things about me that are not true. . . . they have passed the evil rumor that I have prophesied about the day of judgement, which I have certainly never presumed to do. . . . (Migne 45)

She proceeds to tell Hildegard about an angelic messenger who commanded her to tell of what she saw, and to ask for advice and prayer,

> so that you may know my innocence, and that of my advisor, and may demonstrate it to the others. Moreover, I pray that you may make me a part of your prayers, and such as the Spirit of the Lord suggests to you, reply to me with words of counsel..

Again, Hildegard's response is filled with imagery and inspired allusion, but her tone is comforting and humble when she offers this advice from "the most Serene Light":

> Man is a vessel, which God built for himself, and which he imbued with his breath, so that he might complete his works in it. . . . Listen, o troubled daughter, since the ambitious suggestion of the ancient serpent torments somewhat those men whom the breath of God has thus imbued. For when that serpent saw the fine gem,[12] he soon grew dull, asking "What is this?". . . . Now listen again: Let those who wish to complete the works of God always take heed, because they are humble vessels. . . . O daughter, may God make you a mirror of life. (Migne 45r)

Such comforting and supportive language is almost unheard in Hildegard's letters to her male correspondents, but here, in a community of women, she does not hesitate to offer kind and supportive words, which may help a sister in God to deal with her troubles. Her wish for Elizabeth to become a "mirror of life" derives from this otherwise unseen aspect of Hildegard's persona; she is not supplicatory, nor formally humble, nor raging against the world but is sincerely concerned about a sister nun who might, in other circumstances, have been Hildegard herself.

Here, in these letters to women, her tone differs from the letters she presents to men, for now she is no longer dealing with her role as a woman in a man's world but rather as a woman in a community of women, and her language reveals that the abbess has clearly grasped this different situation. She knows her position in the world, and treats it not as a matter of class or political power but as a matter of gender. It is clear that she is aware of a community of women which is separate from the world of men or the community of the Church and that she sees a common plight faced by women in Christendom.

From a study of her letters, one point becomes apparent: Hildegard of Bingen was aware of her social and political position in the world of the twelfth century but also knew how to manipulate her language and her self-representation to further her influence and thereby achieve her aims. Her letters to men move through a continuum of tones, beginning with supplicatory and humble language and gaining in strength and confidence when her wishes are not respected until she bellows with the force and voice of God. Finally, her understanding of her position in a male-dominated world is made manifest through her letters to other women, for in these letters, a softer, more consolatory tone is heard than appears in any of her letters to men. When involved in this community of women, she can talk as a woman, a mother-figure, offering comfort and advice, not needing to resort to the mechanisms she adopts in dealing with men. Nevertheless, what is never absent is Hildegard's great talent for seeing the power that lies in language and for using that power to the best of her considerable ability to secure a modicum of control and influence that a woman in a small abbey in the German heartland could otherwise never hope to achieve.

## NOTES

1. I would like to thank Professor Gregory Johnston, University of Toronto, and Mikael Swayze, University of Toronto, for their helpful and insightful comments on earlier drafts of this paper. Special thanks in particular go to Professor John Carmi Parsons of the University of Toronto. References to

Hildegard's letters are to van Acker's edition unless noted as Migne (referring to Migne's edition, PL 197) or Pitra (*Analecta Sacra*, v. 8). All the translations used in this paper are my own, and I take full responsibility for any errors therein, and elsewhere in this paper.

2. Ferrante comments on just this phenomenon in a discussion of Hildegard, Christine de Pisan and Hrotsvit of Gandersheim when she says that "Instead of rejecting the role of the frail, ignorant woman imposed upon them by their culture, they embraced it and made it work for them"(227).

3. For a discussion of Hildegard's use of authority and rhetoric, see Ahlgren 46-63.

4. For further reading on this subject, see Bullough.

5. Newman deals with this paradoxical inversion of gender and virtue in *Sister of Wisdom*. As part of a detailed and highly influential discussion of this issue, she states that Hildegard "insisted that God had chosen a poor, frail, untutored woman like herself to reveal his mysteries only because those to whom he had first entrusted them–the wise, learned, and masculine clergy–had failed to obey. . . . God had to confound them by making women virile" ( 3).

6. The letter is undated, and addressed simply to the *regina anglorum*; however, since Eleanor became Queen of England a scant two years after Hildegard presented her *Scivias* to the Synod of Trier and remained Queen until after Hildegard's death, it can be directed to none other than Eleanor. In his notes to this letter, Pitra also writes: *Dubio procul non est illa Anglorum regina quam famosa nimis Eleonora. . . .* (Pitra 556, n.1).

7. Flanagan suggests that these letters may not have been solicited, or that if they were, "they must have been very general requests for words of encouragement. . . or at least this is what Hildegard provides" (166). The letter to Henry, discussed later, can be seen in this light, but this letter to Eleanor implies a personal concern and response to a request for guidance.

8. This is an example of Hildegard's inversion of gender roles to assert her authority, as discussed above.

9. It was far from unusual for mystical visions to be accompanied by physical reactions. When Elizabeth of Schönau experienced a vision, she fell into a trance, could not speak and often lost consciousness (Thiébaux 350).

10. Indeed, Hildegard claimed that all of her knowledge was given by God, including her knowledge of medicine, herblore, music and poetry. In fact, she claimed that the music she wrote was that which she heard while experiencing her visions, and thus was sent to her directly from heaven.

11. This is the charismatic illness described above.

12. The devil, according to Hildegard, hated fine gemstones, for they reminded him of his former days of glory in heaven. See the Preface on precious gems in *Physica*.

## WORKS CITED

### Primary Texts

Hildegard of Bingen. *The Letters of Hildegard of Bingen*. Ed. and trans. Joseph L. Baird and Radd K. Ehrman. Vol.I. New York: Oxford University Press, 1994.

————.*Sancta Hildegardis opera omnia*. Ed. J-P. Migne. PL. vol.197. Paris, 1882.

————. *Sanctae Hildegardis opera. Analecta Sacra VIII*. Ed. J-B. Pitra. Monte Cassino, 1882.

————. *Hildegardis Bingensis epistolarium I*. Ed. L. van Acker. CCCM vol. 91. Turnhout: Typographi Brepols Editores Pontificii, 1991.

### Secondary Texts

Ahlgren, Gillian T.W. "Visions and Rhetorical Strategy in the Letters of Hildegard of Bingen." *Dear Sister: Medieval Women and the Epistolary Genre*. Eds. Karen Cherewatuk and Ulrike Wiethaus. Philadelphia: University of Pennsylvania Press, 1993.

Bullough, Vern L. "Marriage in the Middle Ages." *Viator* IV (1973).

Ferrante, Joan. "Public Postures, Private Maneuvers." *Women and Power in the Middle Ages*. Eds. Mary Erler and Maryanne Kowaleski. Athens, Georgia: University of Georgia Press, 1988.

Flanagan, Sabina. *Hildegard of Bingen: A Visionary Life*. London: Routledge, 1989.

Newman, Barbara. *Sister of Wisdom: St. Hildegard's Theology of the Feminine*. Berkeley: University of California Press, 1987.

Shahar, Shulamith. *The Fourth Estate: A History of Women in the Middle Ages*. Trans. Chaya Galai. New York: Routledge, 1983.

Thiébaux, Marcelle, ed. and trans. *The Writings of Medieval Women: An Anthology*. 2nd. ed. New York: Garland, 1994.

# Hildegard as a Medieval "Zoologist"

## The Animals of the *Physica*

*Kenneth F. Kitchell and Irven M. Resnick*

Hildegard's *Physica* is far less studied than it deserves. Moreover when it has been studied, the work has largely been characterized as a parochial or local work, interesting for its magical spells and herbal cures but largely unaffected by the influx of new knowledge that would soon overtake the medieval intellectual world. As Singer puts it so eloquently, "Hildegard lived at rather too early a date to drink from the broad stream of new knowledge that was soon to flow into Europe through Paris from its reservoir in Moslem Spain" ("Scientific Views" 17). We can thus expect little influence in her works from Averroës and Avicenna or from the soon-to-be translated Aristotelian *Historia animalium, de partibus animalium,* and *De generatione animalium.* Instead, these works would soon come together in Albertus Magnus' vast *De animalibus*, a work which integrates all previous threads of animal lore into what might be termed the medieval *Summa zoologica* (Kitchell and Resnick). This 1,598 page tome, incorporating and commenting upon all the new knowledge available on animals serves as an interesting touchstone for Hildegard's natural investigations. While there is debate over exactly when Albertus was born (Weisheipl 17; Entrich; Mandonnet 253), his birth can safely be put within twenty years of Hildegard's death, and thus his work, heralded as the champion of an emerging "modern" science, appeared but one generation after Hildegard's life. As a result, Singer says, Hildegard's "intellectual field was far more patristic than would have been the case had her life-course been even a quarter of a century later" ("Scientific Views" 17). Yet such chronological factors should not rule out our study of Hildegard as an important contributor to the body of knowledge that forms medieval natural science and animal lore. The aim of this paper, therefore, is to refocus study on the *Physica*, with special emphasis on studying the place this work should be accorded in the canon of medieval works of natural history, especially those which deal with animals and animal lore.

While Singer studies in some detail the sources from which Hildegard may have drawn, he generally overlooks the realm of animal lore in his treatment ("Scientific Views" 17-22). Likewise, Thorndike includes Hildegard in his study of natural science, but he is clearly more fascinated by her interest in magic, demons and cures than in a careful study of where Hildegard might fit in with those natural scientists (*physici*) who studied the world of animals (135f). For, if Hildegard was born too early to take full advantage of the new influx of Arabic and Greek learning, she was almost perfectly poised to utilize the traditions of the *Physiologus* and the bestiaries which it spawned. The *Physiologus* was one of the most popular works of the Middle Ages. The name, loosely translated as "The Naturalist," refers not so much to an identifiable author but rather to the work as a whole. It is generally accepted that this collection of stories and legends originated in Egypt at a fairly early date, perhaps as early as the second century A.D. (Clark, "Zoology" 223-26; Curley ix-xxi). Its popularity led to translations into many vernacular languages at fairly early dates (McCulloch 20), and the Latin version played a major role in the rise and spread of the bestiary (Carmody). Bestiaries as such probably began to be written in the late eleventh century and underwent changes and expansions during the subsequent twelfth (Clark, "Zoology" 225; McCulloch 21-44). In their final versions the bestiaries would include well over one hundred animals with some mentions of trees and stones as well. As the number of manuscripts attests, such works were widely read, and it is wise to remember that the anonymous bestiary authors added information from such authors as Pliny, Solinus, Ambrose, and Isidore to the received lore of the *Physiologus*. In so doing they brought older material on animals into play long before the actual works of Aristotle appeared, for the eclectic Pliny in particular freely mined authors as old as Herodotus and as prestigious as Aristotle for his vast encyclopedia. It thus is logical to look at Hildegard's *Physica* for traces of the older *Physiologus*/bestiary lore.

What, then, is a medieval "zoologist?" It is clear that no medieval figure who studied animals, even Albertus himself, the *Doctor universalis*, can be termed a zoologist in the modern sense of the word. Still, Clark has recently pointed out ("Zoology" 223) that there is more accurate observation of animal lore in some of these works than is commonly acknowledged. The problem arises from the fact that the nuggets of what we call "truth" today are surrounded by a multitude of other "facts" which do not meet modern, scientific criteria. Yet to scoff at the beginnings of a scientific movement is to denigrate pioneers merely because they were feeling their way into new, uncharted territories. One focus of this paper, then, is to reassess the progress of these medieval pioneer zoologists by evaluating where Hildegard fits in to their number, and the beginning of the story lies far earlier than the new Aristotelian learning.

Before moving on to such a detailed study, however, it would be well to look at the work as a whole. While Hildegard's scientific views may be discerned throughout her theological and visionary works, her stature as a natural philosopher largely depends on two other works: her *Physica*, otherwise known as the *Book of Simple Medicine* , and her *Book of Compound Medicine* , also known as the *Causae et curae* or *Causes and Cures*, a shorter title provided by a thirteenth-century scribe for the *De causis, signis atque curis aegritudinum.*[1] Although it begins with the history of creation and the Fall of Adam, the *Causae et Curae* is especially valuable for its discussion of medical conditions and cures. It provides remedies for hair loss, migraine headache, toothache, digestive problems, lice, and a host of other afflictions. It prescribes cures for gout, fevers, and intestinal worms (Engbring).

Both the *Causae et curae* and the *Physica* were likely written between 1151 and 1158. Although early in this century the authenticity of these two works remained in doubt (Singer, "Scientific Views" 12), there is now general agreement that they are genuine to Hildegard (Thorndike 2:128-129). Both treatises provide an eclectic and, to modern eyes, rather unsystematic treatment of the natural world, yet for a discussion of the plant and animal worlds one must examine the *Physica*, a work to which we now turn our attention here. While the *Physica* has been translated into both French and German in whole or in part, it is the only one of Hildegard's works mentioned above for which there exists no English translation. Moreover, despite the appearance of French and German translations in the last decade, a critical edition of the Latin text is still wanting. The need for such an edition is all the more pressing in light of the remarkable efflorescence of Hildegard scholarship over the past several decades. Adamson has recently pointed out that as late as 1956 only three manuscripts of the *Physica* were known to scholars.[2] In 1956 a fifteenth-century fragment, Cod. 525 (fols. 18r-23r) of the Burger Bibliothek in Bern, became known. Since 1983, however, five additional manuscript sources have been uncovered.[3] As a result, nine manuscripts of the *Physica* are now known. Five contain the complete text, and two date from ca. 1300. Yet the standard Latin edition remains the nineteenth-century text in Migne's *Patrologia latina*, which is based on only the fifteenth-century Paris manuscript, complemented with additional passages from the first printed edition of 1533. As we shall see, this text is marred by typographical errors and misplaced or misnumbered notes.

In the absence of a critical edition that provides an apparatus comparing all of these manuscript sources, we have been compelled to rely on the edition in the *Patrologia latina*. The translations of Portmann and Reithe were unavailable to us for the completion of this article. We have, however, examined Elisabeth Klein's French translation of Books Five through Eight.[4] Nevertheless, problems with the Latin text will remain until an edition based on all available manuscript evidence is completed. With these caveats in mind, we can proceed to a discussion of the content of the *Physica*.[5]

Hildegard's *Physica* comprises nine books and runs some 223 columns in the Migne edition. Book One is entitled *De plantis* and contains 230 individual chapters on plants. Its eighty-two columns, comprising over a third of the work's entirety, reflect the author's interest in and devotion to medicines and healing. This is Hildegard as she is commonly portrayed—the great healer whose medical skill, in the opinion of Kaiser, contributed more to her popular reputation for saintliness than did all her writings (Thorndike 126). Such was her skill that Engbring entitled her study of the abbess, "Saint Hildegard, Twelfth-Century Physician." In light of this, it is clear that extensive work remains to be done on this book of the *Physica*. Most desired is an accurate listing of the plants mentioned throughout, many of which are mentioned only by their German names. The potential effectiveness of some of these simples also needs to be studied collaboratively with medievalist, latinist, chemist, physician, and pharmacologist all playing a role.

Book Two is entitled *De elementis* and is a very short book, consisting of only 63 chapters and 6 columns in Migne. The "elements" are broadly conceived, for Hildegard starts with air, water, and sea and moves on to rivers (chs. 5-10), classifying them in her pragmatic manner as healthy or unhealthy and as fishable or not. Of great interest is her description of the Nahe River (ch. 9), well known to Hildegard as the river which flowed past her religious house near Bingen. She vividly describes its unpredictability, sometimes placid and at other times turbulent, a description that bespeaks first-hand observation. Its fish are listed as fat and health-producing, and they are said to stay fresh for a long time. The next "element" in Hildegard's list is earth, in several manifestations.

Book Three moves on to trees, and consists of sixty-three chapters covering some thirty-four columns. Hildegard devotes her last eight chapters to such tree-related items as the effect the smoke from trees has on diseases or the uses of moss and pine pitch. The previous chapters, on trees themselves, form a nice corollary to the first book on plants and it is worthwhile, in fact, to notice the simple fact that the trees have their own book. Albertus Magnus would combine trees and plants in his *De vegetabilibus* (Jessen) as does Bartholomew the Englishman, in Book 17 of his encyclopedia. Yet, in Pliny's *Natural History* trees have their own book (Book 12) and Isidore, in his *Origines*, devotes his Book 17 to country matters, treating grain crops, the vine, trees (at some length), plants, and aromatics, each in a separate section of the book. Moulinier has recently studied the sources Hildegard used in her work and decides that Isidore may well have been known to Hildegard, either in a version from a nearby abbey or from a copy owned by Bishop Siward of Upsala ("Encyclopédiste" 127). We will return to the problem of how Hildegard organized the natural world below.

Unsurprisingly, Hildegard's main interest in trees is medicinal. Recipes for simples are found which use every conceivable part of the tree: leaves (new and old); fruit (new and old); outer and inner wood: bark; seeds; roots; and even the earth around the tree. Personal hygiene is addressed with cures for bad breath (ch. 5) and skin blotches (ch. 35) and we are forcefully reminded of the actual state of medieval hygiene by a cure for "cancri" or "crabs" (ch. 53), since context makes it very clear that these are body lice and not any form of cancer.[6] Cures and preventatives for lice are prevalent in the Middle Ages, and often include such odd ingredients as elephant dung and the smoke of burning powdered mercury and lead, a process which might be as dangerous to the human as to his pest. Such nostrums are found in the

works of Albertus *(De animalibus,* 22.99; 23.38; 26.21) and even the
famed *Prose Salernitan Questions* (Lawn 77;175-76). Hildegard is
therefore in good company as she recommends simples with which to
combat the concerns of day-to-day life. In much the same vein, this
book also contains several charms to rid oneself of demons and evil
spirits (ch. 35) as well as a some interesting recipes for beer (chs. 27,
42).

Book Four deals with stones and gems. This book was omitted in
the earlier editions and Thorndike thinks it may in fact be a later
addition (130). This book occupies twenty-six chapters and twenty text
columns but treats over thirty stones.

There is room for much discussion here, but let us move on to the
main substance of the present paper, which lies in Hildegard's chapters
on animals. Space does not permit the sort of in-depth study these
entries deserve, but we will endeavor to show, through the selective use
of examples, what potential for future research lies in their pages. Book
Five deals with fish, describing thirty-seven fish in its twenty-two
columns. There is a great deal of information available to researchers
here. Hildegard, who spent most of her life near rivers, is far more
interested in fresh-water than salt-water fish and this information might
well yield good evidence on the diet of monasteries, which were so
dependent upon fish. She begins the book with a preface where, in a
fairly straightforward fashion, she gives her system of classification or,
to put it in modern terms, her "taxonomy." This provides us with a
useful opportunity to study the methods of classification used in this
work. According to Hildegard, fish vary by where they live, with some
preferring the top of the water, others the bottom, and others the mid-
level. Some prefer mud while others may live among rocks. All of this
affects what they eat, and this, in turn, affects whether their flesh is
good for human consumption. Some fish prefer the day and splendor of
the sun while others prefer night and the moon. Hildegard is also
inordinately interested in how fish breed, concerned with whether they
expel all their eggs and sperm at one time, leaving themselves spent
from the effort or whether they emit at intervals and regain their
strength. In either case, many of the eggs perish. Some fish, she says,
breed outside of their species, much as humans do when they abandon
their nature, and much as beasts do to produce cross breeds. This
matter-of-fact reference to bestiality mirrors the recent investigations of
Salisbury (84-101) but also is an attempt to explain how new breeds
came into existence after the initial act of Creation. The preface ends

with an interesting story which hints at a body of stories which were in existence concerning the time of Adam (Thorndike 136-37). Fish know of certain herbs which, when eaten, make further food unnecessary for up to six months. Hildegard continues: "When Adam was expelled from Paradise, he knew of these herbs and sought them out in the waters. While he ate them he had no other food, but later, when he could have other food, he shunned them" (5.Praef.1269-70). The reason was, she tells us, that such food has an unpleasant side effect of making the flesh tough and knotted.

The odd mixture of taxonomy and folklore presented by Book Five at first seems merely diverting. But let us compare it with the opening words of Albertus Magnus' *De animalibus* 24, on fish:

1. The aquatic animals are then set forth here, each with its own name, and the expositions of names set forth in previous books are considered while each of the animals is described with its characteristics.

We say in general, then, concerning all aquatic animals, that they are of a moist nature and that both their natural habitat and diet show this. For each thing is maintained in a place like-natured to itself and is nourished by food of the same complexion as the principles out of which it is constituted through generation.

It is agreed, then, that such creatures are, in most cases, cold. An indication of this is that they either lack blood or have but little of it. However, a few of them do have a neck, penis, womb, or breasts. Whichever of them also give birth to live young resembling themselves from a womb, have cone-shaped breasts near their pelvic area and also have wombs and penises. But these appendages do not hang down on the outside. They rather have internal penises and emit them at the moment of coitus, as do the dolphin and whale. The breasts are cones of a sort, to which certain milk ducts are led from the body, having a point of interchange with the inferior epigastric vein.

2. Not one of the aquatic animals is ever seen to copulate in an unnatural manner and is never moved to copulate with any other save an animal of its own type. When they lay their eggs, they rub their bellies together or the female leads the way, laying her eggs and the male follows, spreading his milt over them. For this reason, most of the eggs perish, either because they do not exit at the contact of the rubbing or because they descend in such a way that the milt of the

male does not touch them. This is the reason that there the number of fish does not exceed all bounds, even though the fishes' eggs would seem to be exceedingly numerous.

Of the egg layers, the large fish lay their eggs on rocks or in the mud, while the small ones lay them on the roots of aquatic plants. . . .

3. Moreover, although they live in deep water as well as near the land around the shores, the flesh of those which are near the shores is firmer and drier and thus more healthful. The flesh of those dwelling at the bottom is moister and is softer, except for those very large fish with an earthy nature, like those called marine monsters [*beluae marinae*] by some. It is common for all fish to wander about before ovulation, seeking a place fit for it, and that at the time of ovulation to go forth in pairs, male and female, to complete the eggs. . . .

A comparison of the points which interest the two authors is instructive. Albertus clearly differentiates marine mammals from true fish (though he calls each *piscis*) and he will go on to discuss their internal anatomy. But in this selection, brief though it is, we see that he shared many of the same concerns as his earlier fellow German. He is very interested in how fish taste and describes their environment. He considers whether or not they breed outside their genus worthy of discussion. He asks why, if fish produce such prodigious amounts of eggs, they are not more plentiful than they are. Hildegard too, discussing whales, says that both whales and other fish eat fish, "because, if the fish in the sea were not diminished in number by being eaten and devoured, then the sea would be impassable due to the number of fish in it" (5.1.1269) It thus begins to become apparent that while time and the influx of the new learning may separate Albertus and Hildegard, the earlier "Sybil of the Rhine" is clearly part of the same process that led to later, more precise "science" as found in the *Doctor universalis*. In a recent article, Moulinier agrees, claiming that Hildegard, especially through her interest in the reproductive habits of various fish, has made a significant contribution to medieval science and that this book may be the most original and important "de toute la zoologie du Moyen Âge" ("L'abbesse" 461-62). Again, much work remains to be done. For example, while Moulinier is correct in stating that many of the species Hildegard describes were local and that some may be extinct or fished-out by now ("L'abbesse" 468-69) , a careful study identifying Hildegard's fish, many of which bear Germanic names, would be a welcome contribution to our knowledge of local ecology and economy alike. Such a study should also include the observations of Albertus, who in his duties for his order and as a preacher of a crusade traveled throughout Germany and constantly cites fishermen as sources for his lore (*De animalibus* 2.76; 4.38). The late Roman poet Ausonius should also be studied in this context. Ausonius, whose *floruit* was in the latter part of the fourth century AD, devotes a significant portion of his *Mosella* to the fish inhabiting the German river this poem celebrates. Furthermore, while some spawning information may have been available to the abbess from local fishermen, careful study might also reveal that some of this information came to her from those who kept fish ponds to supply the monasteries with this precious commodity.

The sixth book of the *Physica* encompasses twenty-eight columns and contains some seventy-two entries for birds. Much of the book recalls the interests Hildegard evinces in her entries for plants or stones. The beak of a crane, dried and ground to a powder, will help cure pigs being ravaged by a pestilence. Its dried blood, placed on the vulva of a woman undergoing a difficult birth will ease her labor, provided, of course, the bird's right foot is placed on her navel while she looks into the reflecting surface of a bowl of water mixed with that same blood (ch. 4). Likewise, an elaborate ritual involving an ointment made of sparrow-hawk fat and several herbs will cool the ardor of a man or woman in the throes of uncontrollable passion (ch. 20). But let us use this book instead to indicate another fertile source of research the *Physica* might offer.

As stated, there are seventy-two entries for birds in this book. The version used to create the PL edition listed sixty-eight, and four more are added from the earlier printed edition. The following table lists the birds in order as they appear in Migne. The second column indicates any variants that occur between the PL version and the earlier edition and the third column offers the scientific identification offered by F.A. Reuss, who collaborated with Daremberg to produce the PL version. The fourth column provides a probable modern identification for the bird, based either on Reuss' scientific name or, when in parentheses, on Hildegard's Latin. This chart will be used, first, to illustrate the potential for identifying Hildegard's animals and, second, to study her attempts at arriving at a taxonomy for the animals she lists. Please note that scientific notation changes over time. Many of the identifications given in the PL currently have different designations. The common name identifications are thus kept general.

| Name | Variants | PL Identification | Common Name |
|---|---|---|---|
| 1 Griffo | | | (Mythical griffin) |
| 2 Strusz | [Struthio, ed.] | [Struthio camelus] | Ostrich |
| 3 Pavo | | [Pavo cristatus] | Peacock |
| 4 Grus | | [Ardea grus] | Crane |
| 5 Cyngnus (sic) | | [Anas olor] | Swan |
| 6 Reyger | | [Ardeae spec.] | Species of heron |
| 7 Vultur | | [Falconis spec.] | Species of falcon |
| 8 Aquila | | [Falco aquila] | (Eagle) |
| 9 Oderbero | [Ciconia, ed.] | | (Stork) |
| 10 Anser/gans | | [Anas anser] | Goose |
| 11 Halegans | [Grandula, ed.] | | |
| 12 Aneta domestica | | [Anas domestica] | Domestic duck |
| 13 Aneta silvestris | | [Anas boschas] | Wild duck |
| 14 Gallus et gallina | | | (Rooster and hen) |
| 15 Urhun | | [Tetrao urogallus] | Capercaillie |
| 16 Rephun | [Perdix, ed.] | [Tetrao perdix] | Partridge |
| 17 Birckhun | | [Tetrao tetrix] | Black grouse |
| 18 Falco | [Herodius, ed.] | [Falconis spec.] | Species of falcon |
| 19 Habich | [Accipiter, ed.] | | |
| 20 Sperwere | [Nisus, ed.] | | |
| 21 Milvus | | | (Kite) |
| 22 Weho | [not in ed.] | | |
| 23 Corvus | [not in ed.] | [Corvus corax] | Raven |
| 24 Krewa/Kraha | [not in ed.] | | |
| 25 Nebelkraha | [not in ed.] | | |
| 26 Musar | [Larus, ed.] | [Corvus cornix] | |
| 27 Ordumel | [not in ed.] | | |
| 28 Alkreya | [not in ed.] | | |
| 29 Mewa | [not in ed.] | [Columba speciosa] | |
| 30 Columba | | | (Dove/pigeon) |
| 31 Turtur | [not in ed.] | [Columba turtur] | Turtledove |
| 32 Psittacus | | [Psittaci spec.] | Species of parrot |
| 33 Pica | | [Corvus pica] | Magpie |

| | | | |
|---|---|---|---|
| 34 Hera | | [Corvus caryocatactes] | Jay (?) |
| 35 Ulula | | [Strigis spec.] | Owl |
| 36 Huwo | [Rubo, ed.] | | |
| 37 Sisegonino | [not in ed.] | | |
| 38 Cuculus | | [Cuculus canorus] | Cuckoo |
| 39 Snepha | | [Socolopac. spec.] | Snipe |
| 40 Specht | | [Pici spec.] | Woodpecker |
| 41 Passer | | [Fringilla domestica] | Sparrow |
| 42 Meysa | [not in ed.] | [Parus spec.] | Tit |
| 43 Amsla | | [Turdus merula] | Thrush |
| 44 Drosela | | | |
| 45 Lercha | [Laudula, ed.] | [Alaudae, spec.] | Nightingale |
| 46 Isenbrado | | [Alcedo hispida] | Kingfisher |
| 47 Wedehoppo | [Upupa, ed.] | [Upupa epops] | Hoopoe |
| 48 Wachtela | | [Tetrao coturnix] | Quail |
| 49 Nachtgalla | [Luscinia, ed.] | [Motacilla luscinia] | Nightingale? |
| 50 Stara | | [Turnus vulgaris] | Starling |
| 51 Vynco | [Frigellus, ed.] | [Fringilla caelebs] | Finch/Chaffinch |
| 52 Distelwincke | | [Fringilla carduelis] | Goldfinch |
| 53 Amera | | [Emberizae, spec.] | Bunting |
| 54 Grasemucka | | [Motacillae spec.] | Wagtail |
| 55 Wargkrengel | | | |
| 56 Merla | | | |
| 57 Waszersceltza | [Waszersteltza?] | [Motacilla alba] | White wagtail |
| 57a Pelicanus | [ed. only] | | Pelican |
| 58 Beynstercza | | [Motacilla flava] | Yellow wagtail |
| 59 Hyrundo | | [Hirund. spec.] | Swallow |
| 60 Cungelm | | | |
| 61 Vespertilio | | | (Bat) |
| 62 Widdervalo | [widdervalo] | [Pliny <u>HN</u> 30.28] | |
| 63 Apis | | [Apis mellifica] | Honeybee |

| 64 Musca |  | [Musca domestica] | Housefly |
| 65 Cicada |  | [Gryll. Spec.] | Grasshopper/ Cicada |
| 66 Locusta | [not in ed.] |  | (Locust) |
| 67 Mugga |  |  |  |
| 68 Humbelen | [Hunbelen] | [Apis terrestris] | Humble/Bumble bee |
| 69 Wespa |  |  | (Wasp) |
| 70 Glimo |  | [Lampyris noctiluca] | Glowworm/ Firefly |
| 71 Meygelana |  | [cf 1.159] |  |
| 72 Parix | [ed. only] |  |  |

It is evident that many of the "birds" on this list, be they true avians or flying insects, have remained unidentified. Moreover, in many places the casual nature of the editing has created problems of its own. In several places the two problems overlap. Let us take another look at the list with a critical eye.

Number 11, the *Halegans* is given no identification and is only graced with the gloss of *grandula* as found in the editions. This bird is surely the same as Albertus' third kind of goose which he claims is called either the "anser grandinis" (hail goose) or the "anser nivis," (snow goose) (*De animalibus* 7.41). Suolahti, in his admirable study of German bird names (417), and Sanders, who studied Albertus' dialect (435), conclude that this is simply the wild goose which took its nickname from the belief that the appearance of the wild goose was thought to presage cold weather and precipitation. Thus, *grandula*, from the editions, becomes clearly recognized as a form of the Latin *grando*, "hail." A bit later in the list (no. 19) the *Habich* is glossed in the editions as an *accipiter*, a fairly generic term for a hawk (Wood and Fyfe 614). Suolahti traces many forms of the modern German *Habicht*, goshawk, and identifies this animal as *Astur palumbarius*.(359-62). The next name in Hildegard's list is the germanic *Sperwere* (cf. the modern German *Sberber*) clearly related to the Latin *sparvarius*, or sparrow hawk (Wood and Fyfe 626) and whose other name is the *nisus* of the editions, the modern *Accipiter nisus*. This is followed almost immediately by Hildegard's number 22, the *Weho*. The name is unusual, and its use in old Germanic texts seems to refer to several sorts of birds. But Suolahti indicates that at least one use of the name indicates a sort of raptor (340-41). That this is apt here is shown by the context, for as we will show below, Hildegard does indeed group her animals and here the *Weho* is the last of her raptors.

With number 24, the *Krewa* and *Kraha*, we move from raptors to crow-like birds, for it is clear that these are crows (Suolahti 179f.). A new sort of problem emerges with number 25, the *Nebelkraha*, unidentified in the PL edition. This bird is followed by the *Musar*, glossed in the editions as the *Larus* and identified as the hooded crow, *Corvus cornix*. In fact, the previous entry, the *Nebelkraha*, is the hooded crow (Suolahti 181-82) and one suspects a misplaced footnote. The *musar* or *larus*, now left unidentified, admits to two identifications. If *larus* is a valid reading, then we may have the seagull. In the *De animalibus* (24.124) Albertus has the following entry: "LARUS—The sea gull is a bird of the kite genus which both swims in the water and flies in the air in search of prey." Compare Thomas of Cantimpré, Albertus' student and, according to some, the source of some of Albertus' citations in this section (Aiken). In his *De natura rerum* Thomas tells us that the source for his entry on the *larus* is the "Gloss on that place where unclean birds are prohibited in the Law" (5.74). He is referring to Lev. 11:16 where the *larus* is forbidden. Such a gloss is found in the *Glossa ordinaria* (PL 114:814D), itself an epitome of Rabanus Maurus's *Expositiones in Leviticum* 3.1 (PL 108: 357A). Hildegard could have seen any of these earlier texts. What, then, is a *larus*? It transliterates the Greek *laros*, a rather broad sort of term which included, in antiquity at least, several kinds of seagulls (Thompson, 192). Suolahti discusses names which are allied to Hildegard's *Musar* with similar mixed results (5.74). It may be, he concludes, a type of buzzard, or, by being related to the modern German *Möwe*, be related to "seagull." In light of Hildegard's *Mewa*, which follows just below the *larus* in her text and which is almost surely a seagull, the former may be a slightly better choice for the *larus*. It is, of course, possible that the two passages form a doublet, one using the Latin name, the other the Germanic name for the seagull and we thus see further compelling grounds for clarifying the text of this work. Another possibility is that one of the birds is more like a tern and the other the larger seagull.

Chapters 36 and 37 contain two more birds for which no identification is offered in the PL edition—the *Huwo*, offered as *Rubo* in the editions, and the *Sisegonino*, which does not appear in the earlier editions. Suolahti identifies the *Huwo* as an owl, most likely the eagle owl, *Bubo bubo* (307-14), whose distinctive cry has been described as "a dull, descending wúoh" audible over great distances (Grzimek, 8:406). In light of the almost perfect onomatopoeia of the name "huwo" (the German name today is the *Uhu*) the identification as an owl becomes compelling, and "rubo" may well be an ill-informed emendation, correction, or corruption of "bubo." Suolahti identifies the *sisegonino* as the pelican (388-93). Although Hildegard's description of this bird as essentially nocturnal is a bit confusing, her description of the mother pelican's actions toward her children is very familiar from the bestiary tradition. Yet there is a variant involved. In the traditional tale the mother lashes out at her children and kills them because they strike her. Having great remorse, the adult eventually pierces its breast, lets its blood flow over the children, and brings them back to life with obvious christological overtones (Rowland 131; McCulloch 155-57; Clark, *Birds,* 168-71). Hildegard's story is similar but at the same time significantly different. According to her version the mother pelican does not recognize her young when they emerge from their eggs, thinks they belong to some other species (*putat alienos esse*), and kills them. Hildegard also adds some interesting data not commonly found in other versions of the pelican. According to her the bird sometimes hangs in the air, back toward the ground, while it scans the skies to give predictions of the future. If it sees that someone in the area is going to die it gives out with a few cries and is then silent.

Still more identifications are possible. In Chapter 44 Hildegard describes the *Drosela*, but no identification is offered in the PL edition. Comparison with the modern German *Drossel*, however, identifies the bird as a thrush, and this is confirmed by Suolahti (51-54). The *Wargkrengel* of Chapter 5 can also be identified as *Lanius collurio*, the red-backed shrike, known colloquially as the butcher bird. The identification is secured either by reference to Old and Middle High German forms of the name (Suolahti 147-50) or from a most exact description in Albertus' *De animalibus*:

> The *kylian*, a Greek name, is a bird which is called the *warchengel* [butcher bird] in our lands. It has an uncurved beak and does not have hooked talons. The largest of that genus is the size of a blackbird [*merula*] and the smallest is a bit smaller than is the starling. Each genus is grey in color with two black spots near the eyes. They hunt small birds and catch them with their beaks. (*De animalibus* 7.36)

This deceiving bird seems to be, in our lands, the one that we call the *warchengel* in German [butcher bird]. This one preys upon the small song bird which we call the *vinco* [finch] *(De animalibus,*8.82).

The butcher bird is a paragon of violence in the animal world. Both its older Germanic name, which means "hangman" or "executioner" (Sanders 430) and its modern German name, *Dorndreher,* "thorn-swinger," refer to its violent behavior. It has earned its nicknames from its habit of using a sharp thorn to impale its prey, which can reach the size of mice, lizards and smaller birds. Grzimek offers vivid descriptions and pictures to validate the shrike's reputation (9:201-2; 211-12).

The *Merla* of Chapter 56 is also unidentified. Suolahti identifies the *Merle* as *Petrocincla saxatalis* or *Monticola saxatilis* but admits that these birds are rare in Germany (48). Later he indicates the suffix -*merle* may indicate various forms of thrush (56-57). In Chapter 60 Hildegard lists the *Cungelm*, again unidentified. Yet the word's etymology hints at its origin, for in the *kung*-stem we see the root for "king." The bird, then, is the "king bird," in Latin the *Regulus*, i.e., *Troglodytus europaeus*, a wren (Suolahti, 80f. ). The editors of the PL volume refer the reader to Pliny's *Historia naturalis* 30.28 for the *Widdervalo*. Here a bird called the "jaundice bird" (*icterus*) is mentioned, and Pliny identifies it as the one he normally calls the *galgulus*, the golden oriole. More direct is Suolahti's listing of the Middle High German form *Witewal* for the golden oriole (169) . Finally, Hildegard turns to the last of her "birds," viz. flying insects. Among these is the *Mugga* (Chapter 67), unidentified by the editors. The answer lies, once more, in Hildegard's native tongue. Lexer (1:2211) lists several forms of the word *Mücke,* or "fly." Among them are *Mügge* and *Mugga,* all derived from the Latin *musca.* We may not be sure as to which particular variety of fly Hildegard had in mind, and Klein's suggestion of a mosquito or gnat is tempting (177).

With the corrections, emendations, and amplifications just offered (and we may be sure that there are others yet to be made), Hildegard's list of birds may now be printed in fuller, more accurate form. An asterisk denotes an addition or correction to the list.

| Name | Variants | PL Identification | Common Name |
|------|----------|-------------------|-------------|
| 1 Griffo | | | (Mythical griffin) |
| 2 Strusz | [Struthio, ed.] | [Struthio camelus] | Ostrich |
| 3 Pavo | | [Pavo cristatus] | Peacock |
| 4 Grus | | [Ardea grus] | Crane |
| 5 Cyngnus (sic) | | [Anas olor] | Swan |
| 6 Reyger | | [Ardeae spec.] | Species of heron |
| 7 Vultur | | [Falconis spec.] | Species of falcon |
| 8 Aquila | | [Falco aquila] | (Eagle) |
| 9 Oderbero | [Ciconia, ed.] | | (Stork) |
| 10 Anser/gans | | [Anas anser] | Goose |
| 11 Halegans | [Grandula, ed.] | | *Wild goose |
| 12 Aneta domestica | | [Anas domestica] | Domestic duck |
| 13 Aneta silvestris | | [Anas boschas] | Wild duck |
| 14 Gallus et gallina | | | (Rooster and hen) |
| 15 Urhun | | [Tetrao urogallus] | Capercaillie |
| 16 Rephun | [Perdix, ed.] | [Tetrao perdix] | Partridge |
| 17 Birckhun | | [Tetrao tetrix] | Black grouse |
| 18 Falco | [Herodius, ed.] | [Falconis spec.] | Species of falcon |
| 19 Habich | [Accipiter, ed.] | | *Goshawk |
| 20 Sperwere | [Nisus, ed.] | | *Sparrowhawk |
| 21 Milvus | | | (Kite) |
| 22 Weho | [not in ed.] | | *A raptor |
| 23 Corvus | [not in ed.] | [Corvus corax] | Raven |
| 24 Krewa/Kraha | [not in ed.] | | *Crow |
| 25 Nebelkraha | [not in ed.] | *Corvus cornix | *Hooded crow |
| 26 Musar | [Larus, ed.] | | *Seagull? |
| 27 Ordumel | [not in ed.] | | |
| 28 Alkreya | [not in ed.] | | |
| 29 Mewa | [not in ed.] | | *Seagull? |
| 30 Columba | | [Columba speciosa] | (Dove/pigeon) |
| 31 Turtur | [not in ed.] | [Columba turtur] | Turtledove |
| 32 Psittacus | | [Psittaci spec.] | Species of parrot |

| | | | |
|---|---|---|---|
| 33 Pica | | [Corvus pica] | Magpie |
| 34 Hera | | [Corvus caryocatactes] | Jay (?) |
| 35 Ulula | | [Strigis spec.] | Owl |
| 36 Huwo | [Rubo, ed.] | | *Owl |
| 37 Sisegonino | [not in ed.] | | *Pelican |
| 38 Cuculus | | [Cuculus canorus] | Cuckoo |
| 39 Snepha | | [Socolopac. spec.] | Snipe |
| 40 Specht | | [Pici spec.] | Woodpecker |
| 41 Passer | | [Fringilla domestica] | Sparrow |
| 42 Meysa | [not in ed.] | [Parus spec.] | Tit |
| 43 Amsla | | [Turdus merula] | Thrush |
| 44 Drosela | | | *Thrush |
| 45 Lercha | [Laudula, ed.] | [Alaudae, spec.] | Nightingale |
| 46 Isenbrado | | [Alcedo hispida] | Kingfisher |
| 47 Wedehoppo | [Upupa, ed.] | [Upupa epops] | Hoopoe |
| 48 Wachtela | | [Tetrao coturnix] | Quail |
| 49 Nachtgalla | [Luscinia, ed.] | [Motacilla luscinia] | Nightingale? |
| 50 Stara | | [Turnus vulgaris] | Starling |
| 51 Vynco | [Frigellus, ed.] | [Fringilla caelebs] | Finch/Chaffinch |
| 52 Distelwincke | | [Fringilla carduelis] | Goldfinch |
| 53 Amera | | [Emberizae, spec.] | Bunting |
| 54 Grasemucka | | [Motacillae spec.] | Wagtail |
| 55 Wargkrengel | | *Lanius collurio | *Butcher bird |
| 56 Merla | | | *Thrush? |
| 57 Waszersceltza | [Waszersteltza?] | [Motacilla alba] | White wagtail |
| 57a Pelicanus | [ed. only] | | Pelican |
| 58 Beynstercza | | [Motacilla flava] | Yellow wagtail |
| 59 Hyrundo | | [Hirund. spec.] | Swallow |
| 60 Cungelm | | *Troglodytus europaeus | *King bird, wren |

| 61 Vespertilio | | | (Bat) |
| 62 Widdervalo | [widdervalo] | [Pliny <u>HN</u> 30.28] | *Golden oriole |
| 63 Apis | | [Apis mellifica] | Honeybee |
| 64 Musca | | [Musca domestica] | Housefly |
| 65 Cicada | | [Gryll. Spec.] | Grasshopper/ Cicada |
| 66 Locusta | [not in ed.] | | (Locust) |
| 67 Mugga | | | *Fly/mosquito |
| 68 Humbelen | [Hunbelen] | [Apis terrestris] | Humble/Bumble bee |
| 69 Wespa | | | (Wasp) |
| 70 Glimo | | [Lampyris noctiluca] | Glowworm/ Firefly |
| 71 Meygelana | | [cf 1.159] | |
| 72 Parix | [ed. only] | | |

Let us turn now to the next book of the *Physica*, Book Seven, listing only the animals as they appear in order and their most likely identifications. Several of these have been added by the present authors. For example, Hildegard's *lira* (chapter 40), is surely the *loir*, a sort of large dormouse and more commonly the *glis* in Latin (cf. Albertus Magnus, *De animalibus,*1.40; 9.72; 22.103; Klein 257). While some identifications might be challenged, we will use this list for the purpose of discovering Hildegard's taxonomy, occasionally referring back also to the list of birds as emended.

| | | | |
|---|---|---|---|
| 1. Elephans | Elephant | 10. Cervus | Deer |
| 2. Camelus | Camel | | [Cervus |
| | | 11. Rech | caproleus] |
| 3. Leo | Lion | 12. Steynbock | [Capra ibex] |
| 4. Ursus | Bear | 13. Wisant | Wisent |
| 5. Unicornus | Unicorn | 14. Bos | Ox |
| 6. Tigris | Tiger | 15. Ovis | Sheep |
| 7. Panthera | Panther | 16. Hircus | Goat |
| 7a. Pardus | Pard | 17. Porcus | Pig |
| 8. Equus | Horse | 18. Lepus | Hare |
| 9. Asinus | Ass | 19. Lupus | Wolf |

| 20. Canis | Dog | 34. Wasser marth | "Water marten" |
|-----------|-----|------------------|----------------|
| 22. Biber | Beaver | 35. Zobel | Sable |
| 23. Otther | Otter | 36. Harmini | Ermine |
| 24. Simea | Monkey | 37. Talpa | Mole |
| 25. Merkacza | Meerkat? | 38. Wisela | Weasel |
| 26. Luchs | Lynx | 39. Mus | Mouse |
| 27. Dasch | Badger | 40. Lira | Loire |
| 28. Illediso | Polecat | 41. Spiczmus | Shrew |
| 29. Ericius or Swinegel | Hedgehog | 42. Pulex | Flea |
| 31. Eichorn | Squirrel | 43. Formica | Ant |
| 32. Hamstra | Marmot | 44. Helim | Elk (? Klein 263) |
| 33. Marth | Marten | 45. Dromeda | Camel |

At first glance, this list seems to be without any significant order, a charge Thorndike has leveled against the entire work (2:130). Yet to hold this view is to do Hildegard an injustice, for not only is an order present in this section, it bears her personal stamp. Similarly, while Moulinier is correct in stating that Hildegard generally follows what we might call the "Hexaemeron tradition" of the the six days of creation in arranging her chapters ("Encyclopédiste"121-122), we can still discover some of her more detailed thought patterns as she lists the individual animals within those chapters. First, Hildegard shows a tendency to move from the rare to the more common, for the first seven entries in this book are what we might call "exotics," animals from foreign climes. Likewise, in her list of birds, Hildegard began with the mythical/exotic ones (griffon and ostrich).

Hildegard next moves on to a more general group which we might call hoofed animals. These fall into four main groups: equids (the mule is curiously missing) nos. 8-9; cervids, nos. 10-12; bovids nos. 13-14; and farm/food animals nos. 14-18. Note that *bos* is both a bovid, well allied with the *wisant* before it, and a farm animal. This is, perhaps, a clue to how Hildegard's mind works when classifying her animals. The animals are definitely grouped, but there is no ruling scheme at work binding one group to the next. Moreover, almost random association can lead from one group to the next or cause insertions in the overall scheme. Thus, while nos. 10-14 in the list of birds basically form a collection of barnyard fowl, the mention of the goose (*gans,* no. 10) leads to mention of the *Halegans,* the wild goose, in no. 11.

The next group in Book 7 clearly consists of canines (nos. 19-21), but thereafter the list is less clear. The beaver and otter (nos. 22-23) are obviously together as river-dwelling, fur-bearing quadrupeds, but the next group of monkey, *Merkacza,* and cat poses an interesting problem. The first and third animals are secure, but what is the *Merkacza*? Relying on the modern German *Meerkatz,* a monkey, the editors of the PL have identified the creature as a species of monkey. Klein goes so far as to suggest the macaque (235). Yet Hildegard clearly spells out its habits, one of which, she says, is that it has the nature both of a wolf and a cat and that it hides its excrement in the sand. These traits are decidedly un-simian but they do fit a meerkat, much more cat-like and weasel-like than simian. If this is an accurate identification, we once more see Hildegard's mind at work. She groups the animals together, but each group is not part of a general overarching scheme. As wisant reminded her of cow and led her to the farm animals, so too here does *merkacza* move her train of thought into the area of cats and nos. 26-41 are generally taken up with the concept of "mousers." While some may be felines, they are linked to the mustelids by the fact that they all help destroy vermin, a major concern in the Middle Ages. In the middle of this sort of thinking we find the mouse itself, for another way of grouping the mustelids is that they are all "mice." Thus Albertus says: "MUSTELA—The weasel is a familiar animal, sort of a long mouse [*mus longa*] as it were, although in shape it is closer to the marten [*martarus*] than the mouse" (*De animalibus* 22.122; cf. Isidore, *Origines* 12.3.3). Likewise, Hildegard also feels it important to relate which of the fur-bearing creatures she lists provides pelts useful for human clothing. The results are surprising to modern eyes. Thus, the fox is bad to eat but its pelt is healthy and good for clothing (ch. 21). Squirrel fur is good (ch. 31) but that of the *illediso,* most likely a polecat, is not healthy because it brings cold to a person. Marten fur (ch. 33) is good because its sweat does not pass over into its pelt but stays in the flesh, but sable is not recommended for human clothing because the person wearing it sweats too much (ch. 35). Ermine, so valued in modern times, is not good because it is cold in nature. In similar fashion we read earlier that shoes made from whale-skin, unicorn (rhinoceros?) skin, or badger pelt will give you healthy feet and legs (5.1; 7.5, 28) whereas those made of dog skin (7.20) cause foot pain because the dog's inherent uncleanliness has passed out through its sweat into its skin. We thus see another facet of Hildegard's taxonomy, for animals are to be grouped by how useful they are, both for medicinal and clothing purposes. The book then ends with two insects (recall that insects also appear at the end of the previous book) and two animals which, since they only appear in the early editions, may or may not belong to this book.

It is clear that there is order at work in this grouping of animals. A quick glance back at the list of birds shows much the same process at work. Most raptors are close together as are most aquatic birds. We are far from the attempts to form the more elaborate taxonomies which will follow the revival of Aristotle, but we are equally far from the *Physiologus* and the bestiaries where no apparent order informs the listing of the animals. As we have seen before, Hildegard stands somewhere between the *Physiologus*/bestiary tradition and that of the natural philosophers of Albertus' generation.

Book 8 is entitled "De reptilibus" but really deals with a wide variety of vermin. A short book, it covers only eight columns and has eighteen entries. Most interesting is a fascinating story about where vermin came from. In the beginning, we are told, God made every creature good. But after the Devil used the serpent to deceive man and got him evicted from paradise some animals were changed in the divine plan to provide *ultio*, revenge or chastisement, on man and this was done with divine will. Prior to the fall there had been no poisonous animals, but when the earth was corrupted with the blood of Abel a certain cloud arouse and from this cloud all sorts of bad things were let loose on the world in a roiling mass. Moreover, after the flood, the *vermes* arose out of the mud and slime (8.Praef.1337-40). Book 9, consisting of only six columns and eight entries, quickly treats metals and the *Physica* ends on this abrupt note.

Let us close now with a consideration of Hildegard's relation to the *Physiologus* and the bestiaries. Again, Moulinier offers us admirable suggestions as to books to which Hildegard may have had access ("Encyclopédiste" 123f.) . Yet this is a difficult thread to pursue. While Hildegard may have had access to a copy of Pliny, much of his material also finds its way into various bestiaries. It is often very difficult to sort out such threads and be sure that this particular bit of information comes directly from Pliny or via the bestiary tradition. Let us instead concentrate on how Hildegard differs from the existing bestiary lore, for it is here that we find the text of the *Physica* has much to offer the diligent researcher.

If one works with bestiaries for any length of time it is clear that they delight in perpetuating popular and traditional tales about animals. While small details may differ, each bestiary will generally list the same most salient points about a given animal. When one reads Hildegard, therefore, it is surprising to notice that while she preserves some of the traditional lore, she often ignores a great deal of it and equally often substitutes some quite unique bits of her own lore in its place. The potential list of examples is quite large, but we will confine ourselves to a few very clear cases of this phenomenon.

The bear is a frequent bestiary animal. By far the most commonly repeated story about the bear, as old as antiquity, is that it licks its newborn, amorphous cubs into recognizable shape with its tongue (McCulloch 94). Likewise, it was commonly stated that they copulated face-to-face as do humans and monkeys (McDermott 262f.). In Hildegard's treatment of the bear (7.4.1316) we can see that she was aware of the tradition but seems to possess a different slant on her data. In Latin that is frustratingly unclear, she tells us that after Adam ate the apple our natures became somewhat more bestial. As a result bears will often sniff the air and when a person is "in libidine" the bear runs to the human from as far away as half a mile and demands sex. If the human refuses, the bear mauls the human. This is clearly linked to the face-to-face copulation belief mentioned above. In an intriguing aside, Hildegard is at pains to point out that the male bear only approaches human females and the female bear, men. She tells us that the she-bear is so impatient in giving birth that she aborts, and it is for this reason that the young are born unformed, causing the mother to grieve.

We thus see that Hildegard is both in and out of the normal animal-based folklore of her day. Likewise, the story of the self-castrating beaver was ubiquitous in Hildegard's time (McCulloch 95). While she mentions the efficacy of beaver testicles for her beloved medicine, Hildegard spends far more time passing on the unusual information that since the beaver partakes of the nature both of a land and a water animal, it cannot live long away from either element (7.22.1329). The camel does not appear in the *Physiologus* but is fairly common in the bestiaries (McCulloch 101-2), and several facts regularly occur—that there are two-humped and one-humped camels, that they hate horses, endure thirst well but stir up clear water to muddy it to their taste, and females are best for war purposes. Hildegard's treatment (7.2.1313-14) is delightful for the two varieties have merged to form a three-humped camel and each hump has a specific power. The hump near the neck has the strength of the *pardileo*, the middle one has the strength of the *pardus*, and the last one has the strength of a horse.[7]

As Moulinier points out, in Hildegard's list of *animalia* the elephant is listed first, as opposed to the lion, which invariably occupies first place in both the *Physiologus* and the bestiaries("Encyclopédiste" 130) . Yet Moulinier makes too much of this fact. Of more interest are the facts Hildegard has to offer about the elephant which do not appear in the other sources. For we are told that the elephant seeks out a land (or "earth," *terra,* but cf. col. 1318B) which has the "moisture of Paradise" (*succe de Paradiso*), and in that spot it digs for a long time with its foot while it inhales the odor of this moisture (7.1.1313). He does this, Hildegard tells us, to set in motion the mating instinct. Likewise, while she relates the usual story concerning the lion bringing its dead cubs back to life with its roar (McCulloch 137) she typically has an alternate version. In this story the lioness develops a loathing for the male after mating (probably a result of the pain commonly said to accompany their mating, though Hildegard does not mention this directly). Thinking her cubs stillborn, she abandons them. The male, seeing her and smelling the cubs, knows what is afoot and revives them with his roar. The lioness hears the roars, runs back, fights back the male and will not allow him to approach the cubs again until they are full grown (7.3.1314-15). This much is fairly new in the tradition and, moreover, it is somewhat accurate in that dominant males will kill some of their young. But the story immediately expands along the now familiar Paradise model. Hildegard tells us that this story parallels that of Adam and Eve who never had cried out in pain until children were born. When their first child was born, he immediately raised such a cry to the heavens that Adam came running up to see what this new noise was. He thereupon cried out for the first time and was joined by Eve, just as the lion, lioness, and cubs all roar in their birth scene (7.3.1315).

There are many such variants throughout the *Physica.* For Hildegard the hoof of the unicorn and not its horn detects poison, and she relates a fascinating tale about how an unnamed *philosophus* was the first to observe that a unicorn can be captured with a virgin, even conducting tests to prove his theory (7.5.1317-18). She knows that it is important for one's survival as to whether the human spies the wolf first or vice versa (cf. Albertus Magnus, *De animalibus,* 22.114) but she specifically says that it is the wolf's "airy spirits" which cause the mischief, passing over from the wolf to the person (7.19.1327). She knows about the monkey's tendency to "ape" whatever it sees but adds that it has a menstrual cycle based, as is the human's, on the moon and is thus the earliest medieval author to report this fact which is not to be found in the *Physiologus*/bestiary tradition (7.24. 1320; McDermott 78-79). Even the lowly mouse earns an interesting and apparently new story. A mouse who is about to give birth but is in some difficulty, is said to go to the banks of a river where it eats as many pebbles as it can hold (cf. Albertus Magnus, *De animalibus* 22.123). Returning to its hole, it spits these out, blows on them, lies on them to warm them and immediately gives birth. As a result such pebbles are powerful medicine for humans with birthing difficulties as well (7.39.1335).

There are many, many more such examples of this lore, apparently unique to Hildegard, and, as with the many other areas for future investigation suggested above, they all serve to show the treasurehouse of knowledge she possesses for the study of natural science and animal lore in the medieval period. A careful study of her sources will reveal even more. How much material contained in her stories and beliefs results from her local experience as a healer or just as a consumer of goods? How much can be said to be specifically Germanic? Such a careful study would also position her more precisely within the natural science movements of her day, removing any thought that she is a mere naive, local healer. Notice, for example, that we see few overt traces of the religious moralizations so prevalent in the *Physiologus* and bestiary traditions. The closest we get are the parallel stories linking humans and animals through her Paradise tales. She is moving more in the direction of understanding Nature in its pragmatic manifestations. By the same token, if her main aim is not one of moralization, she clearly does not yet possess the intense investigative and experiential drive of an Albertus Magnus in the next generation. She has passed beyond the randomness of the *Physiologus* and bestiary tradition and has imposed further order on the Hexaemeron tradition in an early attempt to see the world in a structured fashion. Yet we are far from the true encyclopedias or the alphabetic listing of animals with the almost modern sounding groupings of such authors as Albertus Magnus. We can thus begin to view Hildegard as a sort of liminal figure who may have been unaware of the new learning that was to sweep Europe but who nonetheless serves as a significant and individualistic bridge between the older learning and that which was to come.

No matter what the ultimate findings of such investigations, it is time for them to begin in earnest. A solid and fully collated text must be established in order to determine what Hildegard's text actually said.

Until that is done, however, much fruitful work is nonetheless possible in the fascinating and challenging text of the *Physica.*

## NOTES

1. The Latin text of the *Causae et curae* is found in Kaiser's edition and, despite its many errors, Kaiser's edition is indirectly the source for the English translation of Madigan and Kulas, who translated not from the original Latin but from Manfred Pawlik's German translation of the Latin text.

2. Cod. 6952 of the Bibliothéque Nationale in Paris (ca. 1425-1450), which formed the basis for the nineteenth-century edition in the *Patrologia latina*; Cod. Guelf. 56, Aug. 4° of the Herzog-August-Bibliothek in Wolfenbüttel (late thirteenth or early fourteenth century); and Cod. 2551 of the Bibliothéque Royale in Brussels (ca. 1450).

3. Ms. laur. Ashb. 1323 of the Biblioteca Medicea Laurenziana in Florence (ca. 1300); Cod. 178a of the Universitätsbibliothek in Freiburg (fifteenth century); Cod. Ferraioli 921 of the Biblioteca Apostolica Vaticana in Rome (end of fourteenth or early fifteenth century); Cod. Oettingen-Wallerstein III 1, 2° fol. 43 (last quarter of the fifteenth century) in the Universitätsbibliothek Augsburg (Weiss-Amer); and a recently rediscovered manuscript containing most of book one of the *Physica* in a German translation from 1456, Ms. germ. fol. 817 (fols. 2r-61v) of the Staatsbibliothek Preussischer Kulturbesitz in Berlin.

4. Klein, like Portmann, consulted the Wolfenbüttel manuscript, Cod. Guelf. 56, Aug. 4°, and Cod. 2551 of the Bibliothéque Royale in Brussels (Klein, 7-8). When these manuscripts help clarify obscurities in the Latin text of the *Patrologia Latina*, Klein supplies in her notes the readings from these other two manuscript sources.

5. References to the *Physica* indicate book, chapter and column in P.L. 197.

6. Albertus Magnus himself speaks frequently of the constant annoyance of such creatures in the *De animalibus.* Lice come in for frequent mention as being produced by the putrescence put forth by our pores, especially among boys who, when very hungry, eat fruit (*De animalibus,* 26.22). It was widely believed, for example, that wool taken from a sheep that had been killed by a wolf would produce lice to torment the garment's owner (*De animalibus,* 7.60; 22.116).

7. The pard is a spotted animal, most likely a cat. It may be a confusion for the panther or leopard which, in some texts, was thought to be the result of the mating of a lioness and a pard. "Pardileo" or "pard-lion" seems to maintain the same two elements of lion and pard. Secure identification is impossible (McCullough 150-151; White 13-14).

## WORKS CITED

### Primary Texts

Albertus Magnus. *Alberti Magni ex ordine praedicatorum de vegetabilibus libri VII.* Ed. Karl Jessen. Berlin: George Reimer, 1867.

_____. Eds. Kenneth F. Kitchell and Irven M. Resnick. *Albertus Magnus' On Animals: A Medieval Summa Zoologica.* Baltimore: Johns Hopkins University Press, forthcoming.

Hildegard of Bingen. *Hildegardis causae et curae.* Ed. Paul Kaiser. Bibliotheca scriptorum medii aevi Teubneriana. Leipzig: B.G. Teubner, 1903.

_____. *Heilwissen.* Trans. Manfred Pawlik. Augsburg: Pattloch Verlag, 1989.

_____. *Holistic Healing.* Trans. Patrick Madigan and John Kulas. Collegeville, MN: The Liturgical Press, 1994.

_____. *Le livre des subtilites des creatures divines: Physique.* Trans. Pierre Monat. 2nd ed. Grenoble: J. Millon, 1988--.

_____. *Physica S. Hildegardis elementorum, fluminum aliquot Germaniae, metallorum leguminum fructuum et herbarum: arborum et arbustorum: piscium denique volatilium et animantium terrae naturas et operationes IIII libris mirabili experientia posteritati tradens .* Argentorati: J. Schott, 1533.

_____. *Physica PL* 197:1117-1352. 1855. Basel: Société bâloise Hildegarde, 1982.

_____. *Physica: livresV-VI-VII-VIII .* Trans. Elisabeth Klein. Basel: Société bâloise Hildegarde, 1988.

*Physiologus latinus.* Ed. Frances Carmody. Paris: Librairie E. Droz, 1939.

*Physiologus .* Trans. Michael J. Curley. Austin: University of Texas Press, 1979.

*The Prose Salernitan Questions.* Ed. Brian Lawn. *Auctores britannici medii aevi V.* London: Oxford University Press, 1979.

Thomas of Cantimpré. *Liber de natura rerum.* Berlin: De Gruyter, 1973.

### Secondary Texts

Adamson, Melitta Weiss. "A Revaluation of Saint Hildegard's *Physica* in Light of the Latest Manuscript Finds." *Manuscript Sources of Medieval*

*Medicine: A Book of Essays* Ed. Margaret R. Schleissner. New York and London: Garland, 1995: 55-80.

Aiken, Pauline. "The Animal History of Albertus Magnus and Thomas of Cantimpré." *Speculum* 22(1947):205-25.

Clark, Willene. *The Medieval Book of Birds. Hugh of Fouilloy's Aviarium.* Binghamton: MRTS, 1992.

_____. "Zoology in the Medieval Latin Bestiary." *Sewanee Mediaeval Studies* 6(1995):223-45.

Engbring, Gertrude M. "Saint Hildegard, Twelfth-Century Physician." *Bulletin of the History of Medicine* 8 (1940):770-84.

Entrich, Manfred, ed. *Albertus Magnus: sein Leben und seine Bedeutung*. Graz: Styria, 1982.

Grzimek, Bernhard, ed. *Grzimek's Animal Life Encyclopedia.* 13 vols. New York: Van Nostrand Reinhold, 1972-75.

Lexer, Matthias. *Mittelhochdeutsches Handwörterbuch.* 3 vols. Leipzig: S. Hirzel, 1872-78.

Mandonnet, Pierre. "La date de naissance d' Albert le Grand." *Revue Thomiste* 36(1931):233- 56.

McCulloch, Florence. *Mediaeval Latin and French Bestiaries.* Chapel Hill: University of North Carolina Press, 1960.

McDermott, William Coffman. *The Ape in Antiquity.* Baltimore: Johns Hopkins University Press, 1938.

Moulinier, Laurence. "L'abbesse et les poissons: un aspect de la zoologie de Hildegarde de Bingen." *Exploitation des animaux sauvage à travers le temps.* XIII^e Recontres internationales d'Archéologie et d'Histoire d'Antibes. Iv^e Colloque international de l'Homme et l'Animal. Juan-les-Pin, APDCA, 1993: 461-72.

_____. "Une encyclopédiste sans précédent? Le cas de Hildegarde de Bingen," *L'enciclopedismo medievale: Atti del convengno "L'enciclopedismo medievale," San Gimignano 8-10 Ottobre 1992*. Ed. Michelangelo Picone. Ravenna: Longo, 1994, 119-34.

Portmann, Marie-Louise. Trs. *Heilmittel: Erste vollständiger und wortgetreue Übersetzung, bei der alle Handschriften berücksichtigt sind.* 6 vols. Basel: Basler Hildegard-Gesellschaft, 1982-84.

Reithe, Peter. *Das Buch von den Tieren*. Salzburg: Otto Muller, 1996.

Rowland, Beryl. *Birds with Human Souls. A Guide to Bird Symbolism.* Knoxville: University of Tennessee Press, 1978.

Salisbury, Joyce. *The Beast Within. Animals in the Middle Ages.* New York: Routledge, 1994.

Sanders, Willy. "Albertus Magnus und das Rheinische." *Rheinische Vierteljahrsblätter* 42(1978): 402-54.

Singer, Charles. "The Scientific Views and Visions of Saint Hildegard (1098-1180)." *Studies in the History and Method of Science*. Ed. C. Singer. Vol. 1. London: Dawson and Sons, 1955, 1-55.

_____. *A History of Biology*, rev. ed. London: Abelard-Schumann, 1959.

Suolahti, Hugo. *Die deutschen Vogelnamen. Eine wortgeschichtliche Untersuchung* . Strassburg: Trübner, 1905,

Thompson, D'Arcy. *A Glossary of Greek Birds*. London: Oxford, 1936.

Thorndike, Lynn. *A History of Magic and Experimental Science*. 2nd ed. Vol. 2 New York: Mac Millan Co., 1929, 124-54.

Weisheipl, James A. "The Life and Works of St. Albert the Great." *Albertus Magnus and the Sciences. Commemorative Essays, 1980*. Ed. James A. Weisheipl. Toronto: Pontifical Institute, 13-23.

Weiss-Amer, Melitta. "Die 'Physica' Hildegards von Bingen als Quelle für das 'Kochbuch Meister Eberhards'." *Sudhoffs Archviv* 76/1(1992): 87-96.

Wood, Casey and Marjorie F. Fyfe. *The Art of Falconry. Being the* De Arte Venandi cum Avibus *of Frederick II of Hohenstaufen*. 1943. Boston: Charles and Bradford, 1955.

# Hildegard of Bingen's
## *Causes and Cures*
## A Radical Feminist Response to the Doctor-Cook Binary

*Marcia Kathleen Chamberlain*

Critic Timothy Valentine once called Hildegard von Bingen a "figure with potential for superstardom in the 1990s," and his prediction has come true (20). During the past few years scholars and enthusiasts in diverse fields have been making valuable new insights and arguments about the life and work of the twelfth-century German abbess. In fact, a cottage industry has literally sprung up around the multi-faceted nun.[1] Religion scholars now note the myriad ways in which Hildegard von Bingen presented herself as a unique mystic and messenger for God. Iconologists highlight the detailed and imaginative symbolism of the religious visions which she recorded. Musicologists praise the innovative manner in which she altered and re-wrote traditional Gregorian chant structure. Linguists argue that Hildegard's *Lingua ignota* is the only imaginary language that still exists intact from the Middle Ages. And an increasing number of homeopathic doctors and herbalists now use Hildegard's medical prescriptions and cures in their daily practices. No one to my knowledge, however, has written yet about Hildegard's tantalizing feminist intervention into the volatile twelfth-century doctor-cook debate. My particular reading of Hildegard's medical text *Causes and Cures*, then, is a contribution to and complication of the growing corpus of scholarship which is stacking up in the Hildegard cottage.[2]

In this paper, I will address Hildegard's rejection of the long-standing doctor-cook binary which tended to uplift what was traditionally thought of as men's work and belittle what was traditionally thought of as women's work.[3] To put her contribution into historical perspective, I will contrast the hierarchical relationship posited so forcefully between medicine and cookery in Plato's *Gorgias* with Hildegard's indirect feminist challenge to it fifteen hundred years later in *Causes and Cures* in order to suggest that a self-described "poor little womanly figure" in twelfth-century Germany made a radical narrative intervention into a long and misogynistic tradition.[4]

Since Carl Jessen's nineteenth-century discovery of a thirteenth/fourteenth-century copy of Hildegard's medical text in the Royal Library in Copenhagen, critics have been hypothesizing about why *Causes and Cures* disappeared from sight for so many centuries. One theory is that Hildegard's work was a part of the old intellectual history which fell out of favor and of use when the new science arrived in Germany (Cannon 60). Another theory is that the book's biting criticisms of the clergy worked against its survival within later religious communities (Cannon 61). I add to the list of possibilities the argument that Hildegard's feminist deconstruction of the doctor-cook binary created a backlash against her text and contributed to its suppression.[5]

Before making clear the particular aspects of *Causes and Cures* I see as feminist, I want to quote briefly from several strong arguments which have been made by contemporary critics about Hildegard's lack of feminism. Bernhard Scholz, for instance, states emphatically that Hildegard was "not a voice. . . advocating a more enlightened attitude towards woman" (380); Sabina Flanagan insists that she "identified with the male literary and theological elite" (44); Andrew Weeks argues that she was a "champion" of "the patriarchal power structure" (47), and Barbara Newman, who first described Hildegard's theology as feminine, nonetheless writes that in terms of feminism Hildegard "did not call for radical change" (20).

Scholz, Flanagan, Weeks, and Newman correctly question the tendency of other scholars such as Samuel Gladden, Gabriele Uhlein, Matthew Fox, and Paula Martin to embrace Hildegard unproblematically as the newest of the old feminists. Gladden, for instance, announces with gusto that Hildegard was "an early proponent of women's rights" (219); Uhlein associates her ideas as part of a powerful "medieval feminist swell" (18); Fox praises Hildegard for a courageous social and spiritual "theology of liberation" (10); and

Martin says that she developed an important "non-misogynistic construct" for medieval women (235). This paper purposefully draws on the insights and enthusiasms of both "sets" of critics. I present convincing signs of feminism in Hildegard's *Causes and Cures*, but I do so in as local and historicized a manner as possible.

Certainly Hildegard's book was radical enough in twelfth-century Germany to have scared men in religious as well as scientific circles. Rather than just elevating the activity of women's cooking to a new level and perhaps reinscribing women within the domestic sphere, *Causes and Cures* actually expands the kinds of roles available for women. First, it authorizes and elevates traditional women's work, specifically the activity of cooking, by making God into the cosmic chef of creation. It was safe theologically and scientifically to see God in terms of the first half of the doctor-cook binary. In the *Scivias*, for instance, Hildegard's God announces outright: "I am the great Physician of all diseases and act like a doctor who sees a sick man who longs to be cured" (104). But representing God as a "mere" cook was another thing altogether. In *Holy Feast and Holy Fast: The Religious Significance of Food to Medieval Women*, Carolyn Walker Bynum points out the radical step taken by religious women of the thirteenth and fourteenth centuries who imagined Christ in the feminine role of food preparer. Hildegard precedes these women by at least a century and even outdoes them by presenting not Jesus but God in that role. In this way, Hildegard identifies herself and other women with a powerful God who during the sacred moment of creation heads not to the laboratory but to the kitchen to mix up a batch of matter and then bake it into human beings.

While raising the status of common cookery in *Causes and Cures*, Hildegard simultaneously attacks the privileged status given to the practice of medicine. She does this by erasing the rigid line separating it from cookery in order to show that its meanings, including what constitutes the practice of it and what does not, are culturally influenced. Her own medical recipes at the end of the treatise boldly declare her to be an accomplished cook as well as healer. Far from being exclusive categories, medicine and cookery are inextricably linked for Hildegard. Thus, *Causes and Cures* exposes the impossibility of the terms in a binary relationship ever staying intact and untouchable on their own sides. Hildegard makes it clear that doctoring, like cooking, is messy business.

Twentieth-century critics are as nervous about this messiness as Hildegard's contemporaries were. Although Hildegard is cited by some contemporary historians as one of Germany's first woman doctors, her medical text is often dismissed as less promising than her complex visionary works (Kraft 117-18). Or, it is treated as idiosyncratic. Newman, for instance, calls *Causes and Cures* " a series of haphazardly compiled jottings" (126); Joan Cadden describes it as "eclectic and unsystematic" (70); Flanagan deems it "raw material" (105). And Peter Dronke, who sees the book as having a "wider outlook," nonetheless suggests that the tension between Hildegard's theological side and her scientific side contributed to a potpourri-like mixture of material and ideas in *Causes and Cures* (172-3).

To their credit, each of these critics disagrees with Charles Singer's 1928 comment that *Causes and Cures* is nothing more than "an interesting relic of Dark Age medicine" whose authorship by Hildegard is dubious (199-239). In fact, they are united in seeking to recuperate Hildegard's text as a significant and innovative twelfth-century medical work. On the other hand, they all seem compelled to apologize in subtle and not so subtle ways for the book's unstructured, unscientific and unfinished format. And it is true that Hildegard's unusual juxtaposition of images and her use of mixed metaphors—such as God as both cook and doctor—create some awkward moments which do not square up with binary thinking. But this is exactly Hildegard's point. The very scrambledness of *Causes and Cures* challenges and mocks the clear distinctions between medicine and cookery, which are presented in an "ordered" and "logical" text such as Plato's *Gorgias*.

Plato's *Gorgias* is one of the earliest and most eloquent proponents for the strict separation of medicine and cookery. Although only some of Plato's texts were circulating in twelfth-century Germany, his ideas about everything from philosophy to cosmology were in the air, literally a "part of the natural 'climate' of the Middle Ages" (Gregory 54). Critics disagree about which specific Platonic texts Hildegard might have read. Dronke, for example, says that there is no evidence that Hildegard ever read the *Timaeus* (183); Sue Cannon, on the other hand, thinks that *Causes and Cures* exhibits a "strong influence of the *Timaeus*" which would have been available to Hildegard in the twelfth century through a sixth-century translation by Boethius (12-13). Newman asserts that whether or not Hildegard herself read Plato, she must have come across commentaries on many of his works in the monastic libraries (68). But even if Hildegard never read the *Gorgias* or commentaries on it, and no one has uncovered yet any convincing evidence that she did, her text *Causes and Cures* curiously responds to the ancient issues regarding medicine and cookery that the *Gorgias* raises. Hildegard refers to the historical figure of Plato in *Causes and Cures* just once, as one of the "pagans" of the past who survived by God-given grace despite the fact that his humors were perpetually out of balance (46). Her description of Plato as an unbalanced man seems to make fun of the philosopher who has Socrates pontificate so confidently in the *Gorgias* about the perfect blend of properties needed in order to maintain balance and order in the individual body as well as the body politic.[6]

The dialogues of the *Gorgias* occur in the private sphere of the home where Socrates, Gorgias, Polus, Chaerephon, and Callicles are gathered. It is no wonder that the first exchange in the *Gorgias* regards feasts and food. Theodore and Lin Humphrey argue that "to understand how food 'works,' how it operates in different 'networks,' how it 'communicates,' then one of the best ways is to look at situations where its power is most heightened" (7). A home, even if it is associated in the dialogue with the masculine presence of Callicles, nevertheless qualifies as one such heightened environment because women's power is linked so intimately to food and to food preparation. Given this setting, it is not surprising that an anxiety about cookery and its place within a structured, balanced society keeps re-surfacing among the men in this dialogue.

Critics George Kennedy and Brian Vickers argue convincingly that Plato's class affiliation in many ways pre-determines his philosophy in the *Gorgias* and that by implication, it also shapes the analogies he draws on to express that philosophy (15: 88-89). They are silent, however, about how Plato's gender affiliation might have affected his choice and interpretation of analogies. Medicine and cookery, for example, were far from gender-neutral categories. This is one reason that Plato's protagonist Socrates becomes so adamant about prying apart the practice of cookery, associated with womanly pleasure, from the practice of medicine, a manly pursuit.

Yet some of the distinctions between medicine and cookery were slighter than the philosophers and the physicians cared to admit. Plato's contemporary, Hippocrates, whose medical works were widely available in the twelfth century, also wanted to put some well-defined distance between the activities performed by doctors and those by cooks. As a physician caught up in the fifth- and fourth- century B.C. struggle to make his profession reliable and respectable, Hippocrates grudgingly has to admit in his book *On Ancient Medicine* that daily food intake is the greatest determinant in one's degree of health or illness because it is the primary way in which the four humors are kept in balance.[7] And since women are disproportionately involved in the daily activity of cooking, it follows that they are also the ones most likely to be in charge of and knowledgeable about the intricate bodily processes of life and death.

This last conclusion panics Hippocrates, who stops short of it by quickly noting that medicine does indeed differ from cookery "in appearance, and that the one is more complicated and needs more study" (74). Predictably, these veiled qualifications bring his views right back to the hierarchical viewpoint of Plato. The term "appearance" might be read broadly to include differences in gender, a factor which automatically limited the category or profession to which one could aspire to or be assigned. The Hippocratic Oath, for instance, prohibited the "complicated" study of medicine by women by emphasizing a teaching and a practicing lineage which passed from father to son. Although there was no official system of medical licensure in Hippocrates' day, women could not qualify as practitioners. Society would not allow a woman even to use the title of physician in conjunction with her name (Lyons and Petrucelli 196).

In contrast, most women were required to practice everyday cookery and so became skilled through hands-on experimentation in the combining of foods and in health-related, humoral matters. Yet Plato's Socrates lectures Gorgias that what women such as these do and know compares meagerly to what real doctors do and know: "[c]ookery simulates the disguise of medicine, and pretends to know what food is best for the body.... [it] is a flattery which takes the form of medicine.... false, ignoble, illiberal, [and] spurious" (355). Socrates later pairs off cookery with cosmetics and depicts both as degraded and illusory forms of true arts because they titillate the appetite and appeal to fleeting tastes.

If philosophical and societal order are to be maintained, it is to Plato's advantage to delimit cookery's sphere of influence and to insist that peril is at hand if cookery overlaps with the practice of medicine. In fact, Socrates tries to convince his listeners that "chaos" will break out if "cookery, health, and medicine ... mingle in an indiscriminate mass" (336). In the*Gorgias*, balance depends upon order, and order depends upon graded distinctions. Plato does not suggest that medicine and cookery have nothing to do with one another; rather he has Socrates elaborate on the inequality of their relationship. This gender-inflected analogy becomes a stand-in for other more abstract binary relationships in the*Gorgias* so that cookery is to medicine what rhetoric is to justice: mere imitation and flattery.[8] In *Gorgias* Plato establishes that only physicians know what is best for the body, that it is the doctors and not the cooks who are the real caretakers of individual bodies and by extension, the body politic and justice itself.

Of course, the idea that cookery was a lesser form of medicine had origins in the body/mind distinction which had already been made by Plato in earlier dialogues. Michel Jeanneret points out that this kind of dualism automatically "provided the general framework for a dichotomy . . . between the stomach and the head" (81). While the head represented reason, the stomach represented the downward pull of the body and its desires. According to Jeanneret, it would not have been unusual to locate the kitchen itself as a dangerous site of temptation where one's ability to reason literally could be clouded and clogged by steam (80). The Christian church later built this concept into its pedagogical narratives. It interpreted Jesus's telling of the Mary-and-Martha story, for instance, to mean that in the kitchen "[c]ooks ministered to bodily needs which by their very nature were inferior to spiritual ones" (Henisch 67). If one valued one's intellectual and spiritual health, one stayed out of the kitchen—this warning was meant on the religious/symbolic level as well as the practical level.[9]

What Jeanneret and Bridget Henisch fail to point out is that this kind of advice could not have been followed by most women from Plato's or Jesus's time period because most of them were tied to the kitchen, bound up in the daily processes of food preparation and distribution. During the past three decades, feminists have managed to re-claim domestic spaces such as the kitchen as important sites of knowledge and interpretation. Some have argued that gender was created at the same time as the kitchen, that it "developed out of the division of labor in food production" (Hastorf 134). Others have analyzed the assumptions behind such dualisms as public/private, culture/nature, mind/body, and male/female, arguing that such dichotomies are never equally paired oppositions, but distinct hierarchical constructs with very problematic gender implications.[10] This paper adds the doctor/cook binary to that list only to show the ways in which Hildegard's *Causes and Cures* deconstructs it.

Fifteen hundred years after Plato and Hippocrates, concern about the relationship between doctors and cooks was still appearing in various kinds of writings of the Middle Ages. Hugh of St. Victor, a twelfth-century theologian like Hildegard, declares the following in his c.1120 *Didascalicon*: "Let no one be disturbed that among the means employed by medicine I count food and drink. . . . the preparing of food belongs to. . . the kitchen, but the strength given by its consumption, to medicine" (79). Like Hippocrates, Hugh of St. Victor expresses his anxiety about the seeming instability of the cultural work roles for men and for women. He wants to reassure men of the important split between the effeminate tasks performed in the kitchen and the virile work performed in the laboratory. In order to do this, he needs to prove that cookery and medicine operate in different spheres.

Reasons for this continued investment in distinguishing between kitchen and laboratory work reflect the massive twelfth-century movements taking place in medicine. It makes sense that twelfth-century men would seek to establish, once and for all, the elusive difference between cooks and doctors at exactly that moment when medicine was moving into the supposedly more scientific and controlled atmosphere of the university. The time for this sort of argument was ripe because for the first time in history there was the beginning of an organized university system in which standardized medicine was taught and degrees conferred.

Hildegard lived during this chaotic transitional time and she witnessed firsthand the push to specialize the field of medicine. The institutionalization of medicine even affected her religious order. The founder of the Benedictines, St. Benedict of Nursia, had established his first order on Monte Cassino in 529—about six centuries before Hildegard's birth. The original monastery was on the site of an ancient temple built to honor the Greek god of healing Apollo (Lyons and Petrucelli 283). St. Benedict, though, wanted nothing to do with the Greeks or their pagan gods; he absolutely forbade the secular study of medicine in his order and instituted instead what he called a Healing Mission. This provided that each monastery would have sick cloisters but that prayer and divine intervention would be the only means employed to cure disease.

By the late Middle Ages, though, the Benedictines had departed widely from their founder's principles. They were well known for their medical contributions and even encouraged their own members in the reading, studying, and copying of certain pagan medical texts from antiquity. A reform movement in the twelfth century tried to purge these secular impulses of the Benedictine order by limiting, and in some cases prohibiting, the study and practice of medicine by its clerics (Cannon 78-9). But even if this internally motivated reform movement had not been successful, outside forces would have come to bear sooner or later. Increasingly, the study and practice of medicine were being reserved for designated spaces and select faces.

This upheaval was difficult for many religious women because the shift in the world of medicine involved its transferal out of the monastic realm, which had allowed them to practice in various approved and non-threatening capacities for over five hundred years, into the university, where women soon were to be excluded altogether (Labarge 174). Outside the monastery, secular women who practiced medicine lacked a religious vote of confidence in their work, so the crackdown on them was particularly severe. Men suddenly felt threatened by the number of secular and religious women, or "lay healers," whose "folk remedies" the general populace seemed to prefer over the scientific cures of the new university-trained doctors (Williams and Echols 49). By the fifteenth century, European women who practiced medicine had been thoroughly discredited on a large public scale; their healing arts had been tied to witchcraft and black magic (Benedek 156).

Hildegard, though, was protected from these scandals, especially during her formative years. Jutta von Sponheim, the Benedictine nun who took Hildegard in at age eight, had some medical knowledge which she imparted to Hildegard, who served in her early years as the infirmarian of the monastery at Disibodenberg. According to Marty Williams and Anne Echols, it is likely that Hildegard not only diagnosed and cared for both male and female patients but that she also grew and experimented with her own herbs (47). Indeed most medieval houses as well as the religious orders had their own gardens which provided herbs for meals as well as for the treatment of disease.[11]

According to Scholz, Hildegard may have shown an early interest in health issues precisely because she was sick so much of the time. He describes her life as "a series of maladies" which constantly spurred her on in her personal studies of physiology and therapeutics (364). Caroline Molina provides a more psychoanalytic interpretation when she posits the thesis that Hildegard learned at a young age "the disruptive potential of disease" and that she summoned up planned illnesses throughout her life in order "to disrupt the notion of the body as a scientifically knowable, controllable object" (90). In *Causes and*

*Cures* Hildegard never mentions her sicknesses, planned or unplanned, but she does represent bodies as coded objects whose mysteries have been revealed to her—and to women in general—by God.

According to Hildegard, the "bowels" and the "elements" of nature "behave in a corresponding manner," and ordinary women are the caretakers and interpreters of this code which Adam scrambles up when he disobeys God (16). In her story, Adam becomes the "man who consumes food like a glutton, who does not eat at the proper times" (16). His lack of control wreaks havoc in his body and in the heavens and sets off an exchange of crazy signals between the two. Suddenly, the rain "does not bring the proper coolness," the sun "cannot bring the proper heat," and the stomach cannot do its "proper" work (125). Eve's and Adam's gluttony in Eden and its far-reaching consequences were both common medieval themes, but Hildegard gives two added twists to the old story. First, she dramatically plays up Adam's sinful behavior and second, she proposes that women are the key to re-establishing right communion between the bowels, the elements, and God. Cookery enables women to crack the three-way relational code because it teaches them how "harmoniously" to maintain the humors in "their correct proportion" and "proper amount" (45).

A number of critics have discussed the ways in which Hildegard's birth into a noble German family and later her entry into the elite Benedictine order with its strong aristocratic ties limited her understanding of class issues and made her immune to her own privilege. Dronke talks about "Hildegard's snobbishness" (200); Scholz says that she "vehemently insisted on the prerogatives of her class" (369); and Newman stresses that she was "[p]roudly aware of belonging to a social and spiritual elite" (9). As accurate as these statements are in a general context, they do not necessarily take into account the message and metaphors of *Causes and Cures*. Terence Scully's in-depth research on hundreds of medieval cookbooks, including medical ones, reveals an aristocratic style and upper-bourgeois content which Hildegard's earthy kitchen vocabulary in *Causes and Cures* works against. Rather than showcasing her knowledge of scented finger-waters, expensive cutlery, and exotic roasting techniques, Hildegard again and again turns to simple images: a small pot, a well-heated oven, some boiling water.[12]

Williams and Echols suggest that the wealthy households such as the one that Hildegard lived in as a small child could have hired chefs to concoct elaborate dishes. But by the time that Hildegard was writing

*Causes and Cures*, she had moved into the Rupertsberg abbey where the nuns were responsible for meeting their own daily needs, including meals. For the first time in her life perhaps, Hildegard was in intimate contact with an all-women community for whom cooking simply was a daily chore. Even if it is not possible to say for certain that Hildegard actually took her turn in fixing meals at the abbey, it is possible to say that in *Causes and Cures* Hildegard uses the idea of cookery to bring women, including those from less privileged backgrounds, into dialogue with God. She crosses a class boundary to raise common cookery to a new status; it becomes a vital process by which many medieval women are able to turn "staple into symbol" (Humphrey 3)— a point which twelfth-century men such as Hugh of St. Victor no doubt found disturbing, regardless of which class of women were doing it.

Indeed the transformation of staple into symbol becomes an important theme in *Causes and Cures*. At creation God uses cookery to show how it is done: matter becomes something other and more when God touches it, just like food. According to Hildegard, God apparently has time to hone his cooking skills before having to create the first human beings. She notes in Part I of her book, for instance, that stormy weather is caused by an unbalanced mixture of fire, air, water, and earth, that it is "like what happens when a kettle is placed over a hot fire. . . [and] boils up and froths over the sides" (3). But God also knows or learns how to cook "upon a mild fire" and to combine the four elements in "ideal proportion" to bring about "good weather" (3).

In Part II of *Causes and Cures* God graduates from making rain and sunshine to making a human being; he mixes just the right amount of fire and elements to make the ideal man. She indicates that Adam's "flesh became hot because of fire" and that "[h]e was cooked" into being (40). God is the expert chef in her story: he knows how to combine the four elements for the perfect amount of time in order to produce a fleshy, fully-done human being complete with all its appendages. Hildegard next imagines something very radical: after the initial act of creation during which God transforms a clump of clay into "a prophet" (40), the descendants of Eve take over for God the human cooking and prophet-making process. Hildegard explains that Eve's body was more moist and airy than Adam's because it was not cooked by hot fires; her creativity, Hildegard suggests, was not dried out. This, in turn, makes Eve's body more suitable later to perform "the artistic work" of human cookery which God invented and engaged in during creation (54).

It is important to note that God's gift to Eve of human cookery gains its significance only after Adam eats the apple in Eden. Hildegard notes that as a result of "this meal," a black, melancholic bile is released into Adam's bloodstream, and it becomes "the cause of all serious disease in humans" (35). The bile disrupts the natural combination of elements in a person and makes him sick. Because of Adam, sickness now can be inherited; men pass on the curse to other generations through their "thin and. . . undercooked" semen (30). Hildegard breaks from tradition when she attributes both men's and women's many ailments to Adam's sinful nature. There are apparently no negative health consequences as a result of Eve's eating of the fruit of the tree of knowledge, except that she begins menstruating. According to Hildegard, after she eats the apple Eve's blood needs to be "periodically cleansed. . . [i]n the same way [that] food cooking in the pot is cleansed when it throws off its foam from itself" (91). Once a woman conceives, her superfluous menstrual foam turns into white milk and is redirected to her breasts (99). Thus, Eve's curse becomes a blessing in disguise. In *Causes and Cures* women are not blamed harshly for their own appetites or sicknesses; instead they are lauded for their abilities to cook and cure. The ability to cook is locked within their own blood and wombs, which are like female pressure cookers, mixing and warming elements together in their "correct proportion" until the meal is ready (45). The biological lessons of human procreation, especially women's part in that delicate elemental balancing process, become Hildegard's basis for the lessons of good health.

Men, on the other hand, are associated from the very beginning of *Causes and Cures* with disease and death. After the serpent food poisons Adam's health and makes his semen cold and bitter, the human elemental state goes awry in everyone, men and women. Eve's postlapsarian responsibilities include overcoming the coldness and bitterness of the corrupted male seed, a feat Hildegard can help Eve to accomplish only through a re-writing of the medical literature passed down from antiquity. This literature insisted that a woman's nature was cold and a man's nature was hot, an idea which Hildegard strategically reverses (Cadden 79). The cold semen of men is "only a poisonous foam until the fire, that is the warmth, warms it" (55). In *Causes and Cures* the woman's womb literally becomes an oven where a child's flesh is concocted "through the warmth of the mother" (55).[13] This cave "holds the flesh [of the unborn child] together with a bloody slime and a constant moisture just as food is cooked in a pot by the fire" (56). Just like God, the divine cook, the woman now is responsible for making sure that the transformation of matter into something "more" continues and that a human being's properties are properly combined and cooked to perfection inside of her.

Hildegard stresses that women's bodies are perfectly created to carry out this task successfully, since "the elements are more active in them than in men, and the humors more abundant" (93). Their wombs are hotter and their stomachs are stronger. Hildegard comments that unlike a man's, a woman's membranes are "thicker and tougher," thus better designed for giving birth and for upholding the stresses of eating all kinds of foods (88). Men, she implies, might have more severe problems with their digestive tracts and intestines because they lack the warmth inside which would cook the food and thus make it digestible. A person who suffers from vomiting, for instance, "is cold within his stomach" and "has nothing warm within himself whereby the foods he eats can be broken down through digestion" (134). For Hildegard, the human body is like a kitchen. Women's bodies contain hotter furnaces than men's, which is why their systems have the best chance of cooking everything properly, whether that be a human being or lunch.

Significantly, Hildegard refuses to say anything about women literally cooking lunch; she keeps women's cookery at the level of abstract symbol and metaphor until the end of *Causes and Cures* when she introduces her set of medical recipes. One way she manages to do this is to emphasize only the internal bodily aspect of women's cooking ability. She then associates the hidden fruit-bearing flame inside a woman's body with another inner force, the powerful spiritual fire. She writes, "Just as ordinary dishes are changed into better-tasting dishes by the addition of seasonings and peppers. . . so is the ordinary nature of a person transformed through the fire of the Holy Spirit into a better sort" (18). In this framework, women become religious cooks who, like the Holy Spirit, know how to use spices and fire to change "cheap food" into "better food."[14] Attention is diverted from women's work in actual kitchens in order to show that their skills are required in other important arenas of transformation—namely, the Christian arena—as well.

By making women into agents who transform sickness and savagery into health and Christian civilization, Hildegard recasts herself and other women as powerful actors—cooks and healers who are integral to the progress of the human race. For instance, Hildegard warns that men who masturbate alone or with animals produce "thin, cloudy, and half-cooked foam similar to skim milk, for it was not heated by the fire" of a woman (122). She explains matter-of-factly that men's juices naturally are more weak and that their desires cannot be satisfied without women's fire. Finally, she instructs skim-milk men that the key to "fat, full marrow" is the participation of women (122). The process of civilization requires that men seek to unite with women in sexual love, thus "stirring and boiling their substances" together (Scholz 375). Men, warns Hildegard, should be more careful to squirt their seed into the proper place, just like "a cooked dish is taken out of a pot and put onto a plate to be eaten"; it is not "throw[n]. . . on the ground" (122). Hildegard invokes basic social rules of stove and table etiquette here to lecture men about their sexual behavior. Paradoxically, it was male writers such as Petrus Alphonsi who in the twelfth century were producing popular compositions on table manners to guide diners in proper behavior (Scully 175).

Fiery, as opposed to foamy, men present a different problem for Hildegard. To deal with them, she still makes use of her cooking metaphor, but she suddenly changes the terms so that now men are the ones with all the fire. Unlike women, though, "hot" men do not use their heat in the service of civilization. She compares their passion to "the fire of a volcano" or "a strongly burning wood fire" (121). In contrast to the potentially destructive blaze raging in them, Hildegard says that women have "a mild warmth that streams out from the sun and brings forth fruit" (121). Women creatively seem able to adjust their internal ovens to compensate for the temperatures of various men. To counteract weak foam, women become fiery furnaces; to counteract masculine fire, women become the tempering forces which keep everything from being burned to a crisp.

Hildegard's claim that women have special expertise in mixing things in their proper proportions has far-reaching ramifications, especially when it comes to their right to the practice of medicine. Hildegard strategically tries to build the confidence of the male monastic community in her medical cookery by prefacing her recipes with a dynamic story about God's and women's work together in the kitchen of creation. This allows her at the end of *Causes and Cures* to translate a symbolic blessing of women's bodies and the work they do into practical advantage; for women, the practice of cookery quite naturally leads to the practice of medicine. By including a set of her own recipes for curing illnesses at the end of *Causes and Cures*, Hildegard drives home her point that women can be doctors too.

In fact, the recipe section seems to imply that not even the move of medicine into universities will alter this fact because the kind of women's knowledge which she has been writing about is God-given and internal. For these reasons, women can never be completely stripped of their natural abilities in the areas of cookery and medicine. Historians are still debating which medical texts and catalogues Hildegard herself may have read or had access to through the monastic libraries in her vicinity. In *Causes and Cures*, though, she refers to none of them. Instead she quotes the Bible and states that her medical recipes are the result of divine inspiration. Putting her ideas into a theological paradigm may have been simply a smart way for Hildegard to present her medical activities. She gives credit to a distant God but completely ignores the male medical community and its texts from which she had probably learned and likely even borrowed.

Among others, Cadden, Newman, and Cannon note that the content of Hildegard's medical recipes closely resembles that of many other recorded herb recipes which were available in the twelfth century.[15] In the context of Hildegard's book, though, the recipes deserve additional comment. Susan Leonardi writes that "the root of recipe—the Latin *recipere*—implies an exchange" and that "like a story, a recipe needs a recommendation, a context, a point, a reason to be" (127). Hildegard's medical recipes are unlike those written down by men, such as Hippocrates' recipes in *On Herbs and Cures,* because as a woman she was involved in a different set of societal exchanges than they were. Even if the ingredients are the same, the larger meanings are not.

I am arguing that Hildegard's creation-centered concoction story at the beginning of her book significantly affects the reception of the recipes which follow. For instance, she prescribes the following cure for digestive problems:

> Take ginger, grind it up, mix it with a little juice from the plant that is called marigold, and then take some flour and make small cakes out of this powder. Bake these cakes in the oven when the heat of the fire has already begun to be tamped down, and consume these small cakes both before and after breakfast. (158)

There is nothing particularly unusual about this formulaic herbal cure, but the practical use of the word *bake* in this section of the medical book resonates with its richer, more metaphoric, uses at the beginning of *Causes and Cures*. It serves to remind readers of God's decision to deliver over the work of cookery, or creation, to women and at the same time it manages to give cookery a concrete meaning which can be used to women's advantage in the everyday world. Because they understand the secrets of keeping things in proportion, women occupy an important position in *Causes and Cures*. They become God's co-partners in the making and the taking care of creation, two activities which Hildegard has gone out of her way to show are intertwined.

The recipe section of her book clearly acknowledges that things in God's creation have gone wrong, and it subtly blames the fallen state of affairs on men. There is carnal lust, for instance, which Hildegard associates with men in the heat of summer and for which she suggests the following cure:

> [T]ake dill and a double amount of stream mint, a little more cowslip
> than stream mint, twice as much from the root of the Illyrium sword
> lily as stream mint, and as much shallot. . . . Cut up these ingredients
> and put them in vinegar, make a seasoning out of it, and then use it
> on every possible dish. (172)

Prescribing this cold dressing or gravy for "every possible dish" is an exaggerated reminder to men that they are out of kilter with themselves and with the universe.

Some of Hildegard's concepts in *Causes and Cures* are innovative; many are not.[16] I think that Hildegard's unique depiction of creation as a process of concoction which is closely tied to women's bodies and women's work stands out, especially when it is tied to the practice of medicine. As various critics point out, Hildegard often managed to upset the rules which were supposed to govern her and determine her sphere. Leonardi points out that the Latin word for "rule" used to be synonymous with recipe (134), and Hildegard bends both to suit her feminist purposes. In *Causes and Cures* Hildegard practices both cookery and medicine and moreover, she links the two in a way that Plato, Hippocrates, and Hugh of St. Victor would have found completely chaotic. Her book gives God's stamp of approval to women's role in the cooking and the balancing of humors, and thus to their practice of theology and medicine—all this at a moment in history when women were supposed to be using hyssop to spice chicken, not discuss creation and cure liver colic.

## NOTES

1. According to the International Society of Hildegard von Bingen Studies, literal cottages are being built to house information about Hildegard and to promote more interest and study in her. Among others, they include the St. Hildegard Center, A House for Hildegard, and the Disibodenberg Scivias Foundation in Germany; the Hildegard Resource Center in Seattle, WA; and a new proposed Hildegard House in Kentucky.

2. In this paper, I will refer to Hildegard's *Causae et curae* as *Causes and Cures*. All other translations are Madigan's.

3. I am not arguing that only women practiced cookery. In fact, although not much information exists about the Cooks' Guilds of medieval Europe, most of it which does exist fails to mention women professional cooks at all (Scully 238-9). Erika Uitz in *Women in the Medieval Town* is one of the few scholars who notes that in places such as the Rhine where Hildegard lived there were independent women who did practice crafts such as Pancake-Baker and Brewer (54). In this paper I hope to decenter the critical attention given to professional cookery done primarily by men and instead focus on everyday cookery which was performed primarily by women.

4. Hildegard frequently referred to herself with phrases such as "poor little creature," "poor little untaught womanly form," "wretched creature . . . being a woman," etc. See Paula Martin's article on Hildegard's self-perception and self-presentation for more on this subject.

5. Sue Cannon states that Hildegard's skill in medicine may have turned off some men and thus contributed to her book's "fall into obscurity" (60). I second this and add to it that Hildegard's deliberate collapsing of medicine with the activity of cookery speeded its decline.

6. In *Women Writers of the Middle Ages* Peter Dronke offers another interpretation. He reads Hildegard's reference to Plato as a serious means for her to identify with an unbalanced yet "gifted" and "exceptional" man (183). He guesses that both Hildegard and Plato were melancholic personalities and for this reason, he states that Hildegard may have been drawn to Plato's unbalanced psychological make-up.

7. For a more in-depth discussion of the humors and their importance in medicine and diet from classical times to the Middle Ages, see Cannon's chapter on "Hildegardian Humoral Pathology" and Joan Cadden's sections

which compare and contrast the views of Hippocrates, Galen, Constantine, and Hildegard regarding the four humors.

8. For a good detailed discussion of both of these analogies (minus, however, any attention to gender), see George Plochmann's and Franklin Robinson's *A Friendly Companion to Plato's* Gorgias.

9. According to the sixth-century *Rule of St. Benedict*, it was preferable to keep one's distance from the areas where food was prepared, except as a kind of spiritual discipline. He noted: "No one is exempt from duty in the kitchen. . . . From this service a monk learns charity and gains a greater degree of merit" (qtd. in Henisch 67).

10. Elizabeth Grosz's introduction to *Volatile Bodies: Toward a Corporeal Feminism* historicizes the philosophic tradition which produced many of these oppositions. Her own book concentrates on the mind/body split.

11. Williams and Echols (19) and Henisch (103) note which spices were available in the twelfth century and how they were used in cookery and medicine. Also Jeffrey Schnapp draws an interesting connection between Hildegard's scientific work and her imaginary *lingua ignota* by showing that a large percentage of her invented words have to do with bodies, herbs and the kitchen (284-6).

12. For a more imaginative look at Hildegard's images, read Ingeborg Ulrich's re-creation of Hildegard's life, as doctor and as cook (28-29, 50).

13. Terence Scully describes the medieval oven this way: "it is a stone cavern that is heated by a fire within it; when the stone of the structure has become hot enough, the coals are removed . . . and the food to be baked is inserted. . . . The heat radiating on all sides is even and moderate" (95-6). Hildegard imagines the woman's womb in this way.

14. Hildegard was interested in both religious cooks and religious doctors. Her book *Liber vitae meritorum* has been described as "a recipe book filled with treatments for spiritual problems" (Walker-Moskop 22). And in a letter to the Rupertsberg nuns, Hildegard talked about the importance of "spiritual medicine" (qtd. in Dronke 153).

15. Newman, for instance, notes that Hildegard would have had access to the recipes of Galen, Pliny, Dioscorides, Isidore, and Strabo (143). Cannon adds to the list Celsus, Marcellus Empiricus, and the *Pseudo-Apuleius* (52).

16. Dronke states that two things which are "new and startling" about Hildegard's medical work are the way in which it re-interprets the four humors and provides descriptions for the four temperaments of women (180). Cadden discusses several other innovations, including Hildegard's use of black bile (70-88). This paper complements their work by suggesting that Hildegard's

discussion of women in relationship to cookery and medicine in *Causes and Cures* is unique too.

## WORKS CITED

### Primary Texts

Hildegard von Bingen. *Holistic Healing.* Trans. Patrick Madigan. Eds. Mary Palmquist and John Kulas. Collegeville, Minnesota: The Liturgical Press, 1994.

———. *Scivias.* Trans. Mother Columba Hart and Jane Bishop. New York: Paulist Press, 1990.

Hugh of St. Victor. *The Didascalicon.* Trans. Jerome Taylor. Records of Western Civilization. New York: Columbia University Press, 1961, rpt. 1991.

### Secondary Texts

Benedek, Thomas. "The Roles of Medieval Woman in the Healing Arts." *The Roles and Images of Women in the Middle Ages and Renaissance.* Ed. Douglas Radcliff-Umstead. Pittsburgh: University of Pittsburgh Publications, 1987. 145-159.

Bynum, Caroline Walker. *Holy Feast and Holy Fast.* Berkeley: University of California Press, 1986.

Cadden, Joan. *Meanings of Sex Difference in the Middle Ages.* Cambridge: Cambridge University Press, 1993.

Cannon, Sue Spencer. "The Medicine of Hildegard of Bingen: Her Twelfth-Century Theories and Their Twentieth-Century Appeal as a Form of Alternative Medicine." Dissertation, University of California, 1993.

Dronke, Peter. *Women Writers of the Middle Ages.* Cambridge: Cambridge University Press, 1984.

Flanagan, Sabina. *Hildegard of Bingen: A Visionary Life.* New York: Routledge Press, 1989.

Fox, Matthew. Preface. *Meditations with Hildegard of Bingen.* Santa Fe: Bear & Company, 1983.

Gladden, Samuel. "Hildegard's Awakening: A Portrait of Disruptive Excess." *Representations of the Feminine in the Middle Ages.* Ed. Bonnie Wheeler. Dallas: Academia,1993. 217-233.

Gregory, Tullio. "The Platonic Inheritance." *A History of Twelfth-Century Western Philosophy.* Ed. Peter Dronke. Cambridge: Cambridge University Press, 1988. 54-80.

Grosz, Elizabeth. *Volatile Bodies: Toward a Corporeal Feminism.* Bloomington: Indiana University Press, 1994.

Hastorf, Christine. "Gender, Space, and Food in Prehistory." *Engendering Archaeology: Women and Prehistory.* Eds. Joan Gero and Margaret Conkey. Cambridge: Blackwell Press, 1992.

Henisch, Bridget Ann. *Fast and Feast: Food in Medieval Society.* University Park: Pennsylvania State University Press, 1976.

Hippocrates. *Hippocratic Writings.* Trans. J. Chadwick and W. Mann. New York: Penguin Books, 1978.

Humphrey, Theodore and Lin Humphrey, eds. *"We Gather Together": Food and Festival in American Life.* Ann Arbor, MI: UMI Research Press, 1988.

Jeanneret, Michel. *A Feast of Words.* Trans. J. Whitely and Emma Hughs. Cambridge: Polity Press, 1991.

Kennedy, George. *The Art of Persuasion in Greece.* Princeton: Princeton University Press, 1963.

Kraft, Kent. "The German Visionary Hildegard of Bingen." *Medieval Women Writers.* Ed. Katharina Wilson. Athens: University of Georgia Press, 1984.

Labarge, Margaret. *Women in Medieval Life: A Small Sound of the Trumpet.* London: Hamish Hamilton, 1986.

Leonardi, Susan. "Recipes for Reading." *Cooking by the Book: Food in Literature and Culture.* Ed. Mary Anne Schofield. Bowling Green, OH: Bowling Green State University Press, 1989. 126-137.

Lyons, Albert and Joseph Petrucelli. *Medicine: An Illustrated History.* New York: Harry Abrams, Inc., 1978.

Martin, Paula. "A Brightness of Purple Lightning: Hildegard of Bingen's Self-Perception." *Representations of the Feminine in the Middle Ages.* Ed. Bonnie Wheeler. Dallas: Academia, 1993. 235-47.

Molina, Caroline. "Illness as Privilege: Hildegard von Bingen and the Condition of Mystic Writing." *Women's Studies* 23(1994): 85-92.

Newman, Barbara. *Sister of Wisdom: St. Hildegard's Theology of the Feminine.* Berkeley: University of California Press, 1987.

Plato. *The Dialogues of Plato.* Trans. B. Jowett. Oxford: Clarendon Press, 1875.

Schnapp, Jeffrey. "Virgin Words: Hildegard of Bingen's *Lingua ignota* and the Development of Imaginary Languages." *Exemplaria* 3:2 (1991): 267-298.

Schofield, Mary Anne. Ed. *Cooking by the Book: Food in Literature and Culture.* Bowling Green, OH: Bowling Green State University Press, 1989.

Scholz, Bernhard. "Hildegard von Bingen on the Nature of Woman." *American Benedictine Review* 31:4 (1980): 361-383.

Scully, Terence. *The Art of Cookery in the Middle Ages.* Suffolk, UK: Boydell Press, 1995.

Singer, Charles. "The Visions of Hildegard of Bingen." *From Magic to Science.* 1928. New York: Dover, 1958.199-239.

Strehlow, Wighard, and Gottfried Hertzka. *Hildegard of Bingen's Medicine.* Santa Fe: Bear & Company, 1988.

Uhlein, Gabriele. "Introduction". *Meditations with Hildegard of Bingen.* by Matthew Fox. Santa Fe: Bear & Company, 1983.

Uitz, Erika. *Women in the Medieval Town.* London: Barrie & Jenkins, 1988.

Ulrich, Ingeborg. *Hildegard of Bingen: Mystic, Healer, Companion of the Angels.* Collegeville, Minnesota: The Liturgical Press, 1993.

Valentine, Timothy. "Hildegard Unplugged." *America* 172.10 (1995): 20-23.

Vickers, Brian. *In Defense of Rhetoric.* Oxford: Clarendon-Oxford University Press,1988.

Walker-Moskop, Ruth. "Health and Cosmic Continuity: Hildegard of Bingen's Unique Concerns." *FCEMN* 11:1 (1985): 19-25.

Weeks, Andrew. *German Mysticism from Hildegard of Bingen to Ludwig Wittgenstein.* Albany: State University of New York Press, 1993.

Williams, Marty, and Anne Echols. *Between Pit and Pedestal: Women in the Middle Ages.* Princeton: Markus Wiener Publishers, 1994.

# Worlds Beyond:
# Poetry, Visions, and Music

# A Poetry of Science
## Relating Body and Soul in the *Scivias*
*Jan S. Emerson*

In everything from hymn to musical drama, practical medicine to abstract theological commentary, personal letters to dramatic exorcistic ritual, Hildegard von Bingen celebrates harmony. So did many of her contemporaries. Medieval thought paired both likely and unlikely to imagine a unified and ordered cosmos, with God as the author, the architect, the ultimate composer. Medieval minds brought together God and man, angel and devil, Good and Bad, healthy and sick, life and death (Pawlik 13) and the topic addressed here, body and soul. Yet many medieval writers, though preoccupied with the relationship between the body and the soul, saw that relationship as a primarily antagonistic one. As debate more than dialogue, animosity more than reciprocity.[1] From medieval to modern times, a similarly problematic relationship has existed between poetry and science, one that was perhaps intensified as university disciplines were defined in the Middle Ages.

In this article I ask how Hildegard understands these relationships, and I seek answers in her use of body-related imagery in the *Scivias*. I want to show how the imagery reveals three major points: 1) The integration of body and soul is total but not without tension. 2) The body and senses can be seduced into evil but are not inherently so. Indeed, they offer the greatest human potential, that of recognizing God.[2] And 3) Even Hildegard's most poetic images of the body are based in observation.

Understanding the body both as the place of her own physical pain and as microcosm to the macrocosm of the universe, Hildegard moves

in the *Scivias* between images of embodiment and abstraction. To the
modern reader there can appear "an almost schizophrenic relationship
between her creative urges and her need to remove them from herself;
between her organic, [potentially] erotic visions,[3] and her reasoned, at
times somewhat forced, analyses of them. She opens the *Scivias* by
declaring the split between her [calm] inner and her [disquieted] outer
being."[4] In the opening Declaration, she has the voice from Heaven
describe how "she suffers in her inmost being and in the veins of her
flesh; she is distressed in mind and sense and endures great pain of
body, because no security has dwelt in her, but in all her undertakings
she has judged herself guilty." But describing the fiery light that came
from Heaven to "permeate [her] whole brain," and "inflame" her heart
and breast, she says at the same time that it "was not like a burning but
a warming flame, as the sun warms anything its rays touch," invoking a
gentle, non-invasive touch that allows her to see with a "pure mind"
(59-60).

Recognizing with other medieval writers a split between inner and
outer sense, she says that Man can know God better "by opening the
inner eyes of the spirit to good, and denying and cutting off the evil that
the outer person can do" (429). At the end of times, according to the
divine commentary on Book 3, Vision 11, many will be deceived by
the magic of the Antichrist, "For they will use their minds to probe this
novelty their outer eyes see and their hands touch, and despise the
invisible things that abide in me and must be understood by true faith"
(503). Clarifying her own experiences in a well-known passage,
Hildegard relates the inner and outer senses to the inner and outer self:
"But the visions I saw I did not perceive. . . by the eyes of the body, or
by the ears of the outer self. . . ; but I perceived them while awake and
seeing with a pure mind and the eyes and ears of the inner self" (60).
Many medieval visionaries must experience a split between body and
soul to gain access to the divine; they cannot have moments of divine
insight unless their souls leave their bodies.[5] Hildegard's visions,
though not perceived with the outer senses of body, are experienced
while she is in the body, which distinguishes her from other visionaries
and grounds her experience in her belief that body and soul are
integrated.[6] This integration she sees as a unity of precisely those
oppositely inclined visible and invisible aspects of the human being,
brought together to serve God, for example in the celebration of the
sacrament of communion:

> The human soul, which is invisible, invisibly receives the sacrament,
> which exists invisibly in that oblation, while the human body, which
> is visible, visibly receives the oblation that visibly embodies that
> sacrament. But the two are one, just as Christ is God and Man, and
> the rational soul and the mortal flesh make up one human being. . . .
> (245)

Like her contemporaries, Hildegard condemns acts of the flesh,
which stem from placing love of the world and the carnal above God.[7]
In Book 2, Vision 6, the Living Light describes how a person's faith
can weaken: "For the body and the soul fight with each other; the soul
seeks to dominate the body, since the desire for sin in the flesh goes
against its wishes, and the body (*corpus*) disdains the righteousness that
is the desire of the life-loving soul. . . . The flesh loves sin (*caro amat
peccatum*), and the soul loves justice, and so they oppose each other
and rarely agree."[8] The pilgrim soul of Book 1, Vision 4, laments of its
body, ". . . alas! Its sensibility gives rise to filth, licentiousness and
wantonness of conduct and every kind of vice. . . . the Devil's
persuasion meets me and ensnares me, and uplifts me in haughty pride,
so that I say 'I want to act according to the joys of earthly fertility.'"
The soul continues, "I condemn all those works that burn with carnal
desire" (113).

Hildegard also condemns her own body and senses: "To my own
inner soul I seem as filthy ashes of ashes. . . . When I think of the
worthlessness of my foolish bodily senses, I deem myself the least and
lowest of creatures. . . ." Her exceeding fear makes her unworthy even
"to be called a human being," nonetheless she asks that the Living
Light not "blot [her] out from the land of the living, for [she] labor[s] at
this vision with great toil." The divine voice tells her that her eyes are
beautiful because the divine counsel dawns in them, and admonishes
her to speak out regardless of any unworthiness: "Though you are
ashes, I will that you speak" (310).

Despite this condemnation of the carnal, Hildegard's work, as
Prudence Allen has suggested, "abound[s] in metaphors for the
complete integration of body and soul." It thus differs from the Neo-
Platonic continuation of the "Platonic tendency to separate the soul
from the body."[9] I want to explore the nature of that integration as
expressed in the images used to portray it. Hildegard stresses again and
again how body and soul, person and senses, spirit and senses are
interdependent, in practical as well as philosophical terms. The

lamenting soul above, though sorrowful over the struggle with its body, also notes its life-giving link to that body: "I am the living breath in a human being placed in a tabernacle of marrow, veins, bones and flesh, giving it vitality and supporting its every movement" (113).

This relationship is a requirement of life, for the soul permeates the human body and blood (416) and rules the body: "The soul is the mistress, the flesh the handmaid. How? The soul rules the body by vivifying it, and the body is ruled by this vivification, for if the soul did not vivify the body it would fall apart and decay."[10] Elsewhere Hildegard adds the senses to body and soul to form a human trinity:

> But a person has within himself three paths. What are they? The soul, the body and the senses; and all human life is led in these. How? The soul vivifies the body and conveys the breath of life to the senses: the body draws the soul to itself and opens the senses; and the senses touch the soul and draw the body. For the soul gives life to the body as fire gives light to darkness. . . . (120)

Hildegard applies anatomical images to the intellect and will, the two principal powers of the soul: "The intellect is joined to the soul like an arm to the body. For as the arm, joined to the hand with its fingers, branches out from the body, so the intellect, working with the other powers of the soul, by which it understands human actions, most certainly proceeds from the soul." It "sifts things" to pick out the useful, the lovable, and that which is pertinent to life (121). The intellect "has true faith in its work, which is the joint of the hand, with which it chooses among the various works wisely as if with fingers" (121). Where the intellect understands, the will activates: "Thus it [the soul] puts its will, like a right arm, as the support of the veins and marrow and the movement of the whole body; for the will does every work . . ." (121).

In the voice of the Living Light, Hildegard urges humans to pay attention to the scriptures because they are "not just a bundle of marrow" (120). But as humans are not simply body, they are also not simply soul. At death, the soul "breaks away lamenting from its abode; for, taking itself out of the body with anguish, it tremblingly allows its habitation to fall, dreading the imminent tribunal of the Celestial Judge" (125). Humans must acknowledge and use both intellect, an arm of the soul, and body correctly: "But you, O human, are blind when you need to see, deaf when you need to hear and senseless when you need to defend yourself, since the intellect and the five bodily senses God gave you are no more to you than filth and emptiness" (127). Not only does the soul permeate and give life to the physical body, but the two cooperate: "the body is the tabernacle and support of all the powers of the soul, since the soul resides in the body and works with the body, and the body with it, whether for good or for evil" (123).

Thus the problem of sin lies not in the senses themselves but in the way humans use them, as the divine voice urges ". . .why do you not serve God, Who gave you both soul and body, for the sake of heavenly wages?" (127). "When you say that you cannot do good works, you speak in unjust wickedness. For you have eyes to see with, ears to hear with, a heart to think with, hands to work with and feet to walk with, so that with your body you can stand up and lie down, sleep and wake, eat and fast. Thus God created you. Therefore, resist the desires of your flesh, and God will help you."[11] Humans simply forget they have their nature so that they can do good, she says (433). But even those whose senses are thrown into disorder by vices still "aspire to eternal reward" (195). In that reward, as in John's Revelations, body and soul will be reunited. In Hildegard, they retain their gender. In the New Heaven and the New Earth, after the call to arise, Hildegard saw that "all the human bones in whatever place in the earth they lay were brought together in one moment and covered with their flesh, and they all rose up with limbs and bodies intact, each in his or her gender. . . ."[12] Also in Hildegard's vision, Christ makes no inquiry or statement concerning their works, and there is no list of works, for their *bodies* are marked with brightness or darkness, indicating their past and their fate. In the commentary which follows immediately, Hildegard emphasizes the integrity of body and gender and the signing of the body-soul unit with its own works: "so all people will rise again in the twinkling of an eye, 'in soul and body, with no deformity or mutilation but intact in body and in gender; and the elect will shine with the brightness of their good works, but the reprobate will bear the blackness of their deeds of misery'" (517). Important to Hildegard also is that Christ will return "with the same appearance He had had in the world and with His wounds still open. . ." so that He too shares the integrity of body and the transparency of His deeds with the risen humans.[13]

Thus Hildegard does not limit her use of body imagery to descriptions of the purely human. She applies it also to describe how humans grasp the dual nature of God: The intellect "is also to the soul as the shoulder is to the body, the very core of the other powers of the soul; as the bodily shoulder is strong, so it understands the divinity and humanity in God, which is the joint of the arm . . ." (121).

The divine voice joins Hildegard in applying bodily imagery to explain much more than human integration. The very workings of the Holy Trinity are those of body and soul. Referring to John 5:6-8 on how the spirit, the water and the blood testify to the Trinity, the voice explains: ". . . these three are one. For the spirit without the bloody material of the body is not the living person, and the bloody material of the body without the soul is not the living person; and these two are not strengthened unto life in the grace of the new Law except through the water of regeneration . . ." (417). The Trinity is inseparable, "like expelled human breath," or "the complete human eye" with its transparent parts that "form one housing for all that is within them" (419). The secrets held by God are described in particularly physical images. They "were, so to speak, just a hand's breadth wide, the distance from the thumb to the little finger of the flat hand; and that was the time ordained in the heart of the Father when He willed to send His Son. He sent Him with a strong hand, and surrounded Him with all the joints of His fingers, which are His works in the Holy Spirit" (338).[14]

If we now turn to the five senses, Hildegard offers a wealth of references. From the very first visions of the first book of the *Scivias*, the vocabulary of physicality and the senses is prominent:

> I *saw* a great mountain the *color* of iron, and *enthroned* on it One of such great glory that it *blinded my sight.* On each side of him there extended a *soft shadow*, like a wing of wondrous *breadth* and *length.* Before him, at the foot of the mountain, stood an *image full of eyes on all sides*, in which, because of those *eyes*, I could discern no *human form*. In front of this image stood another, a *child*, wearing a tunic of *subdued color* but *white* shoes, upon whose *head* such glory descended from the One enthroned upon that mountain that I *could not look at its face.* But from the One who sat enthroned upon that mountain many living *sparks sprang forth*, which flew very sweetly around the images. Also, I *perceived* in this mountain many little windows, in which appeared *human heads*, some of *subdued colors* and some *white.* (Book 1, Vision 1; 67. Emphasis added.)

> . . . And *behold*! A pit of great *breadth* and *depth appeared*, with a *mouth* like the *mouth* of a well, *emitting fiery smoke* with great

*stench,* from which a loathsome cloud spread out and *touched* a
deceitful *vein-shaped form. . . .* And again I *heard* Him who had
*spoken* to me before, *saying. . .* (Book 1, Vision 2; 73. Emphasis
added.)

The emphasis makes clear the presence of images of sight, hearing,
smell, touch, as well as the human form, weight, face, mouth, breath,
veins.[15]

The most negative metaphorical use of the senses appears when
Hildegard refers to the Antichrist in Book 3, Vision 11. She names
desire and pleasure and implies the senses. Hildegard sees five beasts in
the North: "These are the five ferocious epochs of temporal rule,
brought about by the desires of the flesh from which the taint of sin is
never absent." Before the beasts appears "a hill with five peaks," which
symbolizes "the power of carnal desire." Five ropes stretch from the
mouths of the beasts to the peaks, symbolizing the extent of the
temporal powers and "how far people are willing to go in their stubborn
pleasures" (493-95). The Antichrist himself appears within the figure of
a woman that denotes the Church. He is a black and monstrous head
lacking a body, which is interesting because he is the originator of
bodily desire, and is where her womb would be "in the place where the
female is recognized." He appears there because he will come "with the
arts he first used to seduce" (497). Hildegard describes his eyes, ears,
nose and mouth as fiery and animal-like because of his lust and because
he rapes the Church.

But such negative associations of the bodily senses are few.
Describing how God makes himself known to humans, who, weighed
down by their mortality, cannot see His glory, the Living Light says
that He shows Himself "like a painter showing people invisible things
by the images in his painting," making the bodily sense of sight the
access to divinity. Of course Hildegard is not the only visionary to use
sight imagery. Other visionaries see with the eyes of the soul;
Hildegard sees with the "inner eyes" of the "pure mind." What interests
me is how she uses sight and other sense images, how she values the
senses themselves, and the role she assigns them in acquiring
knowledge (503). When compared to the power of angels, it is
precisely the weakness of the human body that enables Man to reach
the heights: "people work more strongly in soul and body than if they
had no difficulty in doing it, since they struggle against themselves in
many perils. . . But an angel, lacking the hardships of an earthly body,

is a soldier of Heaven only in its harmonious, lucid and pure constancy in seeing God; while a human, handicapped by the filth of his body, is a strong, glorious and holy soldier in the work of restoration, which he does in soul and body for the sake of God."[16] After all, God existed in human form.[17]

The five senses are positively related to the Church. In Book 3, Vision 9, Hildegard sees a tower that represents the Church. It is "five cubits across any radius of its interior; for the Church honors the Lamb, her Bridegroom, by giving Him all her inner thoughts and meditations, which ornament her by the inspiration of the Holy Spirit, on what she receives through the five senses" (455). In the same vision appears Justice, leaning against the pillar of Christ's humanity: "She seems to be as broad as five people standing side by side; for she takes in all five human senses and uses them to abide in the law of God. . ." (467). Thus the senses inspire the ornamentation of "thoughts and meditations," which are acts of intellect. Their number supplies an intellectual measurement, breadth. They also make Justice aware of law and enable her to act according to law. Thus, rather than leading to unbridled emotion, they bring knowledge and wisdom, monitoring and guiding behavior.

In another tower image, we learn that if soul and body cooperate towards the good, the five senses will lead to virtues. The passages I turn to now are from Book 3, Vision 3 "The Tower of Anticipation of God's Will," Commentary 3, in which the voice describes the five virtues of Heavenly Love, Discipline, Modesty, Mercy and Victory (*amor caelestis, disciplina, verecundia, misericordia, victoria*) that Hildegard sees in the tower:

> In it you see five figures standing separately, each in its own arch with a conical turret above it. This is to say that in this tower, that is in the strength of the circumcision, there are five strong virtues; not that any virtue is a living form in itself, but a brilliant star given by God that shines forth in human deeds. For humanity is perfected by virtues, which are the deeds of people working in God.
>
> Hence these five virtues stand in this tower in the likeness of a person's five senses. They seized with great zeal upon the circumcision, and cut it off from all iniquity, as the five human senses are circumcised in the Church by baptism. But they [the virtues] do not work in a person by themselves, for the person works with them

and they with the person; just as the person's five senses do not work by themselves, but the person with them and they with the person, to bear fruit together. . . . [18]

Hildegard chooses to relate the virtues to the senses through the image of circumcision, but she moves it from the purely male realm to embrace both male and female. Under the Old Covenant, circumcision, literally and symbolically, signed the male as God's own, and earlier may have been associated with marriage ritual.[19] But already in the Old Testament, it takes on religious and metaphorical significance. When circumcision is "cut off" from its role in Judaism and becomes Christian baptism, at both literal and spiritual levels, the act not only includes, but primarily associates with the female, as an act of birth. The imagery of birth extends to the virtues and the senses "bearing fruit together." This is also one of the many passages in which Hildegard stresses the importance of deeds (Compare below).

In Book 1, Vision 2, Hildegard focuses on two virtues, humility and charity (*humilitas, caritas*), but their relationship to each other is again like that of soul and body, and the emphasis is again on cooperation:

> . . . humility and charity are brighter than the other virtues, since humility and charity are like a soul and a body that possess stronger powers than the other powers of soul and bodily members. How? Humility is like the soul and charity like the body, and they cannot be separated from each other but work together, just as soul and body cannot be disjoined but work together as long as a person lives in the body. And as the various members of the body are subject, according to their powers, to the soul and to the body, so also the other virtues cooperate, according to their justice, with humility and charity. (90)

Hildegard does not present a special hierarchy here. Charity is the greatest of abiding things according to Paul (1 Cor. 1:13), and humility is fundamental to the Benedictine Rule. It makes sense that she require the other virtues to cooperate with these. Her subject seems to be the nature of the relationship between humility and charity rather than the specific equation of either to body or soul, although elsewhere, in the *Causae et curae*, she says that the soul is the more powerful, since it can quiet the body's longing and can live without the body, while the body cannot live without the soul (*Causae et curae* 41-42).

The interidentity of body and soul is perhaps best expressed in Book 1, Vision 4, which reads:

> It is the senses on which the interior powers of the soul depend, so that these powers are known through them by the fruits of each work. The senses are subject to these powers, since they guide them to the work, but the senses do not impose work on the powers, for they are their shadow and do what pleases them. The exterior human being awakens with senses in the womb of his mother before he is born, but the other powers of the soul still remain in hiding. What is this? The dawn announces the daylight; just so the human senses manifest the reason and all the powers of the soul. And as on the two commandments of God hang all the Law and the prophets, so also on the soul and its powers depend the human senses. What does this mean?

> The Law is ordained for human salvation, and the prophets show forth the hidden things of God; so also human senses protect a person from harmful things and lay bare the soul's interior. For the soul emanates the senses. How? It vivifies a person's face and glorifies him with sight, hearing, taste, smell and touch, so that by this touch he becomes watchful in all things. For the senses are the sign of all the powers of the soul, as the body is the vessel of the soul. What does this mean? A person is recognized by his face, sees with his eyes, hears with his ears, opens his mouth to speak, feels with his hands, walks with his feet; and so the senses are to a person as precious stones and as a rich treasure sealed in a vase. But as the treasure within is known when the vase is seen, so also the powers of the soul are inferred by the senses.[20]

Thus the senses are linked not exclusively to bodily functions, but to "reason and all the powers of the soul." As the face manifests the identity of the body, the senses manifest the identity of the soul. To have a body marked with virtuous deeds at the resurrection, a body which has used its senses for their original purpose, the person must cleanse the senses, correcting the transgression of the first man and woman. The individual accomplishes this through the "circumcision" of baptism, enabled through Christ's descent into death and resurrection unto life. The idea of the proper use of the human senses also shapes Hildegard's view of the Fall and *vice versa*. Though she sees the Fall as a result of transgression, it was not a change in Man's nature or a revelation that Man is by nature evil. Man, rather by nature good, was deceived by Satan, who continues to deceive the five senses from their true purpose. Book 2, Vision 7 declares that the Devil inspires the spiritual with carnal desires and pleasures, lust and unclean pollution. Hildegard sees a flame breathing on spiritual people: "This means that the breath of the Devil's persuasion. . . beclouds [the spiritual] with the perversity of its vices, so that they long for the flesh more than for the spirit." She sees six categories of the spiritual, "for the ancient enemy strives to pervert both their five exterior senses and the sixth inner one, the devotion of the heart" (299). Because "the lust of the flesh" clings to the faithful, they can be "ambushed" by Satan, and "because death arose from the fall of the Devil, they must sustain many struggles and sufferings, often hard and adverse for the body, against the Devil's villainies" (403). Thus Hildegard blames Satan, not Eve, for the introduction of death. She speaks more in terms of responsibility than of guilt, and that responsibility is shared by Adam and Eve.

To describe Adam's part in the Fall, that is, his disobedience, Hildegard turns again to the senses. In Book 2, Vision 1, she shows how Adam did not pluck the white flower of obedience that was offered him: "for he tried to know the wisdom of the Law with his intelligence, as if with his nose, but did not perfectly digest it by putting it into his mouth, or fulfill it in full blessedness by the work of his hands" (153). Whereas for most writers, Adam's sin was that he, having been seduced by Eve and her own seduction by the senses and Satan, gave in to the senses, for Hildegard, he did not allow himself to "taste" or "touch" obedience.[21] Hildegard prioritizes the sense of taste over smell here, implying that knowledge comes not simply through intellect, traditionally identified with the male, but through eating, ingestion, visceral images of "taking in," more often associated with Eve and the female by way of lust and sexuality.[22] By emphasizing "the work of the hands," she may be criticizing the Church's decision to deny the active life to monastics as well as justifying her own involvement in founding new houses, caring for the sick, and undertaking public speaking tours. It is also reminiscent of the active role played by the feminine divine in creation (Cf. Newman).

Those who wish to partake of communion are of five modes of being (Book 2, Vision 6; 238), for they "should cleanse the five senses of their body from the dregs of their sins" (266). This is enabled of course through Christ, who combined humanity and divinity in His body. Like other writers, Hildegard understands this to be possible through the Crucifixion, the physical torture and death of Christ's body. She repeatedly links the five wounds of Christ to the five senses, relating humanity and divinity in the human body, and describes the integration of divinity yet again in terms of the body:

> Therefore the human form is to be seen in the inmost nature of the Deity, where neither angels nor any other creatures appear;[23] because My Only-Begotten, to redeem the human race, assumed human form in the flesh of a Virgin. And He will carry in His heart those who are with young. How? My Son carries human beings in His blood, and saves them by His five wounds, for whatever sins they have committed by means of their five senses are washed away by supreme justice when they repent; and He carries them so because He was incarnate, and suffered wounds on the cross. . . . (314)

Elsewhere Hildegard links the wounds and the senses more directly. The armies of the angels and the archangels "are arrayed in the shape of a crown around five other armies. This shows that the human body and soul must, by virtue of their strength, contain the five human senses, purify them by the five wounds of My Son, and lead them to the righteousness of governance from within" (140). And in a related passage ". . . the faithful who direct their body's five senses to celestial things, knowing that they have been redeemed through the five wounds of the Son of God, attain with every turn and working of their mind, because they ignore the heart's pleasure and put their hope in inward things, to love of God and their neighbor" (140, 142).

One of the most interesting and imagistically rich passages connecting the wounds and the senses appears in Book 3, Vision 2, Commentary 21, where the divine light describes the Edifice of Salvation:

> 21. The five wounds of Christ wipe out human sins

> And you see that *the building is fifty cubits wide*, which is to say that the whole breadth of the vices of humanity, which should have built on and revered the work of God but instead followed its own lusts, is mercifully wiped out and forgiven by the five wounds that My Son suffered on the cross. So the wounds of His hands obliterated the

deed of disobedience done by the hands of Adam and Eve, and the wounds of His feet cleared the path of exile for humanity to return, and the wound of His side, from which sprang the Church, wiped out the sin of Eve and Adam after Eve was made from Adam's side. And therefore My Son was nailed to the tree, to abolish what had been done through the tree that occasioned sin; and therefore He drank vinegar and gall, to take away the taste of the harmful fruit.[24]

Hildegard replaces the tree of the first sin by the tree that abolished sin, making the traditional link between the cross and the tree of Adam's perdition as well as implying the family tree of generations that stemmed from the root of Jesse to culminate in Christ (407, 437). But interesting here in terms of interpreting the imagery is that the point of penetration, seen by Hildegard as a wound in not only Christ's death but in the penetration of the female by the male, is the point of birth. According to Hildegard, Mary had Christ with no wound, no penetration, no pain, and from her side (Newman 176). Thus Hildegard links Christ to the female, specifically to Mary, the woman who enabled salvation by giving birth. Sin-tainted human sexuality is redeemed because Christ is the only child born not of sin, in addition to Eve born from Adam's side before the Fall (Cf. Gössmann 28). Thus the Church can enable forgiveness of sin through Him. The imagery of taste can be interpreted almost literally. According to Hildegard, Christ, unlike Mary, suffered the pain of the sword, penetration, to give birth. Elsewhere Hildegard describes male penetration as pollution and stain (Newman 135; *Causae et curae* 60-62). Yet Christ remains pure and gives birth through the side, Mary's place of purity, Adam's place of innocence. He drinks the sour to take away the sin of the sweet, the harmful fruit, to those who sinned. He had drunk wine, the sweet product of fermented fruit, to signify communion with his disciples through his blood. When Christ drinks vinegar, the sourness of fermented fruit, he at once eases his wounds and drinks the sourness of death, restoring sweetness to birth, creation and life. The images are of taste, ingestion, and rather than seeing redemption as a "victory over digestion,"[25] or as a usurpation by the male of female creativity, Hildegard refigures the birth process of the Church, likening Christ to the female, and female to redemption.

Hildegard views humanity and human beings positively. They are a created good and their task is to redeem the self not only in, but through, the body and the senses. As she says, we have eyes to see and

hands to do good works. Yet despite all imagery of cooperation and
integration between the divine and the human, the soul and the body,
God remains impenetrable, distant, unknowable: "the Supreme Power
is so far exalted above the lives of all creatures and above the sense and
intellect of Man, and so incomprehensible in and above all, that no
creature's senses can grasp it, except to realize that this Power is much
higher than it can know" (317). "No human in a corruptible body can
fully understand" God (359). Even the angels "cannot understand or
grasp Him completely" (317). Hildegard often singles out the "height"
(*altitudo*) of Divinity as that which is unattainable. The Tower of the
Church (Book 3, Vision 9) has a height "so great that you cannot make
it out; for the height and depth of divine wisdom and knowledge in the
work of the Church is too great to be understood by the fragile mortal
human heart" (455). In Book 3, Vision 1, the magnitude of the fear of
God is seen as a stone, broad, "because He is incomprehensible," and
high, "because Divinity is above all else and the highest pitch of any
creature's senses cannot understand or attain to it" (311). The only
thing that touches that height are the virtues (326). Yet, a term such as
"height" implies physical measurability, and physical images bring the
unattainable God closer. Humanity is redeemed because the "height of
divinity was contained in the humanity of the Son of God" (338). Hope
comes through the senses, for "the human senses are in the power of
the One True Almighty God, and thus people can know good and evil
and grasp through their intellect whatever is useful for them" (456).
Human beings cannot fully comprehend God, but the senses offer the
greatest human potential, that of recognizing God. Describing the wall
of the Edifice of Salvation, the Living Light speaks:

> The wall is five cubits high, which refers to the virtue of divine
> knowledge of the Scriptures, which imbue Man's five senses for the
> sake of the work of God. The Holy Spirit breathed on them for
> people's good; for with the five senses people can regard [respicit]
> the height of Divinity, and discern both good and evil. (Book 3,
> Vision 2, Commentary 22; 336)

Thus it is precisely because of the senses, the precious stones, gifts
from God, that we have access to God and good at all.

Hildegard uses the body, the familiar, to make her theology
accessible to others, but I think she uses such images also because they
reflect the way she understands the theology. Her images help me

understand what she says, but, like Augustine (XI,3), who wanted to speak face-to-face with Moses, I ask, "How do I know that I understand what she means by what she says? How do I know how Hildegard wants me to take her words?" As an example, I want to leave the *Scivias* to describe my first encounter with the opening pages of *Causae et curae*, the book of medical diagnosis and treatment. Here too, Hildegard integrates the human and the divine, body and soul. In her view (Pawlik14), illness came with Lucifer's Fall and Adam's Fall, which weakened the life energy of humans. Humans thus need healing, and the causes of illness lie in the origins of evil. Healing comes with creation, redemption and the cosmic order. Hildegard stresses the continual dialogue, the relationship, between the winds, the elements, the body, and the behavior of humans. For example, the winds keep the firmament together as the soul the body, and as the bones keep the body from falling apart. In other words, the soul becomes the bones of the body, the skeleton.[26]

I was so struck by Hildegard's imagery I had to write it down. The opening phrase and the interpretation is mine; the images are hers:

she believed
with the heart
of a poet
that the power
of the moon
is greater than
a storm
and the sun
sends its light
to the moon
like a man
making love
in thin air and the
moon is really fire
and stars and planets
gather round
to help the sun
that never stops
til the moon is
full like a woman
with child giving

birth to stars
that warm night air
til its dewsweat
touches the earth
lets it grow fertile
with fruit

These images are poetic. After all, Hildegard was a composer and songwriter. Dronke noted the imaginative power of her lyrics, her push to the limits of expression (179). Her rich visions resulted in visually rich illuminations. She was a creative artist though she did not admit to her own creativity.[27] She saw the entire universe as one great celestial symphony from whose tones one could intuit divinity and life directions. She collected her own songs under the title "The Symphony of the Harmony of Celestial Revelations."

On the other hand, the cosmic symphony was itself based in the ultimate mathematical precision. Its tones reflect divinity because of the distances between planets and stars, perfectly arranged by the Master Architect and Composer. Hildegard's music has also been shown to be based in mathematics. Pozzi Escot has analyzed numerous hymns to reveal their grounding in geometric proportion and the golden section comparable to Gothic architecture. Analyzing Hildegard's antiphon *O quam mirabilis* (Oh how marvelous), Robert Cogan (7-8) "discovered that each of its sixteen phrases is a fractal reflection, an amplification or elaboration, of a single cell. . . . In other words, as God foresaw 'the identity underlying all of creation,' every phrase of the antiphon is foreseen in its originating cell" (Emerson 73). So that in Hildegard's mystic connection to God, integration is not a melting into or blurring between but a mathematically precise basis for the unity of life, the harmony that makes life possible and gives it meaning. Would she, so precisely inclined, have interpreted her images the way I did, with such poetic intent? Or might she have explained:

Using my mind and my senses, I observed that the power of the moon is greater than that of a storm, and the sun sends *its* light to the moon like a man emitting seed in the ether. The sun never stops until the moon is full, like a pregnant woman. When it is full, it sends its light, thus giving birth to stars that in turn warm the night air, until *its* sweat, the dew, touches the earth, and lets *it* grow fertile with fruit.[28]

At the very beginning of the *Scivias*, the voice of the Living Light notes Hildegard's keen insight, her acute observation, almost as though she must be granted her visions on that basis, rather than admit to any creative impulse. But her powers of observation serve her well. Cadden (166) and Allen (237) point out how surprisingly unique, modern and systematic are her methods of inquiry (if not content) into human sexuality. Her treatment of gender differences, sexuality and reproduction is both broader and more serious than other twelfth-century writings on the subject, be they philosophical, medical or theological (Cadden 152-53).

Hildegard saw Christ as the "medicus" of both body and soul; as "salvator mundi," He was savior, healer and priest. Hildegard was herself considered a healer both in physical and spiritual terms (Pawlik 13). She too must have seen herself as following Christ's example. It is no surprise that she chooses images of joints, veins, and blood, thus "incorporating" such concepts as the coexistence of humanity and divinity, or of unity in trinity.[29] It is significant that Hildegard begins to write a decade after the Council of Clermont of 1130 forbade those in spiritual orders to be active, which would include practicing medicine (Pawlik 13). The council's decision, in contributing to medicine's secularization and development as a university discipline, encouraged a split both between science and natural healing and between the care of the soul and the care of the body. Hildegard's teaching, healing, composing and writing proclaim her insistence on the integration of body and soul and offer a counterweight. In the *Scivias*, images of the body permeate her analytical commentary as well as her organic visions. Their presence suggests at once a tension between disparate ways of seeing (also manifested in illness) and an insistence, even celebration, that they are ultimately and intimately one, as joined as the shoulder to the arm.

## NOTES

1. I am thinking of authors such as Brother Marcus, a contemporary of Hildegard, who recorded *The Vision of Tundal* in 1149, in which anything associated with body through flesh, with fertility and sexuality, is linked to the Fall, to sin and punishment through woman. See Jan S. Emerson, "Harmony and Hierarchy in the *Vision of Tundal*," forthcoming in *Imagining Heaven in the Middle Ages: A Book of Essays*, eds. Jan S. Emerson and Hugh Feiss (New York: Garland, forthcoming). Compare Bynum, "Female Body," esp. 222-235,

for thirteenth- and fourteenth-century authors who described the relationship between body and soul as non-antagonistic. See also Bynum, *Resurrection*, for twelfth- to fourteenth-century ideas on the body. Although most of the orthodox writers Bynum discusses agree that "self is by definition embodied" (225), they regret, admit with hesitation or simply do not understand (e.g. Bernard of Clairvaux) the soul's need for body (172-73, 245, 261, 267). Hildegard seems rather to celebrate the need for the body and senses as gifts that offer the person access to God and the rest of creation. Cf. Bynum, who finds "no suggestion at all in the *Scivias* that redemption is escape from body or that salvation could be complete without body" (*Resurrection* 160).

2. Other medieval writers agree with this, but close examination of their writings often reveals that they are reluctant to admit how humans need the senses to know or describe God. Again, a comparison with *The Vision of Tundal* makes this clear.

3. Marilyn R. Mumford has pointed out that the illuminations which accompany Hildegard's visions contain archetypal images of ancient fertility goddesses that celebrate sensuality and sense experience. We need of course to read such images within the context of Hildegard's entire body of work. But that such a statement can even be made already suggests a stark contrast to contemporary visions such as Tundal's.

4. Emerson, "Hildegard," 71. All citations from the *Scivias* are taken from the translation by Columba Hart and Jane Bishop and will be noted by page number only. Corresponding Latin is from the *Corpus christianorum* edition of *Hildegardis Scivias*, eds. A. Führkötter and A. Carlevaris, and is identified by vision number. I would like to thank Hugh Feiss of Ascension Priory, Idaho, for his advice on key Latin passages. Any misinterpretations are mine.

5. See Gardiner for a collection of visions translated from the Latin. For example, Furseus falls into a trance and leaves his body (52). Drythelm returns to his body after having experienced his visions while being held in death (62). Wetti has his visions while asleep and shortly before his death (77-79). The souls of Tundal and Charles the Fat leave their bodies (129, 152). The Monk of Evesham does not know if he is "present in his body or in his spirit," (197) during one vision, and during another is "deprived of all sense of body and mind." (203) Exceptions are Brendan, who takes a voyage to otherworld islands (81-127), and Owen, who enters the purgatorial cave of St. Patrick (135-148). See also Zaleski, 45-52, on exiting the body, and 75-94 on reentry, and Bynum, *Resurrection*, 294.

6. Hildegard's insistence on being awake and aware while having her visions also disassociates her from the excesses of other mystics, such as tears, laughter, extreme action or speech, in Lochrie's terms, from the linguistic and

corporeal rupture that leads to mystical rapture (74-75, 174-75). Compare also her letters to Hazzecha on curbing self-inflicted or excessive behaviors (Flanagan 176-78) and Elisabeth of Schönau (*Epistolarium* 456-57), and Gössmann 24-25 on the contrasting visionary experiences of Hildegard and Elisabeth of Schönau. It is as though Hildegard is situated between the *Ancrene Wisse's* admonition to imitate Christ's suffering in the senses by damming them up, by closing the breached flesh (Lochrie 25-26; also Bynum, *Resurrection* 161 on Hildegard and "bodily breaches."), and, the opposite extreme, excessive rupture/rapture. She often speaks in terms of circumcision, cutting away and denying, seeming to adopt male images and agree with male-associated attitudes of controlling the senses and submitting to reason and authority. In her own life, she suffers extreme illness rather than speaking out (Cf. her doubt before beginning to record the Scivias visions [Hart and Bishop 60-61]). But many of her deeds undermine her admonitions to submission. Even her illnesses bring her independence, such as when she takes to her bed until she receives permission to move her nuns to a new site. She claims the direct authority of God to speak out and undertakes activities considered unsuitable for women and religious, such as preaching tours and caring for the sick.

7. See Bynum, "Female Body" 222-238, on the significance of body in the body-soul relationship, especially in the thirteenth and fourteenth centuries, and *Resurrection*, which includes the twelfth century.

8. 266-67. Hildegard makes the same distinction here between body, flesh and sin that Paul does in Gal. 5:17. To Paul, "flesh" referred more to "sin" than to "body." See Bynum, "Female Body" 223. See Lochrie, 19-27, for a fuller discussion of how flesh relates to body according to Paul, Augustine, Bernard of Clairvaux, and the authors of medieval devotional manuals and rules for women.

9. Allen 234. See Lochrie 26-27, Gössmann 26-27, on gendering body and soul and Bynum, *Resurrection* 145, on metaphorical identifications of intellect (*nous*) as male above sense (*aisthesis*) as female within the soul.

10. 123. To many theologians it was this potential for decay and corruption of the material that is temporal or temporary, not the body itself, nor its physical distinctiveness or gender (Bynum, "Female Body" 230 and *Resurrection* 11-12).

11. 126. Compare the advice Parzival's knightly teacher Gurnemanz gives him: "ir kunnet hoeren unde sehen, entseben unde draehen: daz solte iuch witzen naehen." (You can hear and see, taste and smell: that ought to bring you [closer to] wisdom.) Wolfram von Eschenbach 1: 292.

12. Book 3, Vision 12; 515. See Allen, 235: "The emphasis on the immortality of a sexless soul in the Platonic tradition is overturned by Hildegard's emphasis on the eternality of sexually differentiated men and women. The Platonic emphasis on a sexless soul is further challenged by Hildegard's insistence on the integral place that the body holds in human identity and by the subsequent significance that sexual identification has in human existence. In this way Hildegard separates herself from the sex unity dynamic of the Platonic tradition." See Bynum, "Material Continuity," on medieval discussions of resurrection and reassemblage of the material body. On gendered resurrection, see Bynum, *Resurrection* 143, 154-55.

13. 515. Resurrected bodies thus have no birth or natural deformities, but they do carry signs of experience. It is not clear whether this covers all experience. For example, the ravages of illness would disappear. But if Christ wears His wounds as signs of his glorious martyrdom, we would expect that the saints and martyrs would also wear their wounds, the signs of glorious deeds. This is reminiscent of heroes proudly displaying their battle wounds in Old Irish tales and in the Happy Other World. Cf. Bynum, *Resurrection* 98, 128, 213, 254-55, 265, 338, and Plates 34-35, as well as "Material Continuity" and "Female Body" 229-235. Also Bynum, *Resurrection* 295-329, 341-343, and "Female Body," 224 on the equation of person with body, including in Dante and in modern Western attitudes. See also Christian Moevs, "Pyramus at the Mulberry Tree: De-petrifying Dante's Tinted Mind." Forthcoming in Emerson and Feiss, eds. *Imagining Heaven,* for an example of the mistake of equating person with body.

14. Even Paradise cannot escape Hildegard's focus on body and soul: "Paradise is the place of delight, which blooms with the freshness of flowers and grass and the charms of spices, full of fine odors . . . giving invigorating moisture to the dry ground; it supplies strong force to the earth, as the soul gives strength to the body. . ." (86).

15. Compare the exhortations of the Living Light at the end of each vision of the *Scivias*: Book 1: "Therefore, whoever has knowledge in the Holy Spirit and wings of faith, let this one not ignore My admonition but *taste* it, *embrace* it and receive it in his soul" (69 et al.). Book 2: "But let the one who *sees* with *watchful eyes* and *hears* with *attentive ears* welcome with a *kiss* My mystical words, which proceed from Me Who am life" (157 et al.). Book 3: "But let the one who has *ears sharp to hear* inner meanings ardently love My reflection and *pant* after My words, and inscribe them in his soul and conscience" (321 et al.). Sight, hearing, taste, touch, desire.

16. 335; cf. the view that women's frailty was a weakness that made them more susceptible to temptation as well as to redemption. See, for example, Newman

114-115. Compare Hildegard's description of the creation of the soul at the beginning of *Causae et curae*. Because the soul is given a body and is earthbound yet walks upright, it strives more intensely to look upward to God. Satan, who must crawl since the garden, is jealous of man's upright walk (*Causae et curae* 2).

17. Cf. Bynum "Female Body" 223, where Bynum mentions late medieval attempts to bridge the gap between material and spiritual, body and soul, inspired perhaps by the fact that the "enfleshing" of God is central to Christianity.

18. 345-46. Hildegard describes a sixth virtue, the Virtue of Knowledge of God. See 356-364.

19. *New Catholic Encyclopedia* 3:879: "The metaphorical usage of the concept circumcision seems to strengthen the hypothesis that circumcision in Israel was connected with the rite of marriage. In such places as Dt 10.16; 30.6; Jer 4.4; 6.10; 9.25; Lv 26.41; Ex 6.12, 30, reference is made to 'uncircumcised' lips, heart, and ears as organs that do not fulfill their function; they can do so only when they are, metaphorically speaking, circumcised." Likewise, in Hildegard's view, the senses can begin to fulfill their function when circumcised through baptism. According to the *Catholic Encyclopedia* (3:779), St. Thomas sees circumcision as a figure of baptism, effects of which are "to take away original sin, which comes by generation," and "to restrain concupiscence."

20. 123. The vessel is not a mere vessel in this image. It holds a treasure. It is transparent to allow the treasure to be seen as contained within the vessel, again an image of integration rather than separation. Interesting in this passage is also the likeness of the Law and the prophets, protection and revelation, to the human senses.

21. 149; cf. Newman 107-120, on Eve and Satan, and 167-171, on Eve and Mary, as well as Adam's refusal to pluck the flower of obedience. See also Bynum, *Resurrection* 159: "Indeed Hildegard says that humankind fails when it does not take in and give forth; it fails, for example, when it sees and smells but does not eat and digest obedience. In such metaphors, the organic and bodily processes of germination and nutrition are used unambiguously to describe that which is good, and the person is presented as a psychosomatic unity."

22. On women as food, and fertility as decay, see Bynum, *Resurrection* 221.

23. Compare Canto XXXIII of the *Paradiso*. The Living Light (*vivo lume*) seems to change through Dante's sight. Three circles, one circle, Eternal Light (*luce etterna*). That circle, as Dante watches, seems "painted with our effigy" (*pinta de la nostra effige*). He continues, "I wished to see the way in which our human effigy suited the circle and found place in it" (*veder voleva come si*

*convenne/ l'imago al cerchio e come vi s'indova*). God is like man. This is immediately before the poet's flash of insight. Dante's last image (302-303 in Mandelbaum's translation) is that of a wheel: "my/desire and will were moved already–like a wheel revolving uniformly– by/the Love that moves the sun and other stars." (*ma gia volgeva il mio disio e 'velle,/sì come rota ch 'igualmente è mossa,/l'amor che move il sole e l'altre stelle*). Hildegard describes God the Father as a wheel at the beginning of *Causae et curae* (2). On interpretations of the wheel in the Middle Ages, see Murray, Plates II-IV and 83-84, 98-101.

24. 336. Compare Karma Lochrie's discussions on mystical erotic joining with Christ's wounds (70), wounds as the site of mystical knowledge and speech (82-83) and the five wounds as five vowels in the text of Christ's body (Chapter 5). On the growth of devotion to the Five Wounds in relation to the Crusades and Bernard of Clairvaux, see the *Catholic Encyclopedia* 15: 714-15, and the *New Catholic Encyclopedia* 14:1035-37. Gertrude of Helfta prayed daily in honor of the 5,466 wounds inflicted on Christ (*Catholic Encyclopedia* 15:714).

25. Bynum, *Resurrection* 56; also 111, 149.

26. Cf. *Causae et curae* 5, where Hildegard describes the firmament and the winds: "Firmamentum autem ignem, solem, lunam, stellas et ventos habet, per quae omnia consistit et quorum proprietatibus firmatur, ne dissepetur. Nam ut anima totum corpus hominis tenet, ita etiam venti totum firmamentum continent, ne corrumpatur. . . . Nam terra tota scinderetur et rumperetur, si isti venti non essent, quemadmodum etiam homo totus scinderetur, si ossa non haberet." This particular image of fragmentation seems different from most of those Bynum discusses, which have to do with natural decay or with controlled fragmentation such as the distribution of saints' relics ("Material Continuity"). This is a chaotic flying apart, in modern psychological terms, a fear of loss of control. Such images can express fear of one's own creativity and sexuality. They are also reminiscent of the feared chaos in the opening lines of Yeats's poem "The Second Coming," which is full of biblical and medieval imagery (*Norton Anthology* 2:1582): "Turning and turning in the widening gyre / The falcon cannot hear the falconer; / Things fall apart; the center cannot hold / Mere anarchy is loosed upon the world. . . ." Hildegard's sense of dialogue and interaction between heaven and earth, body and soul extends also to man and woman. In her view, the sexes complement each other (Allen 233) and even share characteristics of the opposite sex (Cadden 166; Allen 240).

27. She did, however, bypass other authorities. See Feiss (11) on her refusal to quote human authorities and Newman (204) on her rejection of all human teaching.

28. ". . .et sol. . . lumen suum in lunam mittit, cum ad eum accedit, ut vir semen suum in feminam mittit. . . . *De luna.* Luna enim ex igne et ex tenui aere est atque in aere stat et habitaculum in ei habet et ipse per eam firmatur. Quae postquam evacuatur, sub solem vadit, et sphaera ab eo extenditur, quae illam ad ipsum trahit, ut achates ferrum ad se trahit. Illam accendit, sed et ceterae planetae et stellae atque aer et cetera luminaria, quae circa lunam sunt, ad eam flagrant et ad accensionem eius ipse succurrunt. . . . Interim enim, dum luna crescendo repletur, sol superiora firmamenti confirmat nec usquam ab hoc cessat. . . . Sed et postquam luna repletur, ita quod velit mulier praegnans efficitur, lumen suum emittit et stellis tradit, et ita stellae lucidiores efficiuntur. *De rore.* Tunc et stellae de eodem calore aerem calefaciunt et roborant, et aer calefactus sudorem suum, scilicet rorem suum, super terram mittit et eam fecundat. Unde et ipsa perfusa fructus gigni. . . . Sed vis lunae tanta est, quod tempestates illas superat et quod iterum splendorem suum emittit, quia vis lunae major est vi tempestatum illarum" (*Causae et curae* 8-9).

29. According to Charles Singer (224), three works containing anatomical descriptions would have been available to Hildegard, including "a series of five diagrams representing respectively the arteries, veins, bones, nerves, and muscles. . . . These diagrams were very widespread during the Middle Ages and were copied in the most servile fashion for centuries." Singer includes a representation of a thirteenth-century anatomical drawing. Barbara Newman (133-35) disputes that at least one of the sources Singer mentions, Constantine the African, would have been known to Hildegard. Hildegard must also be inspired by Paul's discussions of how individuals in the Church must cooperate as members of the body of Christ (e.g., 1 Cor. 12:12-31).

## WORKS CITED

### Primary Texts

Augustine. *Confessions.* Trans. R. S. Pine-Coffin. Harmondsworth: Penguin, 1961.

Hildegard of Bingen. "Epistola CCIr." *Hildegardis Bingensis epistolarium II.* Ed. L. Van Acker. *CCCM* 91A. Turnhout: Brepols, 1993.

————. *Scivias.* Trans. Columba Hart and Jane Bishop. New York: Paulist Press, 1990.

————.*Explanation of the Rule of St. Benedict.* Trans. Hugh Feiss. By Toronto: Peregrina, 1990.

*Hildegardis Causae et curae.* Ed. Paul Kaiser. Leipzig: Teubner, 1903.

*Hildegardis Scivias.* eds. A. Führkötter and A. Carlevaris. 2 pts. *CCCM* 43 and 43A. Turnhout: Brepols, 1978.

**Secondary Texts**

Allen, Prudence. "Hildegard of Bingen's Philosophy of Sex Identity." *Thought* 64 (1989): 231-41.

Bynum, Caroline Walker. "The Female Body and Religious Practice." *Fragmentation and Redemption: Essays on Gender and the Human Body in Medieval Religion.* New York: Zone, 1992. 181-238.

———. "Material Continuity, Personal Survival and the Resurrection of the Body: A Scholastic Discussion in Its Medieval and Modern Contexts." *Fragmentation and Redemption* , 239-297.

———. *The Resurrection of the Body in Western Christianity, 200-1336.* New York: Columbia University Press, 1995.

Cadden, Joan. "It Takes All Kinds: Sexuality and Gender Differences in Hildegard of Bingen's *Book of Compound Medicine.*" *Traditio* 40 (1984): 149-174.

*The Catholic Encyclopedia: An International Work of Reference on the Constitution, Doctrine, Discipline and History of the Catholic Church.* Ed. Charles G. Herbermann et al. 15 vols. New York: Appleton, 1908.

Cogan, Robert. "Hildegard's Fractal Antiphon." *Sonus: A Journal of Investigations into Global Music Possibilities* 11.1 (1990): 1-19.

Dante. *Paradiso.* Trans. Allen Mandelbaum. New York: Bantam, 1986.

Dronke, Peter. "Hildegard of Bingen as Poetess and Dramatist." *Poetic Individuality in the Middle Ages: New Departures in Poetry 1000-1150.* 2nd. ed. London: Westfield College, University of London Committee for Medieval Studies, 1986. 150-92.

Emerson, Jan S. "Hildegard von Bingen." *German-Language Women Writers: A Biocritical Sourcebook.* Eds. Elke Frederiksen and Elizabeth Ametsbichler. Westport: Greenwood, 1997. 69-77.

Escot, Pozzi. "Gothic Cathedral and the Hidden Geometry of St. Hildegard." *Sonus* 5.1 (Fall 1984): 14-31.

Flanagan, Sabina. *Hildegard of Bingen (1098-1179): A Visionary Life.* New York: Routledge, 1989.

Gardiner, Eileen, ed. *Visions of Heaven and Hell Before Dante.* Illus. Alexandra Eldridge. New York: Italica, 1989.

Gössmann, Elisabeth. "Das Menschenbild der Hildegard von Bingen und Elisabeth von Schönau vor dem Hintergrund der Frühscholastischen Anthropologie." *Frauenmystik im Mittelalter.* Eds. Peter Dinzelbacher and Dieter R. Bauer. Ostfildern: Schwaben, 1985. 24-47.

Lochrie, Karma. *Margery Kempe and Translations of the Flesh.* Philadelphia: University of Pennsylvania Press, 1991.

Mumford, Marilyn R. "A Feminist Prolegomenon for the Study of Hildegard of Bingen." *Gender, Culture, and the Arts: Women, Culture, and Society.* Eds. Ronald Dotterer and Susan Bowers. Selinsgrove: Susquehanna University Press: 1993. 44-53.

*The New Catholic Encyclopedia.* Ed. Catholic Universities of America. 14 vols. New York: McGraw-Hill, 1967.

Newman, Barbara. *Sister of Wisdom: St. Hildegard's Theology of the Feminine.* Berkeley: Universty of California Press, 1987.

*Norton Anthology of English Literature.* Ed. M. H. Abrams. 2 vols. New York: Norton, 1968.

Pawlik, Manfred. "Einführung." *Hildegard von Bingen. Heilwissen. Von den Ursachen und der Behandlung von Krankheiten.* Trans. Manfred Pawlik. Freiburg: Herder, 1991. 5-21.

Singer, Charles. *From Magic to Science: Essays on the Scientific Twilight.* New York: Boni and Liveright, 1928.

Wolfram von Eschenbach. *Parzival.* Band 1: Buch 1-8. Mittelhochdeutsch/Neuhochdeutsch. Trans. Wolfgang Spiewok. Stuttgart: Reclam, 1996, 1981.

Zaleski, Carol. *Otherworld Journeys: Accounts of Near-Death Experience in Medieval and Modern Times.* New York: Oxford University Press, 1987.

# Where Is the Body?

## Images of Eve and Mary in the *Scivias*

*Rebecca L.R. Garber*

Eve and Mary represent the two most common role models for medieval women: they appear in contemporary sermons, treatises, medieval texts, romances, sculpture, stained-glass windows, altar pieces, manuscript illuminations. Anywhere that men attempted to define or describe women's roles, one finds references to Eve and Mary. Within texts written by medieval German religious women, however, this most famous feminine pairing is practically absent. Although Mary retains an important role as the mother of Christ, monastic women do not present her as the only positive role model available to women; rather Mary appears as one among several figures considered ideal for imitation, including Christ, the saints, biblical figures and saintly contemporaries. Eve remains significant in her absence: if her name appears within a text at all, it is usually within the formula "daughter of Eve" as a reference to the author, or to women in general. An exception to this general trend, especially with regard to Eve, can be found in the work of Hildegard von Bingen. Her texts present the most complex Mariology of medieval German women writers: Hildegard is the only woman writer to include constructions of Eve within her Mariology, and her comparison of the two women moves beyond a simple oppositional pairing towards a recuperation of Eve through Mary. By offering Eve redemption through Mary, Hildegard offers a means to redeem the female body: Eve's potential yet spoiled fecundity is fulfilled by Mary's corporeal yet non-carnal fertility.

In order to demonstrate just how Hildegard achieves this, I begin with a very brief history of the representation of Eve and Mary to establish a context for Hildegard's portrayals, then I examine two Creation visions from the *Scivias* in which the two women appear symbolically represented. I offer readings of four of Hildegard's Marian lyrics in which Eve, Mary, and a figure of Everywoman appear and conclude with a discussion about Eve and Mary and their possible function as role models for women within Hildegard's texts.

Eve and Mary have appeared throughout Christian history as concurrently parallel and opposite figures. Most authors, theologians and artists, however, present the oppositional nature of the two women more strongly than their similarities. The opposing characteristics of the two women were present at what Ernst Guldan calls "the cradle of Mariology" in the second century C.E. (28), and they remain more numerous than the parallels. In his monumental history of the representation of the two women, Guldan follows several strands of their oppositional portrayal from the patristic period to the twentieth century. These contrasting representations have their roots in patristic writings by such authors as Justin Martyr († circa 165), Irenaeus of Lyon († 202), and Tertullian († post 220), and Zeno of Verona († ca. 371-2). These writers represent Eve as Mary's antithesis more often than as her counterpart in a repetitive cycle of oppositions that was copied down through the centuries. Eve disobeyed, Mary obeyed; Eve lacked faith, Mary remained faithful; Eve appears in the role of *mater morentium*, Mary as *Mater viventium*; Eve listened to the serpent and her actions bore travail, Mary received the angel's words and bore salvation.[1] The palindrome "Eva-Ave" is a well-known lexical symbol for Mary's reversal of Eve's sin. Within visual media, artists often represented Eve as naked, yet unrepentant, as she and Adam are driven from the garden. In contrast, these same painters consistently placed Mary as respectfully clothed, humble, and within an interior space. In these visual representations, the artists contrast the blessed with the punished by means of the physicality of the clothed versus the naked female body. Eve appears as the uncontrollable, sinful female body in contrast with the enclosed, incorruptible Virgin Mary.

Yet for these oppositions to maintain their power to convince, they must spring from a similar root: Eve's shame and Mary's grace can only be fully appreciated if they share an initial identical nature. Thus Eve appears in patristic literature in the role of feminine archetype that finds its perfection in Mary (Guldan 26f.). Both Eve and Mary were created directly by the Trinity,[2] Eve's initial virginity influenced the doctrine of Mary's Immaculate Conception (Guldan 24), and maternal images of the two women nursing their infants often contain similarities.[3] These parallels, however, always serve to underscore the differing nature of the two women: Eve remains always already fallen from Mary's perfection. Although Eve was initially a virgin created by the Trinity, the Fall precluded her retaining her virgin state. Eve as mother remains similarly less wonderful than Mary, as is apparent from the fates of their children. Tertullian eloquently summed up the oppositional nature of the women's maternities: the fallen Eve bore the devil who murdered his brother; Mary bore him who saved his brother and murderer, Israel.[4] Even at those points in which Eve and Mary share the most common ground, Mary must represent the superior position, the perfection of Eve: Eve's lesser and lower nature leads from initial similarity into the oppositional relationship most commonly represented in art and literature.

Hildegard was fully cognizant of the contrasts between the two women. In the majority of her Marian lyrics, Hildegard opposes Eve and Mary. She usually refers to the female actors in the drama of Fall and Redemption by name and makes specific reference to Eve's guilt and Mary's salvific innocence. Within her lyrical corpus, Hildegard sets Eve's specific faults in opposition to Mary's individual virtues: Eve appears "swollen with pride" and "contemptuous of God's order," while Mary is humble.[5] Eve's vice of pride, *superbia*, is found in the responsory "Ave Maria" (110). This sin is further implied in Eve's reaction to God's order: she "despised all things," [*hec omnia Eva contempsit*] in the song "O viridissima virga" (126). Hildegard praises Mary's humility in the antiphon "O quam magnum miraculum" (120). Hildegard also contrasts Mary's perpetual virginity, either implicitly or explicitly, with Eve's role in the sexuality of the original sin. While most poems explicitly mention Mary's virginity, several use metaphors for it instead, such as the *clausa porta* of the antiphon "Hodie aperuit" (116) and the responsory "O quam preciosa" (134). The sexual nature of the Fall is implied in the "mingled blood" found in the antiphon "Cum processit factura" (118). It appears more explicitly in the "laws of the flesh that Eve built" [*carnis iura que construxit Eva*] in the antiphon "O tu illustrata"[6] (136). A further point of contrast remains Eve's role in the origins of human mortality, and Mary's role in obtaining eternal life. Eve is held responsible for the "torment of souls," [*tormenta animarum*], while Mary is the agent of life [*vivificum instrumentum*] in the responsory "O clarissima mater" (112). Eve "gives birth to pain," [*plenum dolorum generi*], whereas Mary "bore the new light for humanity," [*novum lumen humano generi*] in the sequence "O virga ac diadema" (128ff).[7] Along with mortality, Hildegard often mentions the Fall itself, either directly or indirectly, Eve "disturbed the primal matter," [*primam materiam, quam Eva turbavit*] causing the Fall in the antiphon "O splendissima gemma," (114).[8] In addition, Mary's motherhood is explicitly celebrated as loving and radiant, while Eve appears only once as the already fallen mother, whose children are doomed to suffer. Mary is the *amatissima mater* and the *clarissima mater* in the responsories "Ave Maria" (110), and "O clarissima mater" (112), respectively. Eve should have been the mother of all, but fell [*Deus matrem omnium posuit . . . plenum dolorum generi*] in the sequence "O virga ac diadema" (130).

Yet Hildegard's representation of Eve and Mary remains more complex than a simple opposition. Within the illuminations and accompanying text of the *Scivias*, and also within four of her lyrics, Hildegard represents the parallel nature of the two women. Hildegard's images within the *Scivias*, when read against their historical context and her lyrics, appear quite striking. Of the illuminations in which Eve or Mary appears, two are images of the Creation and Fall. This compression of the "earliest history" is quite common in art and literature and has its roots in the Genesis story itself. The story of the creation of humanity, especially as told by the Yahwist author (Genesis 2:7-3:24) is never just the Creation but always already the Creation and Fall.[9] However, the compression of the images and the cryptic nature of Hildegard's representations of Eve and Mary within them require extensive interpretive unpacking on the part of the reader.

The second vision in Book I of the *Scivias,* Vision I. 2 (see Plate 1), presents the Creation, Temptation and Fall of humanity within one register. In contrast with the corporeal humanity of Adam, Eve appears only in symbolic form: she is the stylized cloud, the *candidum nubem* (13),[10] shaped like a wing, rising from Adam's rib. Within the nimbus of the cloud are "many and many stars," *plurimas plurimasque stellas* that represent the children Eve will bear as the mother of the human race, *omnem multitudinem humani generis. . . in suo corpore gestans* (19). The abstraction of the wing contrasts with the actual physicality of sexual intercourse, pregnancy and childbirth and allows Hildegard to bracket questions of Eve's sexuality and sinful nature. By so doing, she removes any "stain" from Eve's progeny, who, according to the divine

Plate 1: The Creation, Temptation and Fall of Humanity. *Scivias* I, 2.

xxi quod uir non mu in uou etate.
non nisi nubilem uxorem ducat.
xxii De uitanda illicita 1 libidinosa
pollutione.
xxiii Quare mulier post partum uel
a uiro corrupta in occulto mane
at 1 ab ingressu templi abstineat.
Qui in coitu pregnantis se pollu
unt. homicide sunt.
xxiiii O see de eadem re.
xxv De commendatione castitatis.
xxvi Johannes de eadem re.
xxvii d expulso adam ds paradysu
minuit.
xxviii d quia homo deo rebellis exsti
tit. creatura ei prius subiecta se
illi opposuit.
xxix De amenitate paradysi que su
cum 1 uim terre tribuit. ut
anima corpori.
xxx Quare ds hominem talem fecit
quod peccare potuit.
xxxi d homo non debet summa p
scrutari cum nec infima ualeat
examinare.
xxxii d homo nunc clarior fulget
quam prius in celo.
xxxiii Similitudo horti. ouis 1 marga
rite ad hominem.
xxxiiii e commendatione humilitatis
1 caritatis. que clariores ceteris
uirtutib exsistunt.

plan, are destined to replace the devil and the fallen angels in heaven: the similarity between the stars within the wing and those shining in the firmament is readily apparent. Adam lies prone, sleeping while Eve is created, yet also awake, as he cups a hand to his ear and listens to the temptations of the flaming hell-mouth. Thus Hildegard portrays Adam as sinful as well as Eve, and lays the blame more equally upon both parents. The black pool that rises up from hell spawns eight arms, *taeterrima nebula se extendens* (13), seven of which assault heaven but are prevented from penetrating by the firmament. The eighth, shaped as a serpent's head, spews black vomit on the cloud-like wing that is Eve and her children [*in ipsa clara regione candidam nubem. . . afflauit*] symbolizing the original sin. The Fall in which the devil cast both Adam (the human form) and Eve (the white cloud) out of that region [*illam eandemque formam hominis de eadem regione ita eiecit*] appears in the disturbance of the elements, which appear in the four corners: *ita omnia elementa mundi. . . in maximam inquietudinem uersa horribiles terrores ostenderunt. . . .*

The Creation and Fall image of the first vision in Book II, Vision II. 1, (Plate 2) concentrates on Adam and his relationship with Christ, the second Adam. Indeed, a multiplicity of Adams appears in the three registers of the illumination. The central roundel contains the six days of creation; Adam first appears at the bottom of the roundel, tinted red, newly formed from clay, *paruam glebam limosae terrae* (110). The Adam of the upper register sniffs [*odorem idem homo naribus quidem sensit*] but does not pick the white flower of obedience: his "turning away," precipitates the Fall (110). Again, Hildegard represents Adam as guilty. The blackness of the central register represents the sin and death into which Adam has fallen, *ad ueram cognitionem eius peccatis grauatus* (117); the reddish tinge to his flesh reflects the physical nature of his sins upon his body. Adam, humanity, is not without hope of salvation, however, which appears in the figures of the stars, representing the prophets: *Quod Abraham Isaac et Iacob et alii prophetae mvndi tenebras significationibvs svis repercvsservnt* (117).[11] Like the stars within the wing-like cloud of Eve, the stars surrounding Adam again represent the progeny of the first parents, here associated with paternity. In acknowledgement of the physical differences between men and women, the stars surround Adam, while they appear within the body of Eve. In the final register, the second Adam, Jesus, the *serenissimum hominem* (111), appears to redeem humanity to the inheritance lost by Adam [*atque eos tactu redemptionis suae ad*

Plate 2: The Creation and Fall of Adam. *Scivias* II, 1.

*hereditatem ipsorum quam in Adam perdiderant misericorditer eduxit]* (119).

Eve does not appear in the second Creation image, nor does Hildegard explicitly mention her in the accompanying textual interpretations. Rather, the symbolic representation of the first woman appears as the white flower, the *candissimum florem*, which Hildegard links with obedience (116). The series of imagesÑ the white flower; the dew on the grass,[*ros pendet in gramine*] and the sweet command of highest obedienceÑ recall Hildegard's hymn *Ave generosa* and confirm that the flower symbolizes Mary, not Eve (Newman, *Symphonia* 122f.). Contemporary theologians, including Hildegard, held that although Mary does not appear in the biblical account of the Creation, she, or at least her soul, was with God in the beginning, in a manner similar to that of Christ.[12] Further, as Vision II.1 includes a representation of the coming of the second Adam, that is, Christ, Mary appears a second time in relation to this event in divine history. In the lowest register she is the radiant light of the dawn, into which the divine flame is absorbed, symbolizing the incarnation, and from which the most serene man (Christ) emerges: *fulgor uelut aurora apparet, cui eadem flamma mirabiliter infusa est, ... de eodem fulgore praefatae aurorae serenissimum hominem egredientem* (118). During the twelfth century, theologians began the association of Mary with the bride in the Song of Songs, whose beauty is compared with the dawn, and Mary appears within Hildegard's lyrics as the dawn.[13] Within the vision, Hildegard carefully separates both symbolic representations of Mary from the blackness of sin which engulfs Adam: Mary remains physically and theologically different from the first parents.

Until the fifteenth century, the most common visual representations of Eve contained the cycle of the Temptation, Fall, and Expulsion (Guldan 56). Thus, it can be said that Hildegard's Creation images both have strong ties with this artistic tradition, as the same series is represented in her illuminations. The image of Eve as the luminous wing forms an especially eloquent statement on Hildegard's part on the participation of the first woman, and thus all women, in the divine plan. The white cloud, created within the "bright region" of paradise, the *clara regione* (13, 19), invokes explicit associations with Eve's innocence [*Evam innocentem animum habentem*] (19) and implicit references to the shining light of divinity, the *lux vivens* (4). The "living light" is both the location within the divinity where

Hildegard saw her visions and the voice of the divine Godhead who interpreted them. Elsewhere, Hildegard associates white garments with the brides of Christ, that is, with the virgin nuns who wed themselves to the heavenly bridegroom, in a partial imitation of both Ecclesia and the Virgin Mary.[14] Hildegard considers white an appropriate color for virgins, as it reflects their purity, chastity and bodily integrity. Likewise, the white color of the cloud reflects Eve's initial virgin state, and her corporeal integrity, which was the original model for women's participation in salvation history.

Within the illumination, the cloud-wing has a distinct green color. Yet both Hildegard's initial report of her vision, and the later interpretation describe the wing as white, a *candidum nubem* (13, 19). This discrepancy with the text must be regarded as deliberate, as there is no similar inconsistency within other illuminations in which virtues are described as appearing in white tunics or veils (specifically Book III, visions 3 and 7). According to both Barbara Newman and Peter Dronke, Hildegard associated the color green with *viriditas*, that is, with "life, growth, and fertility flowing from the life-creating power of God," and the "greenness of paradise which knows no Fall" (Newman, *Sister* 102; Dronke 82, 84). The "fruitful fecundity" represented by the green cloud-wing evokes Eve in her original role as mother of humankind (Phillips 41) yet the associations of this fertility with growth and greeness are distinctly non-carnal. Long before Hildegard, theologians had questioned the possibilities of procreation prior to the Fall: according to Augustine, generation wold have been physical, but not corrupt.[15] Theological readings of God's curse on woman had granted Eve only the pain of child-bearing;[16] of all women, Mary alone was privileged with the "joy of motherhood" (Warner 58, 338; Phillips 141). The presence of the stars within the body of the first Eve, which represent the "whole human race, shining with God's preordination" [*omnem multitudinem humani generis in praeordinatione Dei lucentem*](19) returns the first Eve joyously to her role as mother and addresses one aspect of the bodilyness of procreation which many theologians ignore, that of pregnancy. The description of Eve's prelapsarian maternity found in the *Causae et curae* echoes this illumination: *Prima enim mater humani generis posita erat ad similitudinem aetheris, quia ut aether stellas integras in se continet, sic ipsa integra et incorrupta sine dolore genes humanum in se habebat* [The first mother of humanity was created similar to the Ether; because just as the Ether bears the stars and remains intact, so she, intact and uninjured, and without pain, bore the human race within herself] (104). Hildegard's scientific description of Eve's pregnancy parallels theological discussions of Mary's postpartum corporeal integrity. The colors of the wing within the *Scivias* text and illumination thus invoke associations with divinity, innocence and physical but non-carnal fecundity.

The brightness of the wing is also a rejection of the dualist heresies like those of the Cathars, the Albigensians and the Waldensians. These heresies attempted to grapple with the origin of evil and settled on an extreme view; there were two powers, one wholly good, the other evil, and it was the evil power that created the world. Souls, a creation of the good power, were trapped against their will within the intrinsically evil flesh.[17] Orthodox Catholics distinguished between the material world of the body, which was not inherently evil, and the sinful, carnal appetites of the flesh. Hildegard preached a public sermon against the Cathars in Cologne before an audience of lay- and religious people in about 1163.[18] Hildegard's vision of Eve is consonant with her preaching and shows the souls (the stars) as entering into a body of light; they are not trapped in darkness. Neither the cloud nor the physicality it represents is intrinsically evil. The stars within the wing, which is the body of Eve, shine no less brightly than those in heaven; after passing through this life, they will replace those angels that fell from grace.

Eve is completely absent from the second Creation vision, Vision II. The feminine form represented within the garden appears as a white flower. Like the cloud in the earlier vision, the flower is blessed with *umida viriditate fructuositatis* (116), "fresh green fruitfulness," which for Hildegard represents the fecundity of paradise (Newman, *Sister* 102) and also Mary's salvific pregnancy.[19]

Interestingly, the flower remains completely passive in this image: she neither sins nor is tempted; she neither resists temptation, nor is she attacked. Instead, the interpretation focuses on Adam's actions, or lack of them, and how they relate to the flower. Adam does not taste or touch the flower [*sed gustam eius ore non percepit, nec manibus eum tetigit* ](116). The alimentary nature by which Adam would have come to a fuller understanding of obedience invokes two major associations. One follows a monastic trope, which has roots in Augustinian thought, in which the practice of reading Scripture aloud was considered a "rumination" on God's word and nourishment for the soul.[20] The second accords with the medical practice of ingestion of herbal remedies. The flower of obedience thus can be linked with both Mary and Christ as a means of healing mankind.[21] Hildegard's terminology supports both readings. Although she employs *intromisit* instead of *ruminavit,* she follows this with the statement that whatever so "introduced into the body" will be intimately embraced, *intimae amplexionis* (117), and thus understood.

Yet these images represent not only the Creation but also the Fall: the attack of the serpent on the cloud-wing, Adam's listening to the hell-mouth, his turning away from the flower, his subsequent descent into darkness, and the disturbance of the elements reveal that the future of humanity will not reside within the bliss of Eden but will exist in a fallen state. Within the interpretation of the first vision, Hildegard identifies the original sin and relates it to both sexuality and disobedience. While within the second vision, the sexual nature of the sin is suppressed and only disobedience appears. Both of these readings of the Fall accord with the traditions of the Catholic Church extending back to the patristic period.

The sexual nature of the Genesis transgression was prominent in Jewish writings prior to the composition of the New Testament (Phillips 45). Thus, although the Christian Church Fathers did not originate the reading of the Fall as "a horror story of sexual awareness," they did make it the focus of their interpretations (Phillips 64). If the Fall is read as the awakening of sexuality, or the introduction of lust into the created order, then the actions of the various participants acquire particular sexual resonance. The snake can be read as a phallus; Eve's consumption of the forbidden fruit appears as sexual intercourse with the serpent and the corresponding loss of innocence, and Adam becomes the first cuckold. When read against a backdrop of normative heterosexuality, this becomes a partial explanation as to why Eve was seduced and not Adam. Further lending credence to this interpretation is the Jewish tradition that represents the serpent as a male seducer (Phillips 62). I do not intend to imply that Hildegard may have known the Jewish tradition, only that the tradition of representing the serpent as male existed and that the phallic nature of the snake was an established tradition. Also, although *serpens* appears most commonly as a feminine noun, within ecclesiastical Latin it appears regularly gendered as masculine. Further, its master, the devil, always appears as masculine, and the snake can be seen as an extension of *diabolus*, no pun intended.

Returning to Hildegard's image and texts, the serpent's head which vomits upon the wing appears distinctly phallic. The action (which

appears in the illumination as an attack) is described within the text as a
*seductionem serpentis* (19). Further underscoring the sexual nature of
this event is Eve's loss of innocence: following the serpent's seduction,
she in turn understands how to seduce Adam: suddenly she is able to
"flatter him and thus to win his assent and lead him into
disobedience"(19). The sexual nature of the sin receives further
emphasis through its contextualization within the extended explication
and discussion of the vision. Hildegard interprets the abbreviated
description of the Fall in chapter 9; of the fifteen chapters following
this explication, twelve focus on sexually related topics: marriage,
appropriate and inappropriate sexuality, and chastity.

Within the illumination, the paradisical body of Eve shines without
stain, until the serpent breathes a black poison upon the wing (the Latin
is *afflauit* rather than *vomuit*), in a possible reversal and parody of the
breath of life (Nolan 119). In a curious silence within the text, this
action, which represents the Fall of humanity, receives no subsequent
description or elaboration. In a text filled with interpretations of
specific colors (one thinks, for example, of the meanings attached to the
colored garb of the virtues, or the varicolored zones on the monumental
figures of Ecclesia and Synagoga), Hildegard remains silent about the
black poison. For several reasons, I would identify the substance as
semen. After all, the sin itself is identified within this vision as a sexual
act, as I noted above, in which semen would play a part. Further,
Hildegard held the rather unusual opinion that semen was poisonous
until "it is neutralized by the benign elements of the woman's
womb,"[22] and she also believed that semen first became poisonous as a
direct result of the Fall.[23] Finally, sexual intercourse with a virgin (such
as Eve was before the Fall) destroys the woman's bodily integrity and
is one of two reasons for which Hildegard would deny entry into the
church sanctuary to a woman.[24]

Within the first image, the disobedience of the first parents
receives mention (18f., 31), but the weight of the discussion falls upon
the sexual nature of the sin (19-31). This is not the case in the second
image, in which obedience plays a much greater role: the corporeal
nature of the first woman and her role in physical generation and
human sexuality are made notable by their absence.

In this second image, Hildegard interprets the idea of touching the
flower to gain further understanding according to Christian and
monastic ideals of good works, the manual labor called for in the
Benedictine Rule (chap. 48). However, there is another, less

monastically appropriate interpretation. "Plucking" or 'breaking flowers" was a medieval euphemism for sexual intercourse.[25] As a member of the nobility, Hildegard would have been aware of this metaphor, regardless of her monastic upbringing. Nuns were hardly isolated from the outside world in the twelfth century: secular visitors brought their retinues into the monastery; nuns traveled outside their walls on errands, thus having plenty of opportunity to hear secular lyrics, including this image.[26] As can be seen from my discussion of the other Creation vision, Hildegard knew and agreed with the theology regarding the sexual nature of the Fall. However, no hint of sexuality touches the image of the flower or the interpretation of the Fall within this vision: Hildegard not only refrains from discussing sexuality, marriage, fornication and adultery, she also makes no mention of chastity or virginity.[27] Instead, Hildegard concentrates the interpretation on obedience. Adam "turned his back to the divine command" [*divino praecepto. . . dorsum praebuit*]—that is, he disobeyed.

In opposition to Adam and his act of disobedience, symbolic figures of obedience appear in each of the three registers. Within the first register, Adam kneels before the white flower of obedience. In the middle register, his iniquity appears readily visible as his sin stains his body red. In contrast, the stars representing the prophets shine with the same radiance as the angelic stars in heaven (Visions I. 2 and III. 1) and share a similar divine light with Christ, the second Adam. Although Hildegard does not offer a detailed record of the prophets' "works of faith" [*fideli opere* ](117), she does imply by her choice of prophets that obedience to the divine command distinguishes these remarkable men, *spectabilis viri* (616) from Adam. The first prophet mentioned is Abraham, who, from the time of Augustine, was regarded as an archetype of obedience.[28] Within the final register, two figures of obedience appear, Christ and the Virgin Mary. Christ's obedience to God's command is nowhere more apparent than when he accepts his Crucifixion (Matt. 26: 39-44; Mark 14: 35-41; Luke 22: 42-44; John 18: 11). Mary, the feminine archetype of obedience, appears symbolically within the lower register as the "radiant dawn. . . the purity of unstained virginity" [*fulgore aurorae . . . in candone intermeatae uirginitatis inuiolabiliter* ](119).

Archetypes of obedience thus appear implicitly within all three registers. With regard to the male representatives of the virtue, obedience is presented as an active virtue, related to the concept of the *opere manuum* found in the Benedictine Rule. On the other hand, the feminine symbols of the virtue are quite passive. Neither the flower nor the dawn appears affected by the actions of the men around them: Adam's activities, not the flower's, doom humanity, and Mary's perpetual virginity is by definition unchanged by her pregnancy. Whereas in the previous vision, both disobedience and sexuality form part of the sin of the first parents, here Hildegard posits the original sin as disobedience alone. However, like the flower, the nature of the sin remains curiously passive: while the sexual sin is represented actively, Adam sins here in *not* tasting, *not* reaching out for the flower of obedience. By his inactivity and inattention to God, he falls. In a way, this mitigates the nature of the sin, removing it from the category of commission to omission.

This vision demonstrates the inevitability of the original sin of the first parents. Even though Eve, the woman who, according to much contemporary theology was the source of all sorrow and toil in the world, is absent, Adam still sins. This is not proof that Hildegard was a proto-feminist. Hildegard believed firmly in the doctrine of the *felix culpa*, or fortunate fallÑ that Christ's coming was preordained from before the creation of the world to redeem humanity from sin. The obvious corollary to this belief is that the original sin was also preordained.

Like the Adam of the second image, who turns away from God according to the counsel of the devil, the Adam of the first image is also directly tempted. The temptation finds its imagery in Adam and the hell-mouth in the lower-left corner of the image. In comparison with the attack on the passive wing, Adam actively listens to the flames rising from the hell-mouth. The shape of the wing and the hell-mouth invite further comparison. The edge of the hell-mouth touches Adam's lower shoulder and shapes a concave curve to his left in a wing-like manner. The flames shooting forth resemble stylized feathers. In spite of its appearance, this wing offers no aerodynamic support; in contrast with the wing of light that cups the air beneath it and supports the figure, this fiery wing is broken, and the flier, Adam, falls with it.

In both visions but most explicitly in the second, Adam's actions determine the fall of humanity. The primacy of Adam's sin appears in Hildegard's terminology for the Fall: it is the *casus Adae*, the fall of Adam rather than of Eve. Some modern feminists have interpreted this terminology as a proto-feminist mitigation of Eve's guilt, and Hildegard does tend to assign Eve somewhat less than full guilt for the

Fall. However, I believe it would be highly anachronistic to read any type of feminist agenda into Hildegard's texts.

Several points undermine a reading of this terminology as a feminist stance on Hildegard's part. First, and perhaps most importantly, this was the standard phrase used by theologians to refer to the Fall of humanity. Adam's sin receives the greater emphasis, because, according to patriarchal cultures, Adam's sin is what doomed humanity, not Eve's (Phillips 74). According to this theology, if Adam had not followed Eve into sin, then humanity would still have enjoyed paradise.[29] Thus Adam's Fall received a great deal of theological interest and attempts at explanation. This is in part due to the fact that Genesis 2 contains no justification as to why Adam sinned, and humankind abhors a vacuum. Twenty centuries of male, theological rationalizing has attempted to explain Adam's actions. One of the most enduring reasons was penned by Augustine, who posited that Adam sinned out of love, to avoid being separated from Eve, in an act of heroic self-sacrifice.[30]

It is also important to note that although Hildegard extends blame for the original sin to Adam and most especially to the devil, she does not change the order of the human's entry into sin: Eve always sins first. In most literature on the Fall, including *Scivias* I. 2, the devil approaches Eve first, having ascertained that she is the weaker of the two humans and most likely to believe him, *sciebat mulieris mollitiem facilius uincendium quam uiri fortitudenem* (19). Thus, there is never a question as to the order of sin. However, in a very few texts, the devil approaches Adam directly, as implied in *Scivias* Vision II. 1.[31] In both the Anglo-Saxon biblical interpretation, *Genesis B*, and *Le Mystère d'Adam*, Adam rejects the devil's council, and Satan goes on to tempt Eve, who succumbs and seduces Adam. While the order of the Fall is unclear in Vision II. 1, Hildegard explicitly states in the *Causae et curae* that not only did Eve sin first, but it was necessary for the ultimate redemption of humanity that sin enter the human race through the lesser member, that is, through the female rather than through the male.[32]

Hildegard never denies Adam and Eve's guilt in the question of original sin. The world is obviously fallen, and Christ's coming was necessary for its redemption. However, she mitigates Eve's guilt by sharing the blame: Adam also sinned, not just Eve. Hildegard also lays most of the blame on the devil, which is especially clear in the first image (Newman, *Sister* 112f.). The serpent's head spewing darkness on the wing is an overt attack on the first woman and her children. The cause of the Fall is not an internal, inherent characteristic of Eve; rather, evil comes specifically from the outside.

These two images, when read together, offer a series of commentaries on Hildegard's representation of the Creation and Fall of humanity and woman's place within the divine plan. Within the *Scivias*, Hildegard weaves a complex relationship between the two women most important to salvation history, Eve and Mary. They both appear within the divine light of the initial creation, but only one remains there. Woman appears thus not as intrinsically evil but as holding a prominent and creative place in the divine plan. Eve and her progeny are affected by the black poison of the devil (I. 2), whereas Mary appears unstained by the black pool into which Adam and his descendants fall (II. 1): the images compare Eve's potential yet spoiled fecundity with Mary's corporeal yet non-carnal fertility. Eve's sin involved sexuality and disobedience, whereas Mary appears as obedience incarnate and not as a sexually charged figure. Finally, although Adam shares blame for the Fall, the greatest portion of guilt belongs to the devil.

A similar relationship between Eve and Mary can be found in Hildegard's Marian lyrics: Hildegard both contrasts the negative Eve with the positive Mary yet also compares the initial, pre-lapsarian Eve with Mary in a positive fashion. Hildegard's recuperation of Eve through Mary is more complete in her lyrics than in the *Scivias*, because, at a few points within her lyrical corpus, Mary ultimately redeems Eve's fall so completely that all humankind should celebrate "the exultation of woman per se on account of Mary" and her role in salvation history (Newman, *Symphonia* 273). Hildegard's Marian cycle forms the largest single topic of her lyrics: sixteen of the sixty-three songs focus on the role of Mary in salvation history.[33] Within the majority of these lyrics, Hildegard opposes the two women. However, as in the *Scivias*, Hildegard also celebrates the positive roles that women were destined to play in salvation history.

There are four poems in which Mary redeems Eve in this fashion: the two antiphons, "Quia ergo femina" and "O quam magnum miraculum," the sequence, "O virga ac diadema," and the song, "O magna res." The song "O magna res" does not appear within the *Symphonia* corpus but rather is one of four lyrical passages found within the "Miscellany" section of the Riesenkodex. According to Newman, these should be considered part of Hildegard's musical works, even though the music has been lost.[34] In these hymns, woman initially brings pain; however, salvation also arrives in the "feminine form" of woman. Hildegard claims that, because of Mary, "the feminine form receives the highest blessing" [*et idea est summa benedicta in feminea forma* ] (116). She further finds that "a great felicity is in this form" [*magna felicitas est in ista forma* ] (120) and that "God made the form of a woman into the mirror of all his beauty" [*Deus formam mulieris produxit, quam fecit speculum omnis ornamenti sui* ] (130). Finally, Hildegard declares that "the feminine form is glorious because the mightiest life has arisen in her" [*O feminea forma. . . quam gloriosa es, quoniam fortissima vita in te surrexit* ] (264). The feminine form that these poems celebrate stands as an image of Everywoman, and implicitly includes Eve.

Hildegard's inclusion of Eve within these poems differs markedly from the rest of her Marian lyrics, in which she opposes the two women. Even in these four songs, Hildegard never denies Eve's culpability: instead, Mary works to assuage Eve's guilt so completely that all humanity should rejoice in womankind. That both women can appear in such opposing roles and yet still become a symbol for Everywoman lies in Hildegard's avoidance of their names, a rhetorical strategy that parallels her avoidance of their human representations within the *Scivias*. Instead, Hildegard employs short descriptive phrases to identify the two women. Thus, the "woman who built death" [*femina mortem instruxit* ] (116) obviously represents Eve. Likewise, the "feminine form into which a king entered" [*femineam formam rex introivit* ] (120), refers to Mary. However, the rhetorical repetition of the subject "woman" (*femina* or *mulier*) to refer to Eve and then to Mary within the same poem allows the second *feminea forma* to recuperate the first. This act of recuperation forms the basis for the ensuing celebration of all who partake in this feminine form as Everywoman.

The conflation and recuperation of Eve with and by Mary appear most clearly in the two antiphons. Within the first, "Quia ergo femina," (116) the negative actions of one *femina* are contrasted with the positive deeds of the *virgo*. These two very separate feminine references obviously represent Eve and Mary as oppositional figures. Yet Mary so completely recuperates Eve's actions that the "highest blessing" is found, not only within a virgin and not solely within Mary but in the *feminea forma* itself. Thus all women, as representatives of Everywoman, partake in the blessing of God due to Mary.

Within the song, "O magna res," it is possible to see the beginnings of Hildegard's theory of Mary's recuperative powers. As in the antiphon "Quia ergo femina," a woman causes the construction of sorrow, and this action is "washed away" by another, who is later identified as the familiar *feminea forma*. However, this antiphon alludes to Everywoman through repetition of *femina* within *feminea forma* to refer to both Eve and Mary, which is not the case here. In reference to Eve, Hildegard employs the sexually valenced term *mulier*, "wife" or "married woman": *O luctus! Ach meror! He plantus, qui in muliere edificati sunt* ["O grief, O sorrow, O mourning, that were built in a married woman"] (264). Mary, on the other hand, appears as the theologically oriented *feminea forma*. While this may appear to be quibbling over classical Latin vocabulary, an examination of Hildegard's usage of *femina* versus *mulier* within the *Scivias* reveals that she generally prefers the term *mulier* when discussing sexual matters or marital topics and *femina* when the subject is theological in nature.[35] And yet, in a move similar to Hildegard's placement of Mary in paradise in *Scivias* Vision II. 1, Mary appropriates Eve's formation from the rib. As the dawn, Hildegard's feminine image of the divine light, she washes the faults from the first (Adam's) rib: *O aurora, hec abluisti in forma prime coste*. It is this cleansed "form of the primal rib," that is, Mary in place of Eve, who bears the life that will defeat death. Mary, through the divine time-slippage accessible to the conflated *feminea forma*, both returns to the paradisical state and at the same time returns later to bear the savior in order to retrieve humanity from the Fall. In the role of *feminea forma* it is possible for all women "who were made to adorn all the creatures [of the world]" [ *ita quod omnes creature per te ornate sunt*] according to the original divine plan reflected in the divine light of the dawn associated with Mary.

"O quam magnum miraculum," the second antiphon, contains the most complete conflation of the two women, partially due to the consistency with which the terms *feminea forma* and *femina* are employed: the terminology refers equally to Eve and Mary. Unlike "Quia ergo femina" and "O magna res," in which the terminology changes to reflect the opposing natures of the two women, this antiphon offers a perfect parallelism of terms. Additionally, the conflation succeeds because the poem begins, not with the contrary nature of Eve but with the celebration of Mary, "the feminine form into whom God entered" [*quod in dubditam feminineam formam rex introivit* ] (120). The feminine receives extensive praise so that Eve's transgression appears only as a tangent, an easily dismissed aside as the poem continues in its paean of praise.

The sequence, "O virga ac diadema," contains a similar conflationary maneuver; however, the women also appear as quite separate and opposing beings within the first and third sections of the poem. Newman has ably pointed out the manner in which the structure resembles a triptych: the first and third parts parallel each other in their discussion of the fallen sexuality and frame the central presentation of the divine role of the feminine at the Creation (Newman, *Symphonia* 277). Within the central section, both Mary and Eve are indirectly evoked: Mary appears within the *virga/virgo* punning of strophes 3a and 3b, and God creates Eve, the *formam mulieris*, from Adam's side in strophe 4a. Yet this poem differs greatly from the others. Within this conflationary section, the women are not contrasted: Eve does no wrong here. The conflationary phrase itself is quite unusual; while the other three poems employ the *feminea forma*, here the woman appears as wife, *mulier*. Finally, Hildegard breaks her rhetorical pattern and specifically names Mary in strophe 4b, implicitly defining her as the "form of a woman" made from the side of man. Again, as in the song "O magna res," and in Vision II. 1 in the *Scivias*, Mary replaces Eve at the Creation and returns woman to her divinely ordained role as symbolized by the divine light of the Marian dawn.

Among the more unusual points of opposition in Hildegard's representation of the two women within her lyrics is Hildegard's use of construction metaphors *edifico, reedifico* and *instruo* (110, 112, 116, 120, 264). Of the four poems under specific discussion, only the sequence, "O virga ac diadema," does not contain such references. Newman attributes the "architectural metaphors" in the *Symphonia* partly to Hildegard's immediate historical context: the monastery on the Rupertsberg was under construction at that time (Newman, *Symphonia* 271). One generally associates construction with creation and life; therefore, it is unconventional, but not difficult to envision Mary as a builder, reconstructing salvation, *reedificando salutem* (110). However, while images of Mary as an architect may appear "less conventional" (Newman, *Symphonia* 271), the images of Eve as builder and Mary as destroyer are even less so. In a twist on the concept of construction as positive progress, Eve's "construction" projects are rather negative: "Grief, sorrow, and mourning were built in her," [*O luctus, Ach meror! He planctus, qui in muliere edificati sunt* ] (264). Hildegard extends Eve's involvement in negative fabrication to include the Crucifixion, when Christ received "the sobbing wounds of death that Eve built" [*plangentia vulneria mortis que Eva edificavit* ] (112). Finally, Eve "constructs" the negative endpoint of life itself: she literally "constructs" death: *femina mortem instruxit* (116). Mary's act of destruction thus becomes the positive act of redemption: she "destroys death" by her actions: *Tu destruxisti mortem* (112), Hildegard claims at one point. At another she insists that Mary ended death [*clara virgo illam [mortem] interemit* ] (116). Mary's "destruction of death" and "reconstruction of salvation" evoke Christ's predication in the gospels that he would tear down the temple and rebuild it (Mk. 14: 58).

Newman further associates the building metaphors within the lyrics with the third book of the *Scivias*, which Hildegard recorded at the same time (*Symphonia* 271). Within the third book of the *Scivias*, the virtues both abide in and build the heavenly Jerusalem (the construction aspects are especially apparent in Vision III. 8, in which the virtues appear "descending and ascending, laden with stones" [*ubi omnes virtutes Dei desendentes et ascendentes oneratas lapidus* ] (478). Hildegard's extended use of architectural imagery within the lyrics and the *Scivias* implies a relationship between women who construct Hildegard, Mary, the virtues, the Rupertsberg nuns.

I would extend this association of building and literature to include the *Ordo virtutem*. This is due to a pun, found within the antiphon "O quam magnum miraculum," which refers to the *Ordo*, and is found in one of the construction metaphors associated with Mary/Everywoman as *femina*: *et omnem suavissimum odorem virtutem edificavit* ( 116, l. 11). While *ordo* and *odor* are etymologically quite separate, they are homophonically quite similar, especially with the addition of *virtutem*. Like Everywoman who participates in Mary's construction of the fragrance of the virtues, Hildegard's nuns participated in the creation or construction of the virtues when they performed the *Singspiel*. As a possible form of imitation, Hildegard took the identification of her nuns with the virtues one step further: in Vision II.5, the virtues wear crowns identical to those with which Hildegard adorned her nuns when they received Communion. The nuns thus physically embodied the virtues, not only during the performance of the drama, but repeatedly during the celebration of the Mass. This is not a form of imitation that would have been available to all women qua women: Hildegard and her nuns could recreate the virtues because of their own physical and bodily purity as virgins (Epistle 149).

Bruce Holsinger posits that Hildegard and her nuns would have "experienced the Virgin's body as taste, touch, sight, smell, and. . . sound" when singing Hildegard's Marian hymns (111). I believe that Hildegard created a further means to imitate Mary through these construction metaphors, a form of *imitatio Mariae* that was available to Hildegard and her nuns not only through their building program but also found expression in some of their musical activities, specifically the singing of Hildegard's Marian lyrics, and performing the *Ordo virtutem*. However, these paths to imitation are severely limited in scope: they would not be available to every woman in Germany, only to Hildegard's nuns.

Eve and Mary are the most common paradigms offered to women in the Christian tradition. Eve, according to Hildegard, is remarkably easy to imitate: marry and have children.[36] However, Eve remains a completely inappropriate role model for monastic women. This inappropriateness may have influenced Hildegard's choice of symbolic imagery for Eve: the cloud-wing is so far removed from human experience that it is not available as a model for imitation. Yet this implies that the symbolic is of a lower order than the material world, which was not the case in the twelfth century: Hildegard and her contemporaries considered the symbolic to be of a higher order, endowed simultaneously with multiple, complex and sometimes contradictory meanings. The symbolic representation of Eve allowed Hildegard's positive comparison of Eve with Mary: a human image of Eve would have evoked too many negative associations, such as her nakedness as symbolic of her vice and her unbound hair of lust (Miles 50f., 124, 141, 144). A symbolic image filled with light was the only means by which to represent Eve positively.

Imitation of Mary, on the other hand, is a far more complex matter. Modern feminists and theologians have found Mary an impossible model; no other woman can remain a virgin yet also give birth to a child. The view that "the medieval Marian cult had a negative impact" on the status and lives of real women is prominent in feminist studies.[37] "The inimitability of the Virgin Mother model. . . has left all women essentially identified with Eve" (Daly 81). I will not deny that those in power have employed the Marian cult as a means to control the lives of women; however, to see only the negative aspects of Mariology reduces the complexity that Mary symbolized for medieval people. Mary appeared in medieval images as the queen of heaven  at once celebrated, generous, merciful, and sometimes remote and as the ultimate grieving mother. Yet she also appears as homely and domesticated, a noble woman teaching her son to read, an Everywoman who played with her child and even had spats with her husband. Within the various Marian legends, her miracles vary widely, yet there is almost always a very material component to these miracles. Unlike many saints, whose cures were internal and not easily documented or verified, Marian miracles were often written in the relief of suffering flesh, which made them readily apparent not only to the recipient but also to other witnesses. They demonstrate an intimate concern with the physicality of the human condition, not the abstract blessings of a distant queen.

Hildegard appears untouched by synchronous images in Mariology. Unlike her contemporaries, most notably Bernard of Clairvaux and Elisabeth von Schönau, Hildegard ignored the newer currents in Mariology; she had no visions of Mary, no images of suckling from Mary's breasts, nor did she write a Marian legend. Neither did she encourage her nuns to give birth to Christ in their hearts in imitation of the Virgin (Newman, *Sister* 159). Within the *Scivias* and the Marian lyrics, Mary appears almost exclusively at the point of the Incarnation. This single, historical moment allowed a woman to retrieve for humanity what a woman had lost, and it is this instant feminine renewal within Mary's life that interested Hildegard.

Within the *Scivias*, Hildegard focuses, not on Mary, but on the virtues linked with Mary, such as *Castitas, Humilitas, Oboedientia,* which were most important to monastic women. Images of these and other virtues are presented in the *Scivias* much more concretely and humanly than Mary. In Vision II. 5, the virtues appear, supported by Ecclesia, wearing the same type of costume in which Hildegard dressed her nuns to receive Communion, which clearly indicates a certain level of identification or idealization of the nuns with regard to the virtues. Also, during performances of the *Ordo virtutem*, Hildegard and her nuns would have been able to further "embody" the virtues. These concrete and stable representations of the personified virtues contrast with the complex and mulitvalenced quality of Hildegard's symbolic images of Eve and Mary.

What Hildegard ultimately offers her audience in the *Scivias*, her lyrics, and the *Ordo* is a complicated series of appropriate and inappropriate role models for Christian people in the biblical and allegorical figures who populate her texts. Eve and Mary, the role models very often assigned to women by medieval theologians, remain two among many. They appear as symbols, beyond the material world. Their symbolic appearance renders them prominent and complex, more than a simple opposing pair of "the good versus the bad woman" but also not the only possible role models.

The pervasiveness with which Hildegard disembodies Eve and Mary removes them from such considerations and also contrasts sharply with the embodied character of the personified virtues. Within the *Scivias*, the virtues appear corporeally to construct the City of God on Earth, an action which parallels the nuns and their construction of the Rupertsberg monastery. Within the *Ordo*, the nuns physically assume the bodies of the virtues and actively fight the devil for the Christian soul, this battle mirroring the spiritual one waged by each individual nun. These actions, played out upon the female bodies of the nuns and the femininely embodied virtues, offered Hildegard's nuns and readers access to role models whose activities corresponded with their own. The image of the ideal woman appears, not in the symbolic representations of Eve and Mary but in the human personifications of the virtues, and it appears as the physical female body.

## NOTES

1. Justin Martyr, *Dialogus com Tryphono Judaeo* 100, cols. 709-12; Tertullian, *De carne Christi* 17, pp. 232-33; Zeno of Verona, *Tractatus* 13, 10, col. 352; Irenaeus of Lyon, *Adversus haereses* 3, 22, 4, cols. 959-60.

2. Guldan, 22, Plate, 6, Rome, Museo Critiano im Lateran: Sarcophagas 104, Front side, circa 312.

3. An image of "Eva lactans" appears on the Bernward doors of the Hildesheim Cathedral (completed 1015). In a scene on the left door, Eve sits upon a hill under a poor cloth shelter and nurses her infant son. Wilhelm Pindar labeled this rare image the "original model for all later Madonna sculptures," *Urmutter aller kommenden plastischen Madonnen.* Pindar 127.

4. Guldan, 19, citing Tertullian, *De carne Christi* 17, p. 233.

5. All quotations of the lyrics refer to Newman's critical edition of the *Symphonia*, 1988. Eve appears *cum sufflatu superbie* in the responsory "Ave Maria" (110). Eve "despised all things" [*hec omnia Eva contempsit* ] in the song "O viridissima virga" (126). Mary's humility is praised in the antiphon "O quam magnum miraculum" (120). Her virginity appears in the hymn "Ave generosa," [*intacta puella, tu pupilla castitatis*] (122); in the Alleluia-verse "O virga mediatrix," [*de suavissima integritate* ] (124); and in the responsory "O quam preciosa," [*O quam preciosa est virginitas* ] (134). Finally, Mary appears

as the Virgin, *Virgo*, in the antiphon "Hodie aperuit" (116); in the responsory "O tu suavissima virga" (132); and in the antiphon "O tu illustrata" (136).

6. The sexual guilt of Adam and Eve is implied in the "blushing parents" of the antiphon "Cum erubuerint" (118), and further in the different paternity and guilty maternity found in the sequence "O virga ac diadema" (128).

7. In contrast to Eve's "laws of the flesh" [*carnis jura*] in the antiphon "O tu illustrata, Mary is the "author of life," [*auctrix vita*] in the responsory "Ave Maria" (110); and she, or rather her vital organs, "conquer death" [*mortem superaverunt*] in the Alleluia-verse "O virga mediatrix" (124).

8. The *casus* or, more specifically the *casus Adae*, appears in the antiphons "Cum processit factura" and "Cum erubuerint," (118). The serpent appears in the antiphon "Hodie aperuit" (116); and the devil in the antiphon "O tu illustrata" (136).

9. There are two Creation stories within the book of Genesis. The first, by the so-called Priestly author, (Gen. 1: 26-31, esp. verse 27)) reads, "So God created man in his own image, in the image of God he created him; male and female he created them." The second creation story by the Yahwist author is found in Genesis 2-12. This version contains the familiar story of the creation of Eve from Adam's rib, "So the Lord God caused a deep sleep to fall upon the man, and while he slept took one of his ribs and closed up its place with flesh; and the rib which the Lord God had taken from the man he made into a woman and brought her to the man." (Gen. 2: 21-22) Quotations from the Revised Standard Version of the Bible. For a discussion of the nature of Genesis as an explanation for the fallen state of humankind, see Westermann, 357f.

10. All Latin quotations and page numbers refer to the Latin edition of Hildegard's *Scivias*.

11. The quotation is for the rubric for chapter 9, in which Hildegard interprets the stars within the darkness, *tres magnae stellae. . . in eisdem tenebris apparuerunt.*

12. Hildegard, "Ave generosa," "You are the white lily upon which God gazed before all creation." *Tu candidum lilium quod Deus ante omnem creaturam inspexit. Symphonia* 122. See also Newman, *Sister* 62, notes 50-51; Warner 248, 334, 335.

13. Guldan cites Mary as the "breaking dawn" [*aurora consurgens*] and identifies the image in relation to the bride in the Song of Songs, specifically verse 6: 10, "Who is this that looks forth like the dawn, fair as the moon, bright as the sun." Guldan 108. Honorius Augustoduniensis (of Autun) († ca. 1056) claimed that whatever was said about Ecclesia the bride could be transfered to the Virgin, *Expositio in cantica canticorum*, PL 172, col. 494. Rupert von Deutz († ca. 1130) and other early scholastics used Honorius' idea in their

interpretations of the Canticles. See J. Beumer, "Die marianische Deutung des Hohen Liedes in der Frühsscholastik," *Zeitschrift für katholische Theologie* 76 (1954), 411ff.; F. Ohly, *Hohelied-Studien* (Wiesbaden, 1958), 125ff.; and H. Riedlinger, *Die Makellosigkeit der Kirche in den lateinischen Hoheliedkommentaren des Mittelalters* (Münster, 1958), 202ff; cited by Guldan 80. For Hildegard's use of dawn imagery for Mary, see the antiphons "Hodie aperuit" (116) and "O frondens virga" (120) and the sequence "O virga ac diadema" (130).

14. In the now-famous letter exchange with Tengswich of Andernach, Hildegard defends the costuming of her nuns in white dresses, veils, rings, and diadems as appropriate for the virgin brides of Christ (Epistolae 149).

15. Augustine, *City of God*, Book 14, chapters 21, 23, and 24.

16. Genesis 3: 19, 16. Warner 52, 57, 78. When Dr. James Young Simpson used chloroform to reduce the pain in childbirth in 1847, the practice was fought by the clergy, who believed that relief from pain during labor was women's burden, inherited from Eve, and that release from this pain would be immoral. Eisenberg 226f.

17. For a more extensive discussion of heresies, their tenents, and their proliferation throughout medieval Europe, see Lakeland and Evans.

18. The text of her sermon is recorded in Epistle 48, PL 197, col. 249.

19. The image of "the dew on the grass," symbolizing pregnancy, appears in the hymn, "Ave generosa" (122). Within the song "O viridissima virga," fruitfulness of the Virgin's womb is celebrated in the flourishing and verdure of the spices, *Nam in te floruit pulcher flosqui odorem dedit omnibus aromatibus . . . in viriditate plena* (126).

20. Jager, 154; Augustine, *Confessions* 10.14 and 11.2. On the reading of Scripture during meals as spiritual nourishment, see Augustine, *Confessions* 6.3; Benedict, *Rule*, 38; and Alcuin,*Epistolae* 124 and 173, pp. 123 and 287.

21. Within her lyrical corpus, Hildegard refers to Mary twice as an herbal form of healing: Mary appears as an unguent in "O clarissima mater" (112); references to distillation and the greening of dry spices appear in "O viridissima virga" (126). Occurrences of the *virga/virgo* pun and the branch of Jesse can also be read as references to Mary as a healing substance. Further, Christ appears several times as a blossom within the Virgin's womb (124, 126, 132, 134, and 135), thus furthering the association of herbal remedies with the illuminated flower and with Mary and Christ.

22. Newman describes the neutralization of semen in *Sister of Wisdom* 135. On Hildegard's theory about the poisonous nature of semen, see: *Causae et curae* 59-62. I realize that the black color of the poison contrasts with the natural

color of semen; however, as white symbolizes purity, and the nature of the vomit is poisonous, it must appear, symbolically at least, as black.

23. "At that time when Adam transgressed, the strength of man in his genital member was changed into a poisonous foam" [*Nam in transgressio Adae fortitudo viri in genitali membro versus est in venonosam spumam*].*Causae et curae* 60.

24. The other reason is childbirth, which also breaks the hidden members of a woman's body [*Sed et mulier cum prolem pepererit fractis occultis membris suis templum meum nonnisi* ] (28). The rubric to the twenty-third chapter reads: Wherefore a woman should abstain from entering a temple after childbirth or when corrupted by a man in her secret places [*Qvare mvlier post partvm vel a viro corrvpta in occvlto maneat et ab ingressv templi abstineat*].

25. The Middle High German term is *bluomen brehen*, which appears in the *Minnelyrik* of the twelfth century.

26. In her chapter on "Family Ties," Jo Ann McNamara discusses the various means by which the "world" penetrated the nuns' cloister: through the women's ties to family, through their duties to provide hospitality to travelers, particularly noble retinues, and through their corporate position as landholders, which required their attendance at legal, and sometimes political, courts. McNamara 176-201, esp. 196.

27. The Fall is discussed only in chapter 8. Within chapters 3 and 13, in which Hildegard describes the incarnation of Christ, the virginity that gave birth to Christ is mentioned. It should be noted that *virginitas* appears as a noun and is treated in a manner similar to the virtues of Book III. Virginity does not appear as an attribute of Mary, who is nowhere mentioned.

28. Augustine, *City of God*, book 16, chap. 32.

29. According to Hebrew myths, Eve was not the first woman God had created for Adam: in this case, it is no small step to imagine a sinless Adam waiting for God to create another wife. However, Adam does not have Eve replaced, rather he sins as well. For more on the Hebrew myths of Genesis, see R. Graves and R. Patai, *Hebrew Myths: The Book of Genesis* (New York: McGraw-Hill, 1964); H. Freedman and M. Simon, eds., *Midrash Rabbah* (London: Soncino Press, 1983); Louis Ginzberg, *Legends of the Jews*, Vol. 1 (Philadelphia: Jewish Publication Society of America, 1909).

30. Augustine, *City of God*, Bk. 14, chap.11.

31. On the temptation of Adam prior to Eve in *Genesis B*, see Jager 158-161. For further discussion on this unusual order of temptation, see also Woolf; *Genesis B*, ll. 496-582; and *Le Mystère d'Adam*, ll. 113-314.

32. "Why Eve fell first. But if Adam had sinned before Eve, then the transgression would have been so strong and so incorrigible, that humanity

would have fallen into such a great persistance in incorrigibility, that it [humanity] would neither be able to be saved, nor want to be. Since Eve sinned first, it [the sin] could be more easily erased, since she was more fragile (weaker) than the male." [*Quare Eva primus cecidit. Sed et si Adam transgressus fuisset prius quam Eva, tunc transgressio illa tam fortis et tam incorrigibilis fuisset, quod homo etiam in tam magna obduratione incorrigibilitatis cecidisset, quod nec salvari vellet nec posset. Unde quod Eva prior transgrediebatur, facilius deleri potuit, quia etiam fragilior masculo fuit*]. *Causae et curae* 47.

33. Hildegard's lyrics on the celestial hierarchy and patron saints form slightly smaller percentages; however, I differentiate them because the Marian lyrics focus on the actions of one individual, while the poems about the celestial hierarchy celebrate several of the separate heavenly choirs, and the hymns to the patron saints laud the deeds of numerous saints.

34. The "Miscellany" is found on folios 404rb-407va in the Riesenkodex, Wiesbaden, Landesbibliothek, Hs. 2. Newman discusses her identification of certain passages with the *Symphonia* corpus within her critical edition on pages 11 and 54.

35. This does not preclude Hildegard's use of *mulier* to refer to a consecrated nun (148) or to Mary (498), it merely indicates a preference. In both cases, context is crucial: the nun is about to marry Christ, and Mary, the second wife, is being specifically contrasted with the first wife, Eve. *Quam prima mulier attendit cum plus quam deberet habere uoluit; secunda muliere servitio Dei se subdente.*

36. "And we ourselves have followed her in our own right into exile joining ourselves to her pain" [*et nos secute sumus illam [Evam] in propria causa in exilia sociantes nos illius dolori* ], "O Pater omnium" (224-6).

37. Coletti, 66. For scholars who present Mary as an unattainable model, see Miles, Warner, and McLaughlin.

## WORKS CITED

### Primary Texts

Alcuin. *Epistolae karolini aevi.* Ed. Ernest Dümmler. Monumenta germaniae historica. Berlin, 1895. Vol 2: 18-481.

Augustine. *Confessiones.* Latin. Ed. James O'Donnell. Oxford: Clarendon Press, 1992.

———. *Confessions.* English. Trans. and introd. Henry Chadwick. Oxford: Oxford University Press, 1991.

————. *De civitate Dei*. Eds. Bernardus Dombart and Alfonsus Kalb. Stuttgart: Teubner, 1981.

————. *De civitate Dei*. English. *Concerning the City of God Against the Pagans*. Trans. Henry Bettenson. Harmondsworth: Penguin Books, 1972.

Benedict. *The Rule of St. Benedict in Latin and English with Notes*. Ed. Timothy Fry. Collegeville, MN: Liturgical Press, 1981.

*Genesis B*. Critical Edition. "The Junius Manuscript." *Anglo-Saxon Poetic Records: A Collective Edition*. Eds. George Phillip Krapp and Elliott Van Kirk Dobbie. 6 vols. New York: Columbia University Press, 1931-53. Vol. I: 9-28 (ll. 235-851).

Hildegard of Bingen. *Causae et curae*. Ed. Paul Kaiser. Lipsiae: Teubner, 1903.

————. *Epistolae*. Latin. PL 197.

————. *Ordo virtutem*. Critical Edition. Ed. Peter Dronke. *Poetic Individuality in the Middle Ages: New Departures in Poetry. 1000-1150*. Oxford: Clarendon Press, 1970: 180-192.

————. *Scivias*. English. Trans. Columba Hart and Jane Bishop. Intro. Barbara Newman. New York: Paulist Press, 1990.

————. *Scivias*. Latin. Eds. Adelgundis Führkötter O.S.B. and Angela Carlevaris O.S.B. CCCM. Vols. 43 and 43a. Turnhout: Brepols, 1978.

————. *Symphonia: A Critical Edition of the* Symphonia armonie celestium revelationem *[Symphony of the Harmony of Celestial Relations]*. Ed. Barbara Newman. Berkeley: University of California Press, 1988.

————. *The Letters of Hildegard of Bingen*. Trans. Joseph l. Baird. Oxford: Oxford University Press, 1994.

Honorius Augustoduniensis (of Autun). *Expositio in cantica canticorum*. PL 172.

Irenaeus of Lyon. *Adversus haereses*. English. *Against the Heresies*. Trans. Dominic J. Unger. New York: Paulist Press, 1992.

————. *Adversus haereses*. Latin. PG 7, cols. 959-60.

Justin Martyr. *Dialogus com Tryphono Judaeo*. English. *Dialogue with Trypho*. Trans. Lukyn Williams. London: Society for Promoting Christian Knowledge; New York: Macmillan, 1930.

————. *Dialogus com Tryphono Judaeo*. Greek. PG 6. cols. 709-12.

*Le Mystère d'Adam.(Ordo representacionis Ade)*. Ed. Paul Aebischer. Geneve: Croz, 1963.

*Le Mystère d'Adam*. English. "Le jeu d'Adam." *Medieval French Plays*. Eds. and Trans. Richard Axton and John Stevens. Oxford: Basil Blackwell, 1971. 1-44.

Tertullian. *De carne Christi.* English. *Treatise on the Incarnation.* Ed. and Trans. Ernest Evans. London: S. P. C. K., 1956.

———. *De carne Christi.* Latin. CSE 70, pp. 232-33.

Zeno of Verona. *Tractatus* 13, 10. PL 11, col. 352.

## Secondary Texts

Beumer, J. "Die marianische Deutung des Hohen Liedes in der Frühsscholastik." *Zeitschrift für katholische Theologie* 76 (1954): 411ff.

Coletti, Theresa. "Purity and Danger: The Paradox of Mary's Body and the Engendering of the Infancy Narrative in the English Mystery Cycles." *Feminist Approaches to the Body in Medieval Literature.* Eds. Linda Lomperis and Sarah Stanbury. Philadelphia: University of Pennsylvania Press, 1993.

Daly, Mary. *The Church and the Second Sex.* New York: Harper and Row, 1975.

Dronke, Peter "Tradition and Innovation in Medieval Western Colour-Imagery," *Eranos Jahrbuch* 41 (1972): 51-106.

Eisenberg, Arlene. *What to Expect When You're Expecting.* New York: Workman Publishing, 1988.

Freedman, H. Harry, and Maurice Simon, eds. *Midrash Rabbah.* London: Soncino Press, 1983. Vol. 1. Genesis.

Ginzberg, Louis. *Legends of the Jews.* Vol. 1. Philadelphia: Jewish Publication Society of America, 1909.

Graves, Robert and Raphael Patai. *Hebrew Myths: The Book of Genesis.* New York: McGraw-Hill, 1964.

Guldan, Ernst. *Eva und Maria: Eine Antithese als Bildmotif.* Graz, Köln: Verlag Hermann Böhlaus Nachf., 1966.

Holsinger, Bruce. "The Flesh of the Voice: Embodiment and the Homoerotics of Devotion in the Music of Hildegard of Bingen (1098-1179)." *Signs* (1993): 92-125.

Jager, Eric. *The Temptor's Voice: Language and the Fall in Medieval Literature.* Ithaca, NY: Cornell University Press, 1993.

Lakeland, Walter L. and Austin P. Evans, eds. *Heresies of the Middle Ages.* New York: Columbia University Press, 1963, 1991.

McLaughlin, Eleanor Commo. "Equality of Souls, Inequality of Sexes: Women in Medieval Theology." *Religion and Sexism: Images of Women in the Jewish and Christian Traditions.* Ed. Rosemary Radford Reuther. New York: Simon and Schuster, 1974: 245-51.

McNamara, Jo Ann. *Sisters in Arms: Catholic Nuns Through Two Millennia.* Cambridge, MA: Harvard University Press, 1996.

Miles, Margaret R. *Carnal Knowing: Female Nakedness and Religious Meaning in the Christian West.* Boston: Beacon Press, 1989.

Newman, Barbara. *Sister of Wisdom: St. Hildegard's Theology of the Feminine.* Berkeley: University of California Press, 1987.

Nolan, Edward Peter. *Cry Out and Write: A Feminine Poetics of Revelation.* New York: Continuum, 1994.

Ohly, Friedrich. *Hohelied-Studien; Grundzüge einer Geschichte der Hoheliedauslegung des Abendlandes bis um 1200.* Wiesbaden: F. Steiner, 1958.

Phillips, John A. *Eve: The History of an Idea.* San Francisco: Harper and Row, 1984.

Pindar, Wilhelm. *Die Kunst der deutschen Kaiserzeit.* Frankfurt a. M.: H. F. Menck, 1952.

Riedlinger, H. *Die Makellosigkeit der Kirche in den lateinischen Hoheliedkommentaren des Mittelalters.* Münster: n.p., 1958.

Warner, Marina. *Alone of All Her Sex: The Myth and the Cult of the Virgin Mary.* New York: Knopf, 1976.

Westermann, Claus. *Genesis 1-12.* Darmstadt: Wissenschaftliche Buchgesellschaft, 1972.

Woolf, Rosemary. "The Fall of Man in *Genesis B* and The *Mystère d'Adam.*" *Studies in Old English Literature in Honor of Arthur C. Brodeur.* Ed. Stanley B. Greenfield. Eugene, OR: University of Oregon Books, 1963: 187-199.

# Like a Virgin
## The Problem of Male Virginity in the *Symphonia*
*Maud Burnett McInerney*

Hildegard of Bingen's voluminous correspondence includes a famous exchange with another abbess, Tengswich of Andernach. Tengswich professes herself impressed by Hildegard's prophetic gifts, but she questions the way in which Hildegard directs her convent on two grounds. For one thing, she has heard that Hildegard only admits well-born nuns to her sisterhood, a practice which Tengswich sees as uncharitable and perhaps even unchristian; more disturbing, evidently, was the rumor that Hildegard and her nuns wore elaborate costumes and jewelry on holy days:

> Aliud etiam quoddam de consuetudine vestra ad nos pervenit, virgines videlicet vestras festis diebus pro ornamento candidis quibusdam uti velaminibus, coronas etiam decenter contextas capitibus earum desuper impositas, et his utraque parte et retro angelicas imagines insertas; in fronte autem Agni figuram decenter impressam: insuper et digitos earumdem quibusdam decorari annulis: quae omnia, ut credimus, ad amorem superni Sponsi ducitis, cum justum sit ut sint mulieres cum verecundia se componentes, non in tortis crinibus, neque auro, neque margaritis, aut veste pretiosa. (Migne 336)
>
> Indeed, another thing concerning your habits has reached us; it seems that your virgins on feast days wear as ornaments some kind of white veils, and even elegantly twisted crowns placed upon their heads, bearing the images of angels on either side and in the back; and in the front they have the figure of the Lamb elegantly attached.

And on top of this, their fingers are decorated with some kind of rings. You are encouraging them to do all these things for love of their holy Bridegroom, I suppose, since it is right that women should comport themselves with modesty, not wearing their hair in curls, or gold, or pearls, or precious clothing.[1]

Hildegard's response to Tengswich's rather loaded reference to St. Paul's pronouncements on feminine apparel (". . . women should adorn themselves with proper conduct, with modesty and self-control, not with braided hairstyles and gold ornaments, or pearls or expensive clothing . . ." [I Tim 2:9])[2] is characteristically self-assured and also reveals a great deal about the way she imagines the virgin body:

Forma mulieris fulminavit et radiavit in prima radice, in qua formatum est hoc in quo omnis creatura latet. . . . Sed Paulus apostolus . . . haec attendit: Mulier quae subjacet virili postestati mariti sui, illi conjuncta in prima costa, magnam verecundiam habere debet. . . . Haec non pertinent ad virginem; sed ipsa stat in simplicite et integritate pulchra paradisi, qui nunquam aridus apparebit, sed semper permanet in plena viriditate floris virgae. . . .Virgines conjunctae sunt in Spiritu sancto sanctimoniae et aurorae virginitatis. . . . Quapropter decet per licentiam et per revelationem in mystico spiramine digiti Dei, quod virgo candidam vestem induat, in clara significatione desponsationis Christi, videns quod intextae integritati mens ejus solidetur. (Migne 337-338)

The form of woman blazed forth and glowed in the first foundation, when that form was formed in which all creatures lay hidden. . . . But the apostle Paul . . . understood this: The woman who lies under the masculine power of her husband, joined to him in the primal Rib, must have great modesty. . . . These things do not apply to the virgin; for she stands forth, beautiful, in the simplicity and integrity of paradise, and shall never appear dry, but shall always remain in the full greenness of the flower of the branch. . . . Virgins are joined to the Holy Spirit in holiness and the dawn of virginity. . . . Because of this it is appropriate both according to her privilege and according to the revelation in the mystical breath of the finger of God, that the virgin should wear white clothing, in clear representation of her marriage with Christ, seeing that her will is strengthened by the purity of her clothing.

This passage explicitly identifies the virgin with prelapsarian femininity. Furthermore, in its absolute essentialism, it leaves no space for the virgin to be imagined as anything other than female in body, since her special status is defined by her physical integrity, by the fact that she is not "joined to [her husband] in the primal Rib." For Hildegard, virginity appears to be a condition which is not only gendered feminine, but which is actually sexed female. In this understanding of the term, Hildegard is probably closer to the popular mind of her period than the scholarly mind; compilations of saints' lives such as the *Legenda aurea* assume that virgins are women and in fact establish "virgin" as a category of holiness like "confessor" or "pope" which is peculiar to a single sex.[3] Writers of both the patristic and the medieval period who were more theologically inclined, however, were willing, even eager, to make virginity a state accessible to both men and women, a fact emphasized by several modern writers on the subject. John Bugge, for instance, in his influential monograph, writes that "it would be misleading to allow the inmplication to stand that even at the turn of the twelfth century virginity was only a feminine attribute. Although the concept of spiritual nuptials inclines us to think of it as proper to females, the historical fact is that for centuries virginity was predicable of both sexes" (4). Peter Brown also appears to take for granted the gender neutrality of virginity: "The virgin state of the woman was hailed as a *norma integritatis*: it was both the pinnacle and the model of a state of sexual intactness that men, and especially members of the clergy, should strive to make their own" (397). Brown does not address the problem of how a male body is to imitate a female model and indeed does not appear to recognize this as a problem; it seems to me, however, that patristic and medieval authors, especially male authors, were all too aware of the problem of sexed dissimilarity when it comes to bodily integrity. Hildegard's emphasis on the corporeality and femininity of virginity betrays the problematic nature of the virgin body at every turn, thus running counter to the impulses which characterize theological writing, and inevitably complicating her representation of sanctity in masculine bodies such as those of John and Rupert.

In insisting that the apostolic rules about dress "do not apply to virgins," Hildegard is taking a position directly opposed to that of most of the post-Pauline Church Fathers who addressed the subject. Virginity is never simply a bodily condition for patristic writers, nor is it essentially feminine; rather, it is a combination of physical purity and

spiritual devotion which may allow a shift from one gender to the other.
Jerome wrote that "as long as woman is for birth and children, she is as
different from man as body from soul. But if she wishes to serve Christ
more than the world, she will cease to be a woman and will be called
man" (*In Ephesios* 533). Here the suggestion is that gender need not be
dependent upon biological sex, but may in fact transcend it—and I use
the word "transcend" advisedly, since for Jerome the move from
woman to man is clearly a promotion. The Fathers, however, are not
simply more interested in the moral and transformative aspect of
virginity, they tend to be profoundly suspicious of the physical. In the
*De virginibus velandis*, Tertullian uses the logic of grammar to prove
that virgins were bound by the same rules as women and in the process
renders the term virtually meaningless: "Virgin, like wife or widow, is
a subcategory of the general category . . . the subcategory is subject to
the general category since the general comes before it" (893-894). This
logic allows the definition of woman as "a species of the genre of man,
who literally has engendered her, and to whose substance she merely
returns through marriage" (Bloch 34). Furthermore, it allows Tertullian
to imply that the virgin is a sort of monster, by suggesting that if the
category of virgin were placed upon an equal footing with that of
woman, it would constitute an unnatural third party in the binary
system which put man in charge of woman: "If man is the head of
woman, then he is also that of the virgin . . . unless the virgin is some
monstrous third category with its own head" (898). The possibility
which Tertullian seems so desperate to avoid is that "virgin" might
actually be a third gendered term in a system which, for him, consists
only of man and woman.[4] Similarly, in his letter to Eustochium, Jerome
not only makes it abundantly clear that actual virgins must not have the
liberties and privileges of men and must isolate themselves as
completely as possible from all human contact; he also raises the
possibility of physical virginity only to deny it:

> Nor say "so and so enjoys her own property; she is honoured by all;
> the brethren and the sisters assemble at her house. Has she ceased to
> be a virgin for all that?" In the first place, it is doubtful if such as one
> *is* a virgin. . . . (*Letters* 147-148; emphasis added, Wright's
> translation)

The point here is not that the virgin who lives too much in society
is unworthy of the name but that it is inconceivable that such a virgin

should have been able to maintain the physical integrity which Jerome both fetishizes and disallows. His doubt of her moral virginity is inseparable from his doubt concerning her physical integrity. For Jerome, as for Tertullian, physical virginity is always problematic, always negative, always subject to disproof, violation, defloration, by words if not by deeds.

Later writers were as convinced as Jerome that virgins were no less vulnerable to sin than married women and that virginity in no way liberated them from the restrictions placed by the Apostle upon their sex as a whole. Like St. Paul, Hildegard's contemporary Abelard links the sartorial with the spiritual when he cautions Heloise's nuns against a vanity he considers as characteristic of holy virgins as of women in general and no less dangerous in the religious than the lay. He quotes the first Epistle of Peter, adding his own commentary: "He was right to think it necessary to warn women rather than men away from this vanity, because their weak spirits impel them towards it, since they are more devoted to luxury" (261). The virgin's veil prescribed by male writers thus not only functions to shield her from the public gaze and the inevitable defloration which must follow it (Bloch 100), but also signals a meaning diametrically opposed to that which Hildegard attaches to the veils of her virgins: for the Fathers and Abelard, the veil is a marker of an inalienably female sexual shame; for Hildegard, it is the marker of freedom from that very shame. Hildegard's rhetoric suggests that she may be fully aware that she is resisting both patristic and contemporary authority when she protests that virgins have the right to adorn themselves without the modesty required of married women. She matches Tengswich's Pauline citation (I Tim. 2:9) with one from Revelation, explaining the symbolism of the crowns her nuns wear: "They have his name and the name of his Father written upon their heads," she insists. The reference clearly places her nuns among the heavenly troop of one hundred and forty-four thousand virgins described in Revelation (14:1-5).

In the letter to Tengswich and also in her work more generally, Hildegard not only insists on a moral distinction between virgins and married woman which is founded in corporeal integrity but also that this particular form of integrity is available to women alone. She does acknowledge, occasionally, that there may be a distinction between corporeal integrity and spiritual virginity, but she regularly and consistently emphasizes the corporeal, in sharp contrast to the Church Fathers who expended great effort to make virginity not only a moral condition, distinct from the body and especially the female body, but one available to both men and women, not limited to one sexed body.[5] In their writings certain men are regularly described as *virgo*, a distortion of terminology which would have confounded classical writers, for whom the word described a social condition unique to women;[6] Christ and St. Paul are often called virgins, as is St. John who, in Jerome's treatise on virginity, *Against Jovinian,* becomes the dominant exemplum. "The virgin writer," says Jerome, "expounded mysteries which the married could not, and, briefly to sum up all and show how great was the privilege of John, or rather the virginity in John, the Virgin Mother was entrusted by the Virgin Lord to the Virgin disciple" (366). This use of the word *virgo* to describe men as well as women is adopted by most religious authors of the Middle Ages, even while it generally retains its primary sense in secular usage.[7] Hildegard, however, avoids the word *virgo* when writing of males, even when dealing with John, whom she made the subject of an antiphon and a responsory in the *Symphonia.*

In the first of these, "O speculum columbe," John is described in terms of almost vegetable freshness and fecundity:

| | |
|---|---|
| O speculum columbe | O mirror of the dove |
| castissime forme, | most chaste in beauty |
| qui inspexisti misticam largitatem | who have beheld the mystic largesse |
| in purissimo fonte: | of the purest spring: |
| O mira floriditas | O miraculous blossoming |
| que numquam arescens cecidisti, | who never fell withering |
| quia altissimus plantator misit te: | because the highest gardener planted you |
| O suavissima quies | O sweetest repose |
| amplexuum solis: | of the sun's embraces |
| tu es specialis filius Agni | you are the special son of the Lamb |
| in electa amicicia | in the chosen friendship |
| nove sobolis. | of a new germination. |

In a typically Hildegardian turn of phrase, John is imagined here not as a flower but rather as the process of flowering, an image which links him to the Virgin Mary, whom Hildegard repeatedly describes as a lily or a flowering branch in poems like the "Ave generosa" or "O frondens virga."[8] Here, as elsewhere in Hildegard's writing, the flower is superior to the fruit, because it contains all the potential of fruition without the inevitable decay which must accompany it in the natural world. The last three lines of the song, however, move into a different realm describing John's relationship to the divine in terms which are strictly masculine. Whereas Saint Ursula, for whom Hildegard composed a whole cycle of songs, is consistently represented as the bride of Christ, John is the son of the lamb, *filius agni*, and a member of a chosen group of friends, *electa amicicia*. This last image may recall the Germanic *comitatus*, a group of warriors linked by indissoluble bonds of loyalty. The last word of the poem, *sobolis*, is particularly interesting in this context. It is usually rendered as "generation, race, or lineage," so that the phrase would be understood as "the choice friendship of a new race." The primary meaning of *soboles* (*suboles* in classical Latin) derives from gardening, however; it means offshoot or sprout, the twig or branch which is grafted from one fruit tree or vine to another. The poem thus ends with a word which returns us to the vegetative and fertile images of the second stanza, although in a less explicitly feminine mode and causes me to wonder whether Hildegard's grasp of Latin may not be in many ways more subtle than is generally thought.

Throughout the song, however, the kind of always potential and therefore always undefiled flourishing which Hildegard elsewhere associates with *virginitas* or *viriditas*, the greenness which is for her the symbolic equivalent of virginity (Newman, *Sister* 102; *Symphonia* 304) is never labeled as such. John is instead *castissime forme*, of most chaste beauty, but this language is much less specific than that which informs poems to the virgin like "Ave generosa," to choose a single example among many:

| | |
|---|---|
| Ave generosa | Hail, magnanimous |
| gloriosa et intacta puella. | glorious, intact maiden! |
| Tu pupilla castitatis | You are the pupil of chastity |
| tu materia sanctitatis, | the matter of holiness |
| que Deo placuit. | pleasing to God. |

Here, it is the physically rendered fact that Mary is *intacta puella* which makes her into the stuff of holiness, *materia sanctitatis*. Even the word *castitas*, chastity, is deployed differently. In John's case, he participates in the quality of "chaste beauty"; Mary, in contrast, is described by a bodily metaphor, as the pupil of chastity. "O virga mediatrix" makes the absolute and absolutely bodily quality of Mary's chastity even more apparent:

| | |
|---|---|
| . . . sancta viscera tua | . . . your sacred womb |
| mortem superaverunt | conquered death |
| et venter tuus | and your belly |
| omnes creaturas illuminavit | illuminated all creatures |
| in pulcro flore | in the beautiful blossom |
| de suavissima integritate | of the sweetest integrity |
| clausi pudoris tui orto. | born of your sealed modesty. |

Again, Mary's chastity is described in specific and physical terms, in clear distinction from the general, abstract quality of *castissime forme*.

In the responsory "O dulcis electe," we once again find the emphasis on John as the chosen friend of God, and comparable vegetable imagery:

| | |
|---|---|
| O dulcis electe | Sweet chosen one |
| qui in ardore ardentis | burning for the burning one |
| effulsisti, radix, | you shone forth, root, |
| et qui in splendore Patris | in the glory of the father |
| elucidasti mistica, | you elucidated mysteries |
| et qui intrasti cubiculum castitatis | and entered the chamber of chastity |
| in aurea civitate | in the golden city |
| quam construxit rex . . . | built by the king. . . |
| | |
| Tu enim auxisti pluviam | You increased the rain |
| cum precessoribus tuis, | with those who went before you |
| qui miserunt illam | who sent it upon |
| in viriditate pigmentatiorum. | the greeness of the spice-merchants. |

To see the "root" in this poem as a phallic symbol is probably not simply to betray a post-Freudian mindset; medieval stained glass regularly locates the root of the tree of Jesse in his groin. The action of increasing the rain in order to fertilize the *pigmentarii* (spice-merchants, Hildegard's personal symbol for priests [Newman, *Symphonia* 288]) is also almost stereotypically masculine. It not only recalls the *shoures shoote* which open the *Canterbury Tales*, but also Hildegard's own representation of dew as a fertilizing agent; in "O virga ac diadema," Hildegard uses the falling of dew as a shorthand for the natural process of impregnation which the Virgin escaped (*tu non germinasti de rore,/nec de guttis pluvie*, "you did not spring from the dew, nor from drops of rain"). Besides being characterized in masculine generative terms, John is once again represented as chaste, rather than virginal and as existing in a less than immediate relationship with chastity; he enters into it like a bridegroom into the marriage chamber rather than expressing it through his own body. To translate *cubibulum castitatis* as *chambre de la virginité*, as Hildegard's French translator does, (Moulinier 53) is to distort the sense of the poem: John may be perfectly chaste, but he is not a virgin, because in Hildegard's universe, only women are virgins as we shall see if we turn now to the *Scivias*.

A careful reading of the passages of the *Scivias* which deal with virginity reveals a double impulse on Hildegard's part. On the one hand, she emphasizes the value of virginity as a virtue to which all can and should aspire; on the other, she clearly feels that the state of being virgin is inherently feminine. Throughout the *Scivias*, as elsewhere, she emphasizes the distinct but complementary paths which are laid out for holy men and women: men should be priests; women should be nuns. Both must live chastely, but in women chastity may take a transfigurative form denied to men, virginity; men have access to their own form of transformation deriving from fleshly forebearance and self-denial in the celebration of the Mass, a transformation which Hildegard represents most clearly in her sequence for St. Maximin, "Columba aspexit."

When Hildegard speaks of what we may call universal virginity, the ideal to which all human beings should aspire, she tends to render it in abstract and general terms. Thus, in the tenth vision of Book III, when Christ addresses a crowd of people, encouraging them to avoid the sins of the flesh, he addresses them initially with the gender-neutral *homines* (III. x. 1). Once he begins to address the issue of sexual renunciation specifically, his audience is suddenly divided, according to the heading of part 7: *Admonitio ad virgines et continentes qualiter sanctitatem aggredi debeant* (553), which may be rendered as "Instructions to virgins and continent ones concerning how they may approach holiness." It is not clear from this whether the terms *virgines* and *continentes* are to be understood as gendered; the only use of the word "virgin" to occur in the body of the text, however, is definitely gendered:

> Nam ego sum flos campi: quoniam ut sine aratro campus gignit florem, sic ego Filius hominis sine virili commixtione genitus sum ex Virgine. . . . Sed si idem donum a me fideliter petieris, illud a me fiducialiter impetrabis, tibique dabo ut coram Patre meo consortium mecum habeas in virginitate.(554)

> For I am the flower of the field; just as a field unploughed bears a flower, so I, the Son of Man, was born of the Virgin without commingling with any man . . . but if you faithfully ask me for this gift, you may receive it in good faith from me: I will grant that you may participate with me in virginity, openly before my Father.

Frail humankind is here invited to participate in the quality of virginity, while the only virgin in the absolute sense is Mary. Since being a virgin is implicitly connected here with being female, it is tempting to read the heading as referring to consecrated virgin women and continent religious men, both of whom imitate, in their separate ways, the absolute sanctity and integrity of Christ's body.

Hildegard's description of her fifth vision in Book II conveys the same ambiguous attitude towards the gendering of virginity. She begins with a general statement about "those who devote themselves to virginity" which almost immediately breaks down into two quite separate categories:

> Sed quia virginitas tam gloriosa ante Deum est, ideo qui eam ex voluntate sua Deo obtulerunt eam prudenter conservent; quoniam hoc sanctum propositum cum summa devotione virginitatis susceptum fideliter custodiendum est. . . . Nam ipsi carissimi imitatores Filii mei sunt cum se ita Deo offerunt, ut non sint legati in opinione coniugii nec onerati saeculari causa carnalem copulam respuentes, ne illi cum omni sollicitudine carnis suae subiecti sint, sed hoc cupientes ut gloriosae innocentiae innocentis agni adhaerant. (183)

Because virginity is so glorious before God, those who offer it of their own free will to God must carefully preserve it; because this holy promise undertaken out of the greatest devotion to virginity, must be faithfully guarded. . . . For they are beloved imitators of my Son who offer themselves thus to God, not tied by any demand of marriage nor burdened by worldly cares but rejecting fleshly bonds, so that they may not be subject to the anxieties of the flesh but rather desire to cleave to the glorious innocence of the innocent Lamb.

Up until this point, although the pronouns are (inevitably) masculine, Hildegard seems to have in mind all of humanity. In the paragraph which follows, however, the divine voice which speaks through her is quite clearly concerned only with the male of the species:

Quapropter vir ille qui in animo suo deliberat ne ullam costam sibi copulet, sed hoc desiderat ut in pudore virginitatis propter amorem Filii mei perseveret, sodalitatem eius accipiet, si tamen in operibus eiusdem castitatis perseveravit. . . . Sed si ille postea idem pactum relinquens propter turpem stimulum carnis suae adulterium perpetraverit, libertatem suam in servitutem redegit, quoniam honorem colli sui, ubi Filium meum pudice imitari debuit, per turpitudinem delectationis suae nequiter corrupit, et quia mendacium protulit, vovens se caste vivere, quod non implevit. (183-184)

So that man who decides in his soul not to join himself to any rib, but who desires to preserve the modesty of virginity for love of my Son will become his companion if he only perseveres in the work of chastity. . . . But if he later abandons this pact because of a shameful prickling of the flesh and commits adultery, he reduces his liberty to slavery since he corrupts the honor of his head through shameful pleasure when he ought to have imitated the modesty of my Son, and because he has expressed a lie, making a vow to live chaste and not fulfilling it.

The man, in this passage, does not aspire to virginity itself but rather to something proximate to virginity: *pudor virginitatis*, the modesty of (or associated with) virginity. The result of masculine chastity is companionship with Christ, the same kind of relationship we have seen evoked in the songs to Saint John. The consequences of loss

of chastity are expressed in an almost chivalric register of lost honor
and unfulfilled oaths—a fellowship is here being broken by the
behavior of the incontinent man. It appears that as soon as the subject
becomes male, the discourse of sexual renunciation configures itself as
masculine. This shift is nowhere more obvious than in the final lines of
this section,[9] which describe the position of the repentant sexual sinner:
*non autem ipsum inter sodales suos qui gloria integritatis florent ponit,*
*quoniam societatem illorum deserens libertatem pacti sui abiecit et*
*eam in servitutem peccati redegit* [this does not place him back among
his companions who flourish in the glory of integrity, for he has
deserted their fellowship by casting away the freedom of his oath and
has reduced it to the slavery of sin]. The idea throughout the passage is
that living chastely is something that you do rather than something you
are.

A different kind of integrity entirely is implicit in the parallel
passage devoted to sexual renunciation in women:

> Sed et puella quae ex voluntate sua in sanctissima desponsatione
> eidem Filio meo offertur, ab ipso decentissime suscipitur, qui eam
> hoc modo sibi coniunctam vult habere in consortio suo. Quomodo?
> Ut illum casta dilectione amplectatur, sicut et ipse eam in secreto suo
> diligit; quoniam illi semper amabilis est, quia magis eum quam
> terrenum sponsum quaerit. Quod si pactum eius postea transgressa
> fuerit, tunc coram his qui in caelesti gaudio sunt polluta erit. . . . Ille
> quoque qui eam seducendo violavit, si culpam suam emendare
> volverit, ita paeniteat quasi caelum rupisset. . . . (184-185)

> But a maiden who has of her own free will offered herself to my Son
> in holy betrothal has been taken in by him in the most seemly
> fashion, for he wants her to be joined with him as his consort. How
> may this be? Because she embraces him with chaste affection, and he
> may love her in secret; for to him she is always beloved, since she
> sought him out rather than any earthly spouse. But if she then breaks
> her promise, then she will be polluted in the eyes of those who are in
> celestial joy. . . . And as for the man who violates her by seducing
> her, if he wants to amend his crime, let him mourn as though he had
> broken open the sky itself. . . .

It is clear from this passage that what the man has broken open is
the woman's body, sealed by that curiously hypothetical but always

fascinating organ, the hymen.[10] The physical damage done is represented as irreparable; the corollary to this absolute loss through sexual intercourse of physical integrity is an equally absolute sense of physical integrity in the woman who escapes intercourse.

A final pair of passages from the *Scivias* makes the distinction which Hildegard regularly (if not completely consistently) draws between female virginity and male chastity perfectly apparent:

> Quae dum desiderat Filium meum, in amore ejus cupiens observare virginitatem suam: valde ornatur in thalamo ipsius, quoniam contemnit ardorem quem pro caritate illius sustinet: nolens dissolvi incendio ardentis libidinis, perseverans in pudicitia, quia carnalem virum in spiritali desponsatione despicit; toto desiderio anhelans post Filium meum, recordationem viri carnalis abjiciens.(148)

> She who desires My Son, and wishes to preserve her virginity for His love, is greatly ornamented in his chamber, since she despises the burning which she suffers for love of him. She does not wish to be dissolved in the furnace of blazing lust but perseveres in chastity, rejecting any husband of the flesh for the sake of spiritual betrothal. She sighs for My Son with her whole desire and despises the idea of a fleshly husband.

Hildegard here represents the virgin not as an improbable creature whose sexuality has been eliminated but as fully feminine, a woman whose sexual desires have been redirected towards a supernatural object and who is in fact redeemed not in spite of but because of the essential femininity of that desire.[11] The distinction between awareness of the urgings of carnal human nature and giving way to them is one that Hildegard makes repeatedly, and it is characteristic also of the male counterpart of the woman who chooses virginity:

> Cum etiam fortitudo viri recusat ducere consortium matrimonii, ita quod vir propter amorem Filii mei se coercet in vivida natura sua, cum floret in germine filiorum; ipse tamen constringens membra sua ne exerceant concupiscentiam carnis suae, hoc mihi valde amabile est quia scilicet vir hoc modo vincit se ipsum. (148-149)

> Indeed, when the strength of a man refuses to take a wife, so that that man for love of My Son restrains his own vigorous nature, which

would blossom in the engendering of sons, instead controlling his
limbs so that they may not carry out the lusts of his flesh, this is very
pleasing to me, for in this way indeed a man conquers himself.

The word *virginitas* is conspicuously absent from this passage.
Like the virgin, the chaste man chooses Christ over earthly marriage;
but he restrains himself from action, from "fulfilling the desires of the
flesh" rather than from the more passive sexual pleasure of women who
are acted upon, "dissolved in the furnace of lust." Male chastity
consists of not touching; virginity of not being touched. The two states,
like almost every other aspect of gender in Hildegard, are perhaps
equal, but they are entirely different; the same vocabulary cannot
describe them both. Virginity is clearly conceived as a physical and
social characteristic of women: *Quoniam nobilior est virginitas non
polluta ab initio quam viduitas oppressa virili jugo, cum tamen post
dolorem suum in quo virum suum perdidit, virginitatem subsequitur*
[for virginity unpolluted from the beginning is nobler than widowhood
oppressed under the yoke of man, even if the widow, after the grief of
losing a husband, should follow the example of virginity] (30). A man
who chooses chastity, either before or after marriage, can no more be a
virgin than a widow can; he can only "follow the example" of virginity.
Saint John may be *castissime forme*, but he cannot be *virginea forme*,
because male and female are always distinct in Hildegard's visionary
world, and virginity is something that pertains to the female.

For Saint Paul, the virginal body was sexless, "neither male nor
female." By making virginity the agent of translation from "woman" to
"man," Jerome sought to make it masculine, if not actually male. As
Hildegard imagines it, in contrast, the virgin body is anatomically
female. Virginity in her work is a function already gendered as
feminine before its association with a character of either sex.[12] This
must inevitably alter the body of the male imagined as virgin, and
indeed in the sequence to Saint Rupert called "O Jerusalem," Hildegard
reconstructs the saint's male body according to a female model, in
order to convey the young man's purity and openness to divine
influence.

Hildegard is the only source for our knowledge of St. Rupert. The
*vita* that she wrote for him may have served to authorize her removal of
her nuns to the Rupertsberg, where her new foundation was consecrated
in 1152. The information in the *vita* seems to derive mostly from one of
Hildegard's visions, to which she refers in the third stanza of her

sequence to Rupert (Newman, *Symphonia* 297), but it probably also incorporates folk traditions concerning the church on the site which had stood in ruins for three centuries. One suspects, in fact, that had there been no pre-existing tradition concerning the occupation of the site, the Living Light might have provided Hildegard with a virgin martyr like Ursula as patron saint for her new foundation, rather than a holy young man like Rupert.

Rupert, according to the *vita*, which gives a narrative account of the events rendered imagistically in the sequence, was a Carolingian aristocrat, born of a pagan father and a Christian mother named Bertha. Hildegard's tale of Rupert's childhood provides a rather upsetting vision of early medieval family life. Bertha's husband Roboldus proves to be both unfaithful and tyrannical, and she consoles herself by praying daily for liberation from him—praying in essence for his death, which eventually occurs when Rupert is three years old. Rupert, meanwhile, gives early proof of his divine inspiration by conceiving a powerful hatred for his father and affirming that the duke is both stupid and idiotic. The child is thus represented from the very beginning as embracing Christianity in its feminine form (it comes to him through his mother, like Christ's humanity) and rejecting paganism in its masculine form when he rejects his lecherous and aggressive father. Rupert's body, meanwhile, is particularly apt to divine inspiration or invasion because of its softness and immaturity: *quia Deus miracula sua saepius in iis etiam facit, qui prae mollitia venarum ac medullarum plenam scientiam nondum habent* [because God often performs miracles in those who, because of the softness of their sinews and marrow have not yet attained full knowledge] (1085-86). This softness, *mollitia*, is also typical of women; it is one of the words Hildegard uses where other medical theorists of the Middle Ages use weakness to characterize the way in which the female sex is different from the male (Cadden 82). For Hildegard, feminine softness and impressionability is exactly what makes the female an appropriate recipient for divine grace. Before he hardens into manhood, a little boy is thus capable of the kind of receptivity which women retain all their lives, as long, that is, as they retain their virginity. Whereas centuries later, Freud would imagine little boys as having to triumph over the earliest, feminine state of being and develop into something better, Hildegard sees the femininity of the boy-child as being the peak of spiritual development, something which can only degenerate in later life. Indeed, after having a vision of paradise as an orchard tended by the Ancient of Days, making a pilgrimage to Rome and founding hospices with his mother, Rupert dies at the age of twenty, an age which Hildegard explicitly identifies as premature. God takes his life "lest if he came to full maturity he might follow in the footsteps of his father" [*ne si ad perfectam aetatem perveniret, post vias patris sui incederet*] (1090). Masculine maturity is thus inevitably associated with sexuality; Rupert avoids this fate and dies with his innocence untouched [*fulgentem innocentia*] (1090). It seems possible that Hildegard's conviction that male maturity necessarily involves a loss of innocence is related to the medieval anxiety about nocturnal emissions. There was an ongoing debate as to whether ejaculation during sleep was sinful and required abstinence from the sacrament; Jean Gerson wrote a tract on the subject called *On Pollution*, and Constantine the African and Thomas Aquinas both deal with the subject at some length (Cadden 142).[13] If non-ejaculation is the criterion, or even part of the criterion, for male virginity, then it is easy to see why the male virgin must have been as rare as hen's teeth, and why virginity and chastity come to be exchangeable terms for men as they are not for women.

Like the *vita*, Hildegard's songs to Rupert emphasize his purity and incorruption, characteristics she would surely have described as *virginitas* had they occurred in a woman, and in fact she represents his body repeatedly in feminine terms, using images of viridity and fruitfulness which she elsewhere applies to the Virgin. Thus Rupert is the *dulcis viriditas pomi*, the sweet greenness of the apple (st. 4b),[14] Mary the *viridissima virga*, greenest of branches (no. 19). Stanzas 4b and 5 imagine Rupert's body as both hollow and intact:

| | |
|---|---|
| O vas nobile, | O noble vessel |
| quod non est pollutum | unpolluted |
| nec devoratum | undevoured by |
| in saltatione antique spelunce, | the dance in the ancient cave |
| et quod non est maceratum | unharmed by |
| in vulneribus antiqui perditoris: | the wounds of the ancient |
| | traitor |
| | |
| In te symphonizat Spiritus sanctus, | the Holy Spirit rings in you |
| quia angelicis choris associaris | you join the angelic choirs |
| et quoniam in Filio Dei ornaris | adorned with the Son of God |
| cum nullam maculam habes. | for you are without stain. |

Mary Douglas reminds us that "both male and female physiology lend themselves to the analogy with the vessel which must not pour away or dilute its vital fluids. Females are correctly seen as, literally, the entry by which the pure content may be adulterated. Males are treated as pores through which the precious stuff may ooze out and be lost. . . ." (150) In other words, while either kind of body can be imagined as a container, they are imagined as containers which operate differently and which are differently threatened, the emphasis for the female being on remaining sealed in order to prevent the entrance of alien substances, for the male, in order not to allow the escape of any native substance. Hildegard represents Rupert as an uncontaminated vessel and aligns that vessel with an ideal of feminine purity by means of a series of images elsewhere associated with the Blessed Virgin. The "dance in the ancient cave" is the same "olde daunce," presumably, in which the Wife of Bath was so proficient; Rupert's purity is thus identified as sexual innocence. The following stanza confirms this with a deliberately Marian echo (*nullam maculam habes* ) and again emphasizes the hollowness of Rupert's body, this time in a musical sense, as though he were the bell of a trumpet or the cavity of a drum; in other poems (no. 17, and the unnumbered "O Fili dilectissime") Mary will similarly be represented as containing the heavenly symphony. Rupert's virginity expresses itself through the feminization of his body.

This feminization is obliquely underscored in the *vita*, which not only depicts Rupert according to the images of fruition we have so often seen applied to the Virgin, but which concludes with a curious echo of the creation scene from Genesis. When Rupert reaches the sinister age of twenty and begins to be tempted by his friends *ad voluptatem saeculi,* towards the pleasures of the world (1089), his mother has a significant dream, in which she sees one of the ribs fall from her side, a sight which terrifies her. Shortly afterward, Rupert is stricken with what will prove to be his final illness. It is difficult not to escape the conclusion that Hildegard is deliberately if not satirically revising the creation of Eve here. While Hildegard herself never represents Eve as in any way essentially inferior to Adam,[15] she was certainly aware of the tendancy of many other writers to see Eve as secondary, a feeble imitation of the perfection of the pre-lapsarian Adam; in her account of the life of Rupert, which is full of Edenic echoes and visions, Hildegard redresses the balance, representing her youthful saint as nothing more than a fragment of his mother's body, his holiness deriving entirely from hers. In this context, it is not insignificant that it is Bertha, not Rupert, who builds the church which Hildegard and her nuns will reconstruct several hundred years later.

The sequence to St. Rupert ends with a cosmic evocation of the city of heaven and its inhabitants:

| | |
|---|---|
| Et ita turres tue, | And so your towers |
| O Ierusalem | O Jerusalem |
| rutilant et candent per ruborem | burn and glow with the crimson |
| et per candorem sanctorum | and the pure white of the saints |
| et per omnia ornamenta Dei, | and through all the ornaments of God |
| que tibi non desunt, o Ierusalem. | which fail you not, O Jerusalem. |
| | |
| Unde vos, o ornati | And so, O you ornamented ones |
| et o coronati | you crowned ones |
| qui habitatis in Ierusalem, | who live in Jerusalem |
| et o tu Ruperte, | and you, O Rupert |
| qui es socius eorum | their companion |
| in hac habitatione, | in that dwelling place |
| succurrite nobis famulantibus | help us, your servants |
| et in exilio laborantibus. | laboring in exile. |

This final vision of Rupert betrays some of the same ambiguity which characterizes the relationship of John to the ideal of virginity; Rupert is not directly represented as crowned with either the red of martyrdom or the white of virginity. He is *like* a martyr, although he died in bed, the verse implies, and *like* a virgin, although male.

The evocation of apocalyptic crowns and garments brings us back to our point of departure, the rings and crowns Hildegard's nuns wore to celebrate special occasions. The costumes and behavior of the Rupertsberg nuns clearly demonstrate the extent to which the power of Hildegard's virginal and explicitly feminine ideal could be enacted through real female bodies, and, in exceptional cases, upon imagined male bodies such as that of Rupert. For a man to participate in virginity, as we have seen in the case of Rupert, involves a transcendence and transformation of his male body in a way which seems almost deliberately to invert the kind of honorary masculinity bestowed by the Fathers of the Church upon virgin women. Hildegard's invention or re-invention of the physical female as the ground of sanctity allows her to imagine a female subject existing in a state of separate equality—the term is deliberately loaded, of course. Hildegard's utopian vision did not attempt, as many writers before me have noted, the subversion of patriarchal authority. Her visionary rhetoric does, however, permit her to occupy (when it suits her) a strategic position "outside" of the hierarchical structure of the medieval sex-gender system, as a virgin rather than a woman. Whereas most nuns remained bound by the prohibitions directed against women by the Fathers and later authorities, Hildegard effectively freed herself from these by insisting that such prohibitions did not apply, since she, although female, was not a woman, but something more and better: a virgin. This carefully constructed position undoes the traditional hierarchies according to which medieval authority was usually produced while it refigures the female body as normative and authoritative rather than other and lacking in authority.

## NOTES

1. All translations from the Latin are my own.

2. This letter is now generally recognized as pseudo-Pauline.

3. As Barbara Newman reminds us, "the meaning of virginity in [the virgin's] own eyes was not necessarily the same as its meaning for her male directors." *From Virile Woman to WomanChrist*, 6.

4. It is interesting that, while Tertullian's argument begins with grammar and makes use of the categorical distinctions between general and specific nouns, it nonetheless maintains the fiction of only two genders in a language (Latin) which has three: masculine, feminine, and neuter.

5. See for example Augustine, who, in *The City of God* argues that there can be no violation of virginity without some degree of consent, "because it may be believed that an act, which perhaps could not have taken place without some physical pleasure, was accompanied by a consent of the mind" (I.ch.16.26, quoted in Schulenberg 36). As Schulenberg notes in her discussion of this passage, Augustine uses it to establish a hierarchichal relationship between body and soul in which "corruption of the soul necessarily precedes corruption of the body" (35). Augustine goes on to imply that physical integrity is largely irrelevant, even though its loss (a loss which only women can suffer) is always a bad thing.

6. As Giulia Sissa points out, the Greeks at least made no clear distinction between physical virginity and the social fact of being an unmarried woman (76-86). Hippolytus, the tragic hero determined to preserve his chastity at all

costs, is so complete an exception to the rule that his virginity renders him almost monstrous.

7. Vernacular equivalents of the word generally indicate unmarried, intact women. See Schulz, 25-31 for a discussion of the Middle High German words *kint* and *maget,* "child" and "maiden." These are the words and connotations with which Hildegard would have been familiar from her own childhood.

8. For extended discussions of Hildegard's Marian poems, see Newman, *Sister* 156-195, and Holsinger.

9. The edition by Führkötter places these lines at the beginning of the next chapter; I have followed Hart and Bishop, who restore them to the end of the previous chapter, where they clearly belong.

10. On the invention of the hymen, see Giulia Sissa.

11. Hildegard's eroticization of divine desire prefigures the even more corporeal metaphors which will dominate the writing of women mystics of the next generation and beyond. It is also, of course, akin to the rhetoric of St. Bernard's famous sermons on the Song of Songs.

12. "Sex, in this universe, proceeds from gender, not the other way around. A figure does not cry and cower because she is a woman; she is a woman because she cries and cowers. And a figure is not a psychokiller because he is a man; he is a man because he is a psychokiller." Clover 13.

13. Involuntary manifestations of sexuality were a subject of concern in the female as well as the male; Hildegard herself argued that women should not be excluded from church while menstruating (*Scivias* I.ii.20). See also Wood, "The Doctor's Dilemma" for an extended investigation of the moralization of involuntary sexual processes.

14. The numbering of stanzas is Newman's.

15. On Hildegard's representations of the creation of Eve, see Newman, *Sister*, especially chapter 3, "The Woman and the Serpent"; see also the article by Rebecca Garber in this collection.

## WORKS CITED

### Primary Texts

Abelard. *Lettres complètes d'Abélard et d'Héloise.* Ed. M. Gréard. Paris: Garnier, 1904.

Augustine. *The City of God Against the Pagans.* Trans. George McCracken. Cambridge, MA: Harvard University Press, 1957.

Hildegard of Bingen. *Epistolarum liber.* PL197. 143-382.

———. *Scivias.* Eds. Adelgundis Führkötter and Angela Carlevaris. CCCM XLIII-XLIIIa. Turnhout: Brepols, 1978.

———. *Scivias*. Trans. Columba Hart and Jane Bishop. New York: Paulist Press, 1990.

——— . *Symphonia: A Critical Edition of the* Symphonia armonie celestium revelationum [Symphony of the Harmony of Celestial Revelations]. Ed. and trans. Barbara Newman. Ithaca and London: Cornell University Press, 1988.

Jerome. *Against Jovinian.* In *A Select Library of the Nicene and Post-Nicene Fathers.* Eds. Philip Schaff and Henry Wace, vol. 6. Grand Rapids, MI: Eerdmans, 1952.

———. *In Ephesios.* PL. 26. 467-588.

———. *Select Letters of St. Jerome.* Trans. F.A. Wright. Cambridge, MA: Harvard University Press, 1933 rpt. 1991.

Tertullian. *De virginibus velandis.* PL 2.

## Secondary Texts

Bloch, R. Howard. *Medieval Misogyny and the Invention of Western Romantic Love.* Chicago and London: University of Chicago Press, 1991.

Brown, Peter. *The Body and Society: Men, Women and Sexual Renunciation in Early Christianity.* New York: Columbia University Press, 1988.

Bugge, John. *Virginitas: An Essay in the History of a Medieval Ideal.* The Hague: Martinus Nijhoff, 1975.

Cadden, Joan. *Meanings of Sex Difference in the Middle Ages: Medicine, Science and culture.* Cambridge: Cambridge University Press, 1993 rpt. 1995.

Clover, Carol. *Men, Women and Chainsaws: Gender in the Modern Horror Film.* Princeton: Princeton University Press, 1992.

Douglas, Mary. *Purity and Danger*. Harmondsworth: Penguin, 1970.

Holsinger, Bruce. "The Flesh of the Voice: Embodiment and the Homoerotics of Devotion in the Music of Hildegard of Bingen (1098-1179)." *Signs* (1993): 92-125.

Moulinier, Laurence, trans. *Hildegarde de Bingen: Louanges* . Paris: Orphée/La Différence, 1990.

Newman, Barbara. *From Virile Woman to WomanChrist: Studies in Medieval Religion and Literature.* Philadelphia: University of Pennsylvania Press, 1995.

———. *Sister of Wisdom: St. Hildegard's Theology of the Feminine*. Berkeley: University of California Press, 1987.

Salisbury, Joyce E. *Church Fathers, Independent Virgins.* London and New York, Verso, 1991.

Schulenberg, Jane Tibbets. "The Heroics of Virginity: Brides of Christ and Sacrificial Mutilation." *Women in the Middle Ages and the Renaissance: Literary and Historical Perspectives.* Ed. Mary Beth Rose. Syracuse, NY: Syracuse University Press, 1986.

Schultz, James A. *The Knowledge of Childhood in the German Middle Ages, 1100-1350.* Philadelphia: University of Pennsylvania Press, 1995.

Sissa, Giulia. *Greek Virginity.* Trans. Arthur Goldhammer. Cambridge, MA: Harvard University Press, 1990.

Wood, Charles T. "The Doctors' Dilemma: Sin, Salvation and the Menstrual Cycle in Medieval Thought." *Speculum* 56,4 (1980): 710-727.

# A Musical Reading of Hildegard's Responsory "Spiritui Sancto"[1]

*Kathryn L. Bumpass*

Peering into any particular corner of Hildegard von Bingen's creative life is somewhat like walking through a hall of mirrors. Though images are clear and distinct, the boundaries between them are difficult to locate in any real space, physical or mental. In ways that defy easy description, her music is wondrously intertwined with her mystical visions, the fount from which all her remarkable gifts flowed, with her poetry and theological views, with her piety and her vanities, with the divine and the mundane, with the spiritual and the patently political. And, like all other aspects of her life, the music both reflects and projects her position as a woman in her society.

Because of her fame as an abbess, a mystic and an artist, we have more information about Hildegard than practically any other woman musician in the twelfth century. Hence, an attempt to understand her as a *woman* musician is at least founded on a large and plausibly authoritative body of documentation.[2] So widely known among medievalists are the details of Hildegard's biography that I need here refer only to a few watershed dates and events in her life.

Early in her childhood she began to have extraordinary experiences she later would describe as visions, but she did not make them public until 1141, when divinely commanded to do so. Some of the visions were specifically musical, and it is these which have come down to us as her compositions. She herself reported, "untaught by anyone, I composed and chanted plainsong in praise of God and the saints, although I had never studied either musical notation or any kind of singing" (*Vita* PL 197, quoted in Newman, *Symphonia* 17; see also

Dronke's translation in *Women Writers* 145). We should attempt to
understand both Hildegard's compositions and this comment in the
light of twelfth-century notions of musical composition[3] and of
religious experience.

Over the course of Western music history, particularly since
around 1600, musical "composition," as distinct from improvisation
has been tied to the *writing down* of the musical work, to such an extent
that *de facto* if not in theory, most people today assume virtually an
ontological relationship between the "piece" and a record of that piece
written in musical notation. Such was not the case in the Middle Ages.
Only gradually did a perceived need for some kind of notation emerge
in the centuries prior to 900 C.E. These earlier systems of notation
differed drastically from those of later times, so much so that even
today's specialists in medieval music often cannot determine precisely
or with certainty what the older notation means.

Whereas in modern times musicians have come to regard a score
as a fairly precise and reasonably complete set of directions of what to
perform and how, recent scholarship has shown that early music
writing functioned more as a general reference to a "piece" that was by
no means fixed as to details of melody and rhythm; further, both
medieval composition and the notation adapted to it combined what we
now conceptualize as memory, improvisation and composition.[4] The
situation was more like that of the relation between a raga and any of
its realizations, or between a notated version of a folk song (such as
"Amazing Grace") and any of its realizations.[5]

Men and women in cloisters sang the Divine Office daily and, as in
Hildegard's case, from childhood. They learned liturgical chant by
hearing and doing it rather than by reading from notation. In so doing,
they absorbed the grammar, syntax and vocabulary of chant much as
young children learn language, and were thus able to create new
melodies, drawing on the conventions of their familiar musical
"language." Thus, even someone who had not studied notation or
theory of modes would be able to "compose" on the spot.

Applying this understanding to Hildegard's pieces, her confession
to a lack of musical education assumes an import different from what
one might at first attach to it. She obviously knew how to sing (indeed,
to judge from her surviving melodies one would guess she was an
accomplished singer) and even how to compose, in the sense noted
above, without having formally studied theory of music and notation.

By her own testimony Hildegard composed her melodies in an altered, apparently heightened state of awareness. Clearly, she understood them as fruits of her visions, as divinely given. These songs generally are more complex than most Gregorian chant, often made up of long asymmetrical phrases with frequent melismas, passages in which one syllable of text is set to many musical tones. Such melodies require great breath control and vocal agility. Moreover, her melodies tend to have wider ranges than the melodies recorded in the medieval Church's liturgical books, typically spanning at least one and one-half, sometimes as much as two and one-half octaves (about what would be expected of an opera singer today), and using both the high and low ends of the singer's range. All these features place Hildegard's songs well beyond the singing ability of most monastics of her day. Further, she seems to have devised her own distinctive modal system, differing in several important ways from the traditional eight ecclesiastical modes.[6] These idiosyncratic features may well have been connected in some way with Hildegard's visionary states. At the same time, close analysis reveals a remarkable degree of stylistic consistency, as Marianne Richert Pfau has demonstrated ("Mode and Melody" 53).

Many of her contemporaries knew Hildegard's songs, and several noted their unusual features, indeed their strangeness, compared to the prevailing style of liturgical chant. From the terms they used in describing the songs, it seems likely that they, as well as Hildegard herself, regarded them as inseparable from her mystic experiences (*Symphonia* 17). Indeed, Barbara Newman has suggested that Hildegard's music may be closely associated with her development and use of a *lingua ignota*, an "unknown" mystical language:

> The *Lingua ignota* might have been a kind of secret language for the initiated, used to create an atmosphere of mystical intensity in the convent. The fact that Hildegard and her associates spoke of it in the same breath with her music suggests that these works served a common function. Both were revealed from heaven and had arcane significance. . . . (*Symphonia* 18)

Hildegard's songs were apparently written over a number of years. The monk Odo of Soissons wrote her a letter in 1148, referring to her *modos novi carminis,* her "songs in a new style"; from this it may be deduced that she had been composing long enough for her songs to have become known in monastic circles well beyond her own community. Newman concludes that most of Hildegard's songs now preserved must have been written by 1158 and later collected under the title *Symphonia armonie celestium revelationum* (*Symphonia* 8). The songs of the *Symphonia* would thus have spanned the years when Hildegard's fame began to spread and when she undertook the lengthy and often tortuous process of establishing a separate and independent monastic foundation for her nuns on the Rupertsberg, moved the community there and struggled to put the new convent on a sound footing. The songs were written, in short, during a time of great activity, achievement and increasing fame, but also a time of great controversy, struggle and pain for the abbess.

Hildegard's compositions are preserved with musical notation in two principal manuscripts; this description is briefly summarized from Newman's exhaustive study of the sources. The earlier of the two, D or Dendermonde, dates from ca. 1175 and now contains 57 songs; it is thought to have been compiled under Hildegard's supervision. The other manuscript is the Wiesbaden Riesenkodex or simply R. It is thought to have been compiled ca. 1185, after Hildegard's death and perhaps, as Newman suggests, as a kind of "complete works." Manuscript D shows some gaps; R appears to be complete (*Symphonia* 6-12). These two manuscripts appear to have been arranged in a theologically hierarchical order rather than liturgical order, a matter which Newman discusses in great detail (*Symphonia* 51-73). Although the placement of the Ursula songs differs slightly in the two sources, the order in both links St. Ursula with martyred innocence, virginal purity and with the idea of the virgin as a special representative, indeed embodiment of the Church. This powerful emphasis on virginity lies at the root of Hildegard's "theology of the feminine," which Newman has so eloquently and convincingly delineated in her study *Sister of Wisdom*.

Legend tells that Ursula, a Christian noblewoman, was betrothed to a pagan king. Unwilling to marry a pagan, she asked three years' delay, during which time she traveled across the seas, to Rome and other places, in the company of eleven thousand virgins. In some versions of the legend, her betrothed was undergoing conversion during this time. At the conclusion of her three years' sojourn, she returned by way of Germany—Cologne—where she and her eleven thousand companions were martyred.

Not by coincidence does St. Ursula occupy an especially important place in Hildegard's theology and art. One of the great sources of personal struggle for the abbess, both during the years of the *Symphonia* compositions and throughout her life was the tension between her view of herself as a "poor little female" and her contradictory independence in both thought and action. St. Ursula, the divinely inspired and martyred virgin, seems to have been a kind of alter ego, a projection of Hildegard's contradictory affirmation of and resistance to feminine roles of her day and a symbol through which Hildegard transformed her personal conflict into spiritual insight. I will speculate that this conflict probably was in some way bound up with her impressive achievements. Indeed, her theology of the feminine might be regarded as a life long work of reconciling the conflict, and accordingly I assume it as critical to an understanding of Hildegard's musical creations, no less than her other achievements.

The *Symphonia* includes 13 compositions on the St. Ursula legend, including antiphons, sequences, responsories and an extraordinary hymn; "Spiritui sancto" is one of two responsories. Though the form shows considerable variation, the basic framework for responsories is fairly straightforward. A longer section called the Respond typically consists of several musical phrases (2-5) and concludes with 1-2 lines of text and music that will be repeated several times during the course of the piece. This refrain usually carries the most important liturgical-theological idea. The Respond is followed by a short versicle, with different text and music; then comes the refrain. There is often another versicle, employing the shorter doxology as a text and using the same music as versicle 1; it, too, is followed by the refrain. A model of this form appears below.

**Figure 1.** General Form of Responsories

Respond
2-5 phrases with refrain of 1-2 lines

Versicle 1
2-4 phrases

Refrain from Respond

Versicle 2 (shorter doxology)

Refrain from Respond

"Spiritui sancto" shares with other Ursula settings several characteristic themes and images as well as the musical complexity typical of Hildegard's more elaborate compositions. It stands out, though, in several ways: both text and musical setting emphasize the martyred virgin's rejection of conventional marriage with what I take to be a certain violence; the virgin's sacred marriage to Christ is conveyed in one of Hildegard's more sensuous images; a reference to the Old Testament hero Abraham provides what I believe to be a pointed gloss on both Ursula's faith and sacrifice and on Hildegard's personal experience. My following translation, which is literal rather than poetic, reflects the significance I attach to these distinctive points. The Latin texts are taken from Newman's critical edition of the *Symphonia* (230).

**Figure 2.** Text and Translation

| | |
|---|---|
| Spiritui sancto honor sit | Honor to the Holy Spirit, |
| qui in mente Ursule virginis | who, in the mind of the |
| virginalem turbam | virgin Ursula, gathered a |
| velut columbas collegit. | throng of virgins, as doves. |
| Unde ipsa patriam suam | And she left her own country |
| sicut Abraham reliquit. | just as Abraham did. |
| Et etiam propter amplexionem Agni | And she also tore herself away from |
| desponsationem viri sibi | her pledge to a man, for the sake of |
| abstraxit. | the Lamb's embrace. |
| | |
| Nam iste castissimus | Thus, that most chaste |
| et aureus exercitus | and golden army |
| in virgineo crine | with maidenly hair |
| mare transivit. | crossed the sea. |
| O quis umquam talia | O who ever heard |
| audivit? | such things? |
| | |
| Et etiam propter amplexionem Agni | And she also tore herself away from |
| desponsationem viri sibi | her pledge to a man, for the sake of |
| abstraxit. | the Lamb's embrace. |

| | |
|---|---|
| Gloria Patri et Filio<br>et Spiritui sancto. | Glory to the Father and the Son<br>and the Holy Spirit. |
| Et etiam propter amplexionem Agni | And she also tore herself away from |
| desponsationem viri sibi | her pledge to a man, for the sake of |
| abstraxit. | the Lamb's embrace. |

The biblical story of Abraham is about faith, trust in the divine. It is this trust that made Abraham the Old Testament archetype of the righteous man, indeed the man divinely chosen to enter into covenant with Yahweh. Abraham was a pilgrim, a wanderer whose sense of direction came from divine inspiration. He was a man who, by the standards of his culture, had no reason to pull up stakes and set out for an uncertain destination and future, had no reason to believe Yahweh's promise that he would have a son and become a father of nations. By the standards of the ancient world, he was foolish to trust Yahweh. By the standards of her society, Hildegard was foolish and, as a woman, a "weaker vessel." Quite consistently she accepts her own unworthiness, particularly her unsuitability as a *woman* to make judgments and decisions on her own; she was, again in her own words, a "poor little female." Like Abraham, however, she trusted in divine inspiration and acted on it; her actions consequently carried divine authority. She might certainly have found in Abraham a kindred spirit.

The verb *abstraxit* seems quite strong in this context. Although various English equivalents are possible, the literal "tore away" seems most to capture the spirit of both the complete text and the extravagant musical flourish on this word. This is to be contrasted with the verb for Abraham's leaving, *reliquit*, which suggests leaving in the sense of giving up or leaving behind. In Hildegard's poem, St. Ursula does not merely "give up" the comfortably familiar and safe idea of marriage, but "tears herself away" with a certain violence. To appreciate more fully the force of *abstraxit*, we may compare a similar passage from Hildegard's sequence in honor of St. Ursula, "O Ecclesia":

| | |
|---|---|
| In visione vere fide<br>Ursula Filium Dei amavit<br>et virum cum hoc seculo reliquit. . . . | In a vision of true faith<br>Ursula loved the Son of God<br>And gave up/left behind a<br>man [her betrothed] |

along with all things of
this world. . . .

*(Symphonia* 238-243)

Even in this piece, which is poetically and musically more
elaborate than "Spiritui sancto" and which is remarkable for its
rhetorical parody of the most erotic passage from the Song of Songs,
the abbess employs the milder verb *reliquit.*

Hildegard's hymn in honor of St. Ursula, "Cum vox sanguinis,"
employs the Abraham reference to serve the abbess' exegetical
wizardry. This hymn is apparently meant to link the sacrifice of Ursula
and martyred virgins generally with the main line of salvation history,
beginning with the patriarch's willingness, as an act of trust in Yahweh,
even to sacrifice his own son, and concluding with God's willingness to
sacrifice his. These heroes and heroines of faith are linked to Christ's
sacrifice by the image of sacrificial blood. The seventh stanza of the
hymn is quite close in language to the responsory "Spiritui sancto";
indeed Newman calls it an "echo" and believes that this hymn and
"Spiritui sancto" were probably intended for the same liturgical
occasion *(Symphonia* 313).

Newman's research suggests that "Spiritui sancto" was not written
until after the conflict over Hildegard's move to the Rupertsberg had
begun. The Abraham reference thus invites comparison with
Hildegard's decision to move her convent. Acting on what she claimed
was divine inspiration, she left her home and entered into an uncertain
future. Faced with fierce opposition from the monks at Disibodenberg,
especially Abbot Kuno, she took to her bed, paralyzed by divine
affliction, until she won her point and the abbot capitulated. In short,
this responsory may be, among other things, a specific reference to her
struggles to move to the Rupertsberg.

Such ideas are consistent with patterns in the poetry, and I believe
that an inclusive text-music analysis of the song further supports such a
reading. In this connection, Ritva Jonsson and Leo Treitler have offered
particularly illuminating insights into medieval text-music relations.
There are, as they observe, many writings on music from the Middle
Ages. Some of these are basically about the more technical side of
music, such as theory of modes and learning how to sing from notation.
Another body is about *cantus*—song—a term which in medieval
writings applies indistinguishably to speech and sung text, or by
extension, to spoken or sung melody. If we want to understand how

words and music together created expression, Jonsson and Treitler insist, we must look at what the treatises say about *cantus*. (2-23)

One of the best extant sources dealing with such matters is the writer known simply as "John" (Johannes), whose treatise *De musica* is thought to have originated ca. 1100, and which was widely known in the later Middle Ages. Following is an important passage, in the translation by Warren Babb. It comes from Section 10, in which John discusses the terminology of modes: ". . . very likely, the modes are called 'tones' from a resemblance to the tones that Donatus calls *distinctiones*. For just as in prose three kinds of *distinctiones* are recognized, which can also be called 'pauses'—namely, the colon, that is, 'member'; the comma or *incisio*; and the period, *clausula*, or *circuitus*—so also it is in chant. In prose, where one makes a pause in the reading aloud, that is called a colon; when the sentence is divided by an appropriate punctuation mark, it is called a comma; when the sentence is brought to an end, it is a period" (Babb and Palisca 116).

The gist is this: there is a main note for every mode, called the "final"; a melody in that mode will generally begin and will invariably end there. There is another note of almost as great importance, which is usually 4 or 5 scale degrees higher than the final and which is called the "dominant." John says that when a musical phrase (a "pause") falls on the dominant, there is a colon; whenever the melody touches on the final, there is a comma; when it concludes on the final there is a period. It should be noted that John reversed the usual relationships between colon and comma; from the entire context it appears he meant the comma to be the stronger mark of punctuation.[7]

John's discussion implies a rhetoric of text and music different from the one that has dominated composition in more recent times. Since at least the sixteenth century, expression in music has come more and more to depend on a perceived correspondence between words and musical representation of the words, a phenomenon called either "text painting" or "word painting." Thus, one commonly hears (and sees in the musical score) melodic lines that rise from lower to higher pitches at the word "ascend"—or the inverse when texts refer to descending or falling. By contrast, medieval *cantus* related music to text primarily by means of grammar. This grammar is precisely what John refers to in the passage cited above.

Following John's guidelines I scanned just the Respond, the main section, of Hildegard's "Spiritui sancto." The following example shows with the appropriate punctuation marks where the melody rests on the final or dominant. I have omitted a few touches on the final or dominant that are simply decorative in nature and not anchor points of the melody. Pfau assigns this song to Hildegard's distinctive "a" mode; its melody makes a very effective, if unconventional use of the subfinal pitch (the one just below the final), in concluding phrase 1b. In this particular place it functions as a strong attractor to the final. My parsing of the text is based on Newman's critical edition and on the score published by Otto Mueller Verlag. In carrying out this exercise I hope to divide the text into sense units as medieval musicians might have understood them.

Text parsed: *Spiritui sancto, honor sit: qui in mente Ursula, virginis vigirinalem turbam, velut columbas collegit. Unde ipsa patria suam sicut Abraham reliquit. Et etiam propter amplexionem Agni, desponsationem viri sibi, abstraxit.*

**Figure 3.** Music-Text Phrasing in "Spiritui sancto"

| Melodic phrase | Text | Ending on Final or Dominant |
|---|---|---|
| 1a + 1b; 2 | Spiritui sancto | F + subfinal; F |
| opening of 1a | honor sit | D |
| 3 | qui in mente Ursule virginis virginalem turbam | F |
| 4 (starts with 1a) | velut columbas collegit | F |
| 5 | Unde ipsa patriam suam sicut Abraham reliquit. | F |
| 6 | Et etiam propter amplexionem Agni | subfinal F |
| 7 | desponsationem viri sibi | F |
| 1a + 1b | abstraxit. | F |

Hildegard's text begins with honor to the Holy Spirit [*Spiritui sancto honor sit*], placing first the theme of divine inspiration; the divine name is set to melodic phrases 1a + 1b, which as the piece unfolds, prove to be the most frequently repeated, and arguably the most musically distinctive, and phrase 2; "honor sit" repeats phrase 1a. The next sense unit introduces St. Ursula, in whose mind the Holy Spirit acts to gather other virgins, like "doves" [*columbas*]. The image of the dove in Christian thought is associated not only with virgins, but with ritual sacrifice and, most importantly in this context, with the Holy Spirit. All this is set to musical phrases 3-4, the latter combined with a repetition of phrase 1a; the rounding of this sense unit with phrase 1a and a slightly modified version of phrase 1b confirms, with musical rhetoric, the conflation of the Holy Spirit's inspiration with the idea of virginal sacrifice. This opening text-music unit concludes with an extended melisma on the verb *collegit*, the specific action of the Holy Spirit.

The following couplet brings a new melodic configuration; so the reference to Abraham is set apart in both the Latin text and in the musical setting. This is melodic phrase 5. The Respond closes with a refrain carrying the burden of Hildegard's thought in this responsory and divides into the melodic phrases 6 and 7, and a closing repetition of 1a + 1b. *Et etiam propter amplexionem Agni* concludes on the final. The betrothal to a mortal man gets a new melodic idea and is set off from the final word of the refrain, the strong verb *abstraxit*. Hildegard has set this verb to the opening melody (phrases 1a + 1b), relying on musical repetition to invoke the Holy Spirit's inspiration yet again at this point. The entire melodic phrase on "abstraxit" is, in fact, a complete musical period in itself, beginning and ending on the final and recapitulating in a slightly ornamented form the opening sense unit.

Overall the structure of this Respond shows marked similarities to a general plan that Pfau has discerned in the majority of Hildegard's songs and associated particularly with pieces in the "e," "d" and "a" modes ("Mode and Melody" 54-57). The plan unfolds as a series of three key phrases and/or sections of a song that comprise its melodic "matrix"; Pfau notes these phrases are often elided and/or compressed and, further, that "motion through the matrix is by no means limited to the beginnings . . . [but ] occurs more than once in a piece, notably at internal articulations." One of the main points of such recurrence in responsories is the *repetenda* [refrain] ("Mode and Melody" 55). The matrix of "Spiritui sancto," following Pfau's scheme, is highly compressed and encompasses my melodic phrases 1a, 1b, and 2. (See Figure 3 above.) The thrice-repeated melodic phrase 1a + 1b is the most distinctive in the entire song, mainly because of its successive leaps, each bounded by the final or dominant. It thus rhetorically links the inspiration of the Holy Spirit with Ursula, with virginity, with the action of gathering other virgins and, finally, with the forceful rejection (*abstraxit*) of marriage to a mortal man, that the virgin might become the bride of Christ.

The versicle is set apart in numerous musical ways. Most obviously, its text setting is more syllabic than that of the Respond, and it lies generally lower in the mode. Then the refrain is repeated. Manuscript R tacks on a shorter doxology followed by the refrain yet again; MS D omits the second versicle and refrain statement.

Overall, the Respond presents the following train of thought: invocation of the Holy Spirit who inspires the actions of the virginal St. Ursula; comparison of Ursula to the archetypal man of faith, Abraham, who gave up the comfort and safety of home to undertake a risky but divinely ordained journey; Ursula's wrenching herself away from her home and the safety of marriage to a mortal in order to bind herself to Christ. The versicle that appears in both surviving manuscripts refers to these actions as "tales"—implying foolishness. Direct or indirect references to foolishness occur in most of the Ursula songs, and these references in turn recall the language and tone of an important autobiographical passage from Hildegard's *Vita*, restored and translated by Dronke. Here the abbess describes her move to the Rupertsberg, and the conflicts which attended it:

> . . . with a vast escort of our kinfolk and of other men, in reverence of God we came to the Rupertsberg. Then the ancient deceiver put me to the ordeal of great mockery, in that many people said: "What's all this—so many hidden truths revealed to this foolish, unlearned woman. . . . Surely this will come to nothing." (*Women Writers* 150)

In fact, "foolish" is one of Hildegard's favorite adjectives to describe her own unworthiness; she repeatedly refers to herself as a "poor" or "foolish woman."

It is possible without forcing the issue to read this responsory not only as a statement of Hildegard's theology of the feminine but also as a musical artifact bearing some remarkable parallels to her own life. Throughout her recorded life she seems to have wrestled with her own independence, her pride as a woman and a virgin and her own sense of authority, accepting as she did the quite different view of women pervasive in the Church and in her society generally. Thus she always defended her decisions, her judgments, her writings and music on the basis of divine revelation, which consistently inspired her to contradict social norms circumscribing the role of women. The reference to Abraham is quite possibly a justification of her decision, bitterly opposed by her ecclesiastical superior Abbot Kuno, to remove her community to the Rupertsberg. Such a reading helps account for the violence of expression in the verb *abstraxit*, a verb which is inescapably emphasized by the musical-rhetorical setting. The setting, moreover, links this unusually pointed rejection of marriage and, by extension, male authority to the power of divine inspiration. If such a reading is correct or even plausible, Hildegard's responsory is at one and the same time an exquisite decoration of the liturgy for St. Ursula, a concrete example of her theology of the feminine and a personal justification of an important decision that brought her into bitter conflict with male authority.

Yet even more is implied here, particularly in the context of Hildegard's theology of the feminine. The conventional metaphor of the virgin as bride of Christ overlaps that of the Church as bride of Christ, and Hildegard's thought gives a particular emphasis and character to it. Particularly illuminating are the distinctions she makes between the sanctified chastity of widows and that of virgins. I here refer to two examples from the abbess's writings. This first is a letter cited by both Dronke and Newman and written by one Tengswindis (Tengswich), abbess of another German women's community. Tengswindis taxes Hildegard with the seeming presumption of allowing her nuns to wear fine clothes and tiaras, invoking Pauline admonitions for women to dress and behave modestly. In justifying this practice, Hildegard distinguishes between the requirements imposed on married women and virgins' freedom from such requirements. The married woman has known sex, which Hildegard apparently, like most Christian thinkers of her day, regarded as the emblem of the Fall. Hildegard says the virgin, however, "remains in the simplicity and beautiful integrity of paradise"(*Women Writers* 166; *Sister* 221); she remains the paradisal virgin, indeed the only remaining link between humanity before and humanity after the Fall. She is the only representative of humanity remaining worthy to be the bride of Christ, to embody the Church. She thus may deck herself in "bridal splendor" (*Women Writers* 166; *Sister* 222). In fact, virginity is the very sign of redemption and the true mark of the Church; the Church collectively constitutes a "new race" of beings born into a restored Paradise. Newman observes, "This newness belongs mystically to the entire Church, but literally only to virgins" (*Sister* 220).

In comparing two of Hildegard's lyrics—the "Symphony of Virgins" and the "Symphony of Widows" (*Symphonia* 220-225)— Newman finds additional possibilities. She suggests the pieces were written "for choral performance by the two categories of nuns in her care" and reveal Hildegard's "perceived difference between the 'penitent' widows and the more exalted virgins, who had taken Christ as their first and only lover" (*Symphonia* 305). Here again the virgins enjoy the more elevated status, in that they have never known human sexuality, only the spiritual love of Christ. On the other hand, the widows enjoy a freedom from men, an independence in action, that differs from that of virgins, whose freedom is rooted in the perfection of Paradise, of never *having* to act. The widows have borne the subjugation of marriage, a social necessity from which they are now free. They may be spiritually less exalted, but they enjoy greater independence. Newman observes that the "sense of monastic widowhood as a liberation from marriage was expressed even in the rite of consecration. A virgin becoming a nun had to receive her veil from the bishop's hands, but a widow was entitled to place it on her own head 'because she is freed from the rule of man'" (*Symphonia* 306).

Woman's exaltation stems from virginal purity, which links her to the original state of humanity, in Paradise; it is an abstract ideal essential to her salvific role in Hildegard's theology of the feminine. Yet Church and the larger society grant her personal independence only as a monastic widow, who by her former marriage, has placed herself outside the gates of Paradise. I believe this contradiction may reflect Hildegard's view of herself as a type, the Virgin, and as a particular woman who enjoys an independence remarkable for women in her day. It is a view made the richer and more suggestive precisely because of the contradictions; indeed, only in such contradictions, I suggest, does the fullness of Hildegard's ideal of Woman reside.

No surprise, then, that the figure of St. Ursula proved a particularly potent vehicle for exploration of the central tension in the abbess's life. Ursula, second only to the Virgin Mary, stands as representative of a universal and abstract principle—female Virginity—which is humanity's only remaining link to its angelic purity prior to the Fall and, embodied in Ecclesia, the essential partner of Christ in the divine work of salvation. At the same time, Ursula is a divinely inspired individual who suffers ridicule and ultimately martyrdom at the hands of men for her decisions and actions. Thus in Ursula, Hildegard has fused the personal and the universal so as to justify to herself and her society her own actions. This may all be read back into "Spiritui sancto", I think, for throughout this song, as in many of her compositions and writings, Hildegard seems to say that only God—no mortal male—has authority over her, over the divinely inspired virgin, who by action of the Holy Spirit, is elevated to a status approaching that of Christ.

*Note to the following Transcription of the Respond: The transcription shows the main pitches of the melody in stemless note heads, and what I take to be ornamental tones in small note heads tied to the notes to which they are applied. In the interest of making the transcription as easy to read as possible, particularly to readers who are not conversant with the technicalities of chant notation, I have omitted the marks indicating ligatures. My transcription is based on Otto Mueller Verlag's published score of Hildegard's* Lieder, *which presents the songs in modern chant notation, and on the recording by Sequentia. I have included all the* musica ficta *B-flats shown in the published score, though in view of Pfau's analyses of Hildegard's idiosyncratic modal types, particularly the "a" mode to which "Spiritui sancto" belongs, I do not necessarily concur with the all the B-flats added. In two places I have indicated what I believe to be necessarymusica ficta B-flats in square brackets; flats in parentheses, as well as those written above the staff without any editorial marks, are those from the published score.*

# Respond from Hidegard von Bingen's
## "Spiritui sancto"

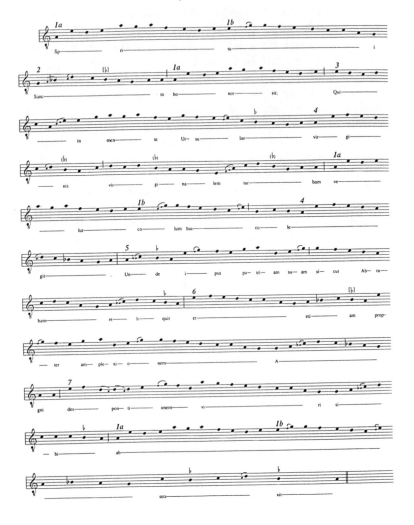

## NOTES

1. An earlier version of this article was read at the International Medieval Congress, University of Leeds, July 10, 1995, as part of the session "Regendering the World: Medieval Women Reinscribe Male Tradition," sponsored by the Center for Early Women Writers at California State University, Fresno.

2. This paper is heavily indebted to studies by Peter Dronke, particularly *Poetic Individuality in the Middle Ages* (Oxford: Oxford University Press, 1970), and *Women Writers of the Middle Ages* (Cambridge: Cambridge University Press, 1984), especially the chapter "Hildegard of Bingen," 144-201; and to Barbara Newman's research, and particularly her critical edition of Hildegard's song texts, *Symphonia. A Critical Edition of the Symphonie armonie celestium revelationum.* Ithaca and London: Cornell University Press, 1988) and *Sister of Wisdom. Saint Hildegard's Theology of the Feminine* (Berkeley and Los Angeles: University of California Press, 1987)

3. Our present Western notion of "composition" as a distinct activity with no logically necessary connection to performance would have been foreign to medieval musicians. The role of "musician" encompassed what we would now call composition, music theory and analysis, performance, and speculative philosophy, particularly systems of thought in which concepts of number and proportion were key elements. For Hildegard to declare herself untutored was roughly equivalent to her saying she was not a philosopher as then understood.

4. This is a complex story in its own right. The subject has been most fruitfully investigated by Leo Treitler in "Homer and Gregory: The Transmission of Epic Poetry and Plainchant", "Oral, Written, and Literate Process in the Transmission of Medieval Music" and "The Early History of Music Writing in the West." See also Helmut Hucke, "Toward a New View of Gregorian Chant."

5. Consider, for example, the folk tune "New Britain" [familiarly known with the words of the hymn "Amazing Grace"], which can readily be found in notation. What I see in the Episcopal Church's Hymnal 1982 is more a reference to a general melodic shape I—and millions of others in the English-speaking world—know as "Amazing Grace" than a precise record of a fixed tune. I do not sing exactly what is notated, and have rarely heard anyone sing just what is notated; we sing, rather, a combination of what we remember of that shape and the many different ways we've heard it played and sung, mingled with anything "new" we happen to make up on a particular occasion.

6. The most extensive discussion of Hildegard's modal system is to be found in Pfau's unpublished dissertation.

7. The passage above is also quoted and interpreted in Jonsson and Treitler, 8. John's point is even clearer in context; see chapter 10, "On the Modes" in Babb and Palisca, 115-117. John's chapter 19, "On the best plan for ordering melody," 139-144, provides further insight into the relationship between medieval musical-poetic rhetoric and composition.

## WORKS CITED

### Primary Texts

Hildegard von Bingen. *Lieder.* Salzburg: Otto Mueller Verlag, 1969.

———. *Symphonia. A Critical Edition of the Symphonia armonie celestium revelationum.* Ed. and trans. Barbara Newman. Ithaca and London: Cornell University Press, 1988.

———. *Symphoniae.* Sequentia, dir. Barbara Thornton Harmonia mundi, D-7800, 1989.

### Secondary Texts

Babb, Warren, trans. and Claude V. Palisca, ed. *Hucbald, Guido, and John on Music. Three Medieval Treatises.* New Haven and London: Yale University Press, 1978.

Dronke, Peter. *Poetic Individuality in the Middle Ages.* Oxford: Oxford University Press, 1970.

———. *Women Writers of the Middle Ages.* Cambridge: Cambridge University Press, 1984.

Hucke, Helmut. "Toward a New View of Gregorian Chant." *Journal of the American Musicological Society* XXXIII (1980): 437-467.

Jonsson, Ritva and Leo Treitler. "Medieval Music and Language: A Reconsideration of the Relationship." *Music and Language.* Studies in the History of Music. New York: Broude, 1983. 2-23.

Newman, Barbara. *Sister of Wisdom. St. Hildegard's Theology of the Feminine.* Berkeley and Los Angeles: University of California Press, 1987.

Pfau, Marianne Richert. "Hildegard von Bingen's *Symphonia armonie celestium revelationum:* Analysis of Musical Process, Modality, and Text-Music Relations." Diss. State University of New York at Stony Brook, 1990.

———. "Mode and Melody Types in Hildegard von Bingen's *Symphonia.*" *Sonus* 11 (Fall 1990): 53-71.

Treitler, Leo. "The Early History of Music Writing in the West." *Journal of the American Musicological Society* XXXV (1982): 237-280.

————. "Homer and Gregory: The Transmission of Epic Poetry and Plainchant." *Musical Quarterly* LX (July 1974): 333-372.

————. "Oral, Written, and Literate Process in the Transmission of Medieval Music." *Speculum* LVI (1981): 471-491.

# Echoes of Hildegard:
# The Fourteenth Century and
# Beyond

# Rhenish Confluences
## Hildegard and the Fourteenth-Century Dominicans
*Leonard P. Hindsley*

At first glance there seems to be little to recommend the thesis that the thought and writings of Hildegard of Bingen (1098-1179) influenced fourteenth-century Dominicans such as Meister Eckhart (c. 1260-c.1329), John Tauler (c. 1300-1361), Henry Suso (c. 1295-1366), Margaret Ebner (c. 1291-1351), Adelheid Langmann (c. 1312-1375) and Christina Ebner (1277-1356). The Benedictine Hildegard lived by a different monastic rule and according to a more ancient spirituality than did the Dominicans who adopted the Rule of St. Augustine and their own constitutions to define their way of life and spirituality. Benedictine monasticism sought to reestablish the "garden of Eden" or rather to create an ordered society which foreshadowed the kingdom to come. Dominicans, although inspired by the Western monastic tradition and greatly influenced by the Cistercians, saw the monastic way of life as preparation for an active ministry. The friars went forth to preach and hear confessions, and the nuns often engaged in counseling and spiritual direction. Hildegard wrote voluminously on all sorts of topics, whereas the Dominican nuns wrote autobiographies, monastery chronicles and personal letters while the friars preached homilies or wrote theological tracts. Scholars have written of Hildegard as an apocalyptic prophet with, as Barbara Newman puts it, a "startling lack of interest in her own subjectivity" (17). On the other hand Dominicans produced numerous documents showing their abiding interest in the details of the personal spiritual life as a lived experience upon which they could reflect theologically. All of them, men and women, were concerned with their personal relationship with Christ. The nuns, and even some of the friars or chaplains, understood themselves almost exclusively in ecstatic bridal mystic categories. Margaret and Christina Ebner as well as Adelheid Langmann each wrote an autobiography (entitled *Revelations*) which dealt primarily with her own relationship with Christ. They interpreted this personal and passionate relationship with Christ in terms of the love shared between the Bride and the Bridegroom in the Song of Songs.

In this last respect, the Dominican nuns differ markedly from Hildegard by degree. For Dominicans of the fourteenth century, bridal identification ranked first in their self-understanding, and it gave them an entire set of symbolic references to image what was a deeply personal, interior and mysterious union with Christ. Hildegard's use of bridal imagery appears to be more external, public and ritualized. She prefers the image of the undefiled virgin as bride in a never-to-be-consummated love relationship with the High Priest:

> [The Virgin] stands in the simplicity and the wholeness of a beautiful paradise that will never fade but remain forever green and ripe as a branch in blossom. . . . Virgins are wedded in the Holy Spirit to holiness and the dawn of virginity; therefore it befits them to come to the High Priest as a whole burnt offering consecrated to God. (Epistle 116, quoted in Newman, *Sister* 222-3)

Hildegard dresses up her nuns quite literally in bridal raiment, which remains symbolic attire for the wedding feast but not for the mystical marriage bed. The Dominican mystic, Adelheid Langmann (d. 1375) recorded her imaging of union with Christ in more intimate terms:

> The Lord now approached the bed. In all his joyous beauty he knelt down before the bed and his face was turned toward mine. I looked up and gazed at him. He was so beautiful that I could not bear it and it seemed to me that my soul would dissolve from true love. He said, "My Beloved!" With the same word that so sweethly came out from his mough he drew my poor, sinful soul into his Godhead and I can say nothing about this vision. . . . (Strauch 65:23-30)

Despite these differing emphases in spirituality, one still suspects that Hildegard influenced the Dominicans. This is an important point since Dominican spirituality and mysticism reached a climax in the fourteenth century. It could be argued that it was the greatest mystical era in the history of Christianity. What role did Hildegard of Bingen play in it?

Previous scholarly research has shown that there are certain similarities in teachings and use of images between Hildegard and Meister Eckhart. Any confluence here is important to note since Eckhart was called "Master" by younger Dominicans whom he taught at the studium in Cologne. John Tauler, among many, recognized Eckhart as his teacher and mentor and extended his teachings into the next generation. However, because of the condemnation of Eckhart's ideas in 1329, any direct influence he exerted over his pupils is always expressed by them in very cautious and oblique terms.

Oliver Davies has already shown instances of Hildegard's writings and thought in the sermons of Meister Eckhart (Davies 51f.). He argues that there is good reason to suspect that the young Eckhart knew some of Hildegard's texts. Especially in his sermons in a collection called *Paradisus animae intelligentis,* Davies finds evidence of Hildegard's influence linking the two by their use of themes, particularly "the belief that humanity is both the 'work' and the 'tool' or 'instrument' of God, and the idea that the Holy Spirit underlies both the vitality of living things and the fruitfulness of spiritual grace . . ." (Davies 54-55). Also, Eckhart's use of Hildegard's term *viriditas* or "greenness" is developed in sermon 72. Davies goes on to state that, "They are both keenly interested . . . in the original point of creation from the Godhead, and in the genesis of creatures through the Word" (58), and to claim that Eckhart and Hildegard had in common their interest in the "fertility" of God (59). What these examples show is that the Master considers Hildegard as a valid theological source and authority, an attitude which his student John Tauler also adopts.

John Tauler exerts a much greater and longer-lasting influence on the Dominicans than had his mentor. What is more important, he explicitly mentions Hildegard of Bingen in three sermons. Louise Gnädiger asserts the following: "In addition Tauler uses the 'Book of Revelation' (*Scivias*) of Hildegard of Bingen (1098-1179). In one of his extant sermons Tauler expressly refers to two illustrations from the Rubertsberg Codex, namely, the representation of the personification of Holy Fear of God and Poverty of Spirit; he also refers to an attempt to represent the unknowable God in symbols. Tauler knows these images from the manuscript and also from frescoes or paintings in the refectory of the Dominican convent of St. Gertrud am Neumarkt in Cologne" (Gnädiger 37).[1]

This same sermon (*In domo tua oportet me manere*, Hofmann 68; Vetter 69) Tauler preached on the anniversary of the dedication of the Cathedral of Cologne. The text upon which Tauler bases his sermon he takes from the Gospel appointed for that celebration, namely, Luke 19:1-10, the story of Zachaeus. Tauler uses the verse, "For I must stay in your house today" (Lk 19:5 RSV), as his thesis. He incorporates various themes in his text beginning with the observation that outward structures, such as churches, and outward activities, such as liturgical celebrations, must benefit the human soul so that it will become the true temple of God. To accomplish this end Tauler emphasizes the necessity for discipline in all its manifestations. The believer, having curbed disorderly appetites in eating and drinking, seeing and hearing, talking and acting, can become the sweet odor of sacrifice to God (2 Cor. 2:15). Tauler, speaking directly to his audience, asserts that the believer may become so altered by God that these words of Psalm 104:3 may be applied to describe him or her for it is God, "who makes the clouds your chariot, who rides on the wings of the wind" (377). The psalm text poetically describes the victory of the believer, who by self-discipline is raised to new spiritual heights. Lest Tauler be accused of Pelagianism with reference to the disciplined believer accomplishing such a godlike end, he immediately speaks of the interior aspects of the process of discipline which are brought about, not by human effort but by the will of God. Such a believer receives the "wings of a dove," that is, simplicity of heart, the "wings of the eagle," that is, wisdom and love, and the "wings of the wind," and "this wind represents the most contemplative human being, the hidden, most perfect one transformed into the image and likeness of God. He far exceeds the power of reason and all that reason is able to accomplish. He goes beyond the senses. Such a human being flies back to its origin, into its uncreatedness and becomes a light in the Light" (377). Tauler then applies this progression to the story of Zachaeus who climbed the sycamore tree to see Jesus. From this comparison Tauler asserts that the believer must climb above human passions and natural inclinations by means of mortification and discipline in order to become a spiritual, rather than a carnal being. In opposition to the opinion of the worldly who view such efforts as foolish, Tauler paraphrases the text from Luke: "Father, I thank you that you have hidden these great things from the great and the wise of this world and have revealed them to the little ones" (Lk 10:21) (379).

Precisely at this point Tauler refers explicitly to Hildegard. "Because of this many lovely things were revealed to the noble creature St. Hildegard, and these are painted in St. Hildegard's book and also in two small paintings in the refectory of our sisters" (379). Tauler expands on his themes using the text and the paintings contained in Hildegard's manuscript and from copies of the paintings in the Dominican sisters' convent. He then describes the two paintings in his sermon linking them with Hildegard's portrayal of the Fear of God in Vision 1 of Book I.2. where she writes:

> And before him at the foot of the mountain stands an image full of eyes on all sides. For the Fear of the Lord stands in God's presence with humility and gazes on the Kingdom of God, surrounded by the clarity of a good and just intention, exercising her zeal and humility among humans. And thus you can discern no human form in her on account of those eyes. For by the acute sight of her contemplation she counters all forgetfulness of God's justice, which people often feel in their mental tedium, so no inquiry by weak mortals eludes her vigilance. ( 68)

Tauler describes this fear as "a careful self-scrutiny of a human being . . . in places and ways, words and works . . ." ( 379). He uses Hildegard's reference to humility to speak of true self-knowledge and self-discipline with the goal of the kingdom of God, or rather the establishment of that kingdom as the dwelling place of God in the temple of the soul. Tauler also uses the detail of the lack of human form to mean that, having no face and head, Fear of the Lord shows "self-forgetfulness, whether one loves or hates it, praises or blames it. And it has no hands; and this shows true detachment from all things" (379). Tauler adapts Hildegard's vision and text to speak of the virtue which will both place the soul constantly in the presence of God and guide the soul in the ways of the Lord through self-awareness and acts of self-discipline. These, in turn, will dispose the soul to the attainment of the kingdom of God. This goal and its required methods of attainment feature importantly in Dominican spirituality. One of the Order's fondest reminiscences of Dominic shows him at his nine ways of prayer. Jordan of Saxony, in his *Libellus*, describes the source for interpreting Dominic's manner of praying: "He loved to read the book called the *Conferences of the Fathers*, which deals with the vices and with all the matters of spiritual perfection. The paths of salvation outlined therein he carefully studied and tried to imitate with all the strength of his soul. Along with the help of grace, this book refined the purity of his heart, intensified the light of his contemplation, and raised him to a high level of perfection" (Lehner 13). The goal of the attainment of the kingdom of God, along with the presribed attitudes, disciplines and prayer methods to attain it, come from the Egyptian desert tradition via the writings of John Cassian (c. 360-435) whose *Conferences* and *Institutes* were among Dominic's favorite texts. On his journeys Dominic always carried Cassian's works, the Gospel of Matthew and the Letters of St. Paul with him. The teachings contained in the "Nine Ways of Prayer" based in part upon the writings of John Cassian promote the acquisition of certain virtues, four of which are particularly pertinent to Tauler's understanding of Hildegard: humility as the basis of the spiritual life, and compunction, penance and gazing upon Christ as elements of the disciplining of the believer.

Both Tauler and Hildegard stress the importance of humility for real progress on the part of those who fear the Lord. Hildegard states that this is so because God himself "submitted himself humbly to poverty," and it is when human beings "truly fear God and ardently embrace humility of spirit" that they receive virtues from God and therefore may progress in the way of holiness (68). Tauler uses his description of a second Hildegardian picture in the sisters' refectory in his sermon to convey a similar message: "This picture represents poverty of spirit whose head is God. The whiteness of the garment means the simplicity of the path, the absence of presumption, and also true abandonment. Both go barefoot. This means the naked following of the true image of our Lord Jesus Christ. The blue dress means steadfastness, not that one practices today and then sleeps tomorrow but rather it should be a constant practice to the end with hands upraised ready to accept God's will, works and sufferings" ( 379-380). Tauler concludes his sermon and reinforces the idea of humility using the words of Christ to Zachaeus as his source: "This day I must abide in thy house." He interprets that phrase to mean: "You must come down. You should hold all things as nothing except to go down to your very nothingness without power or possessions; and so I must come into your house today—that is necessary" (380).

In this way, Tauler makes use of Hildegard's artwork and writings in the sermon, citing her teaching as authoritative and then expanding on the key concepts of "Fear of God" and "Poverty of Spirit" while preaching to a monastic audience which he addresses as "Kinder" (children).[2] Whether he was preaching to young male novices or to nuns, the message of the homily is to see the value of outward things to transform the inner reality. "Fear of God" is the beginning of wisdom and applies to any Christian spirituality. "Poverty of Spirit" must be the fulfillment of real mendicant poverty. The disciplines he mentions which foster spiritual progress are all monastic virtues: fasting, praying and watching. Tauler's reference to Hildegard thus joins his audience to an ancient spiritual tradition, the distinctive elements of which can be applied in the contemporary situation, for the validity of these elements is linked with the humanity of the believer and the call to be transformed, to be made perfect (Mt 5:48).

Tauler also explicitly mentions and quotes Hildegard in his second sermon for the Feast of Corpus Christi (*Qui manducat meam carnem*, Vetter 60f). He bases the sermon on the text "He who eats my flesh and drinks my blood abides in me and I in him" (Jn 6:56). In speaking of the mystery of the Eucharist, Tauler once again thanks God that this mystery has been revealed to the little ones (Lk 10:21). He urges his audience to view this glorious gift of God with enlightened reason and ardent love. He sees the ingestion of the body and blood of Christ as yet another instance and means by which God unites himself with humans and is "made one with us" ( 310-311). Speaking of the glory of this miracle, Tauler again resorts to the authority of Hildegard: "But St. Hildegard writes that this happens invisibly every day" (311). He bases this statement upon Hildegard's sixth vision in Book Two (Christ's sacrifice and the Church). There Hildegard reports a vision of the celebration of the Mass: "Hence when a priest clad in sacred vestments approached that altar to celebrate the divine mysteries, I saw that a great calm light was brought to it from Heaven by angels and shown around the altar until the sacred rite was ended and the priest had withdrawn from it" (237). The mystical vision intensifies as the Mass progresses. When the priest sings the *Sanctus*, ". . . Heaven was suddenly opened and a fiery and inestimable brilliance bore it on high to the secret places of Heaven and then replaced it on the altar, . . . and thus the offering was made true flesh and true blood, although in human sight it looked like bread and wine" ( 237). Later in the same vision Hildegard hears a voice which foreshadows the thesis of Tauler's sermon: "Eat and drink the body and blood of my Son, to wipe out Eve's transgression, so that you may be restored to the noble inheritance" (237). The commentary on these passages stresses the presence of God in light during the sacrifice of the Mass and portrays it as a holy event in which God and humans communicate ( 241). The celebration of the Mass also reminds God of the passion of Christ beginning with the institution of the Eucharist on the night before he died. In the vision God says, "For He too offered Me bread and wine in the outpouring of His blood, when he cast down death and raised up humanity" (241). The offering of the bread and wine recalls all the events of the Paschal Triduum—the Last Supper, the Crucifixion and the Resurrection. This offering of the Mass extends the effects of Christ's sacrifice. Just as this *Urmesse* establishes the New and Everlasting Covenant in the offering of bread and wine, in Christ's obedience to the Father's will, by the shedding of Christ's blood along with his death on the cross and his Resurrection from the dead, so every celebration of the Mass in every age and every place re-presents those saving events and likewise raises the believer up.

Hildegard's visions supply powerful affirmation of the Dominican stress on the importance of the Eucharist. Hildegard's thought may well be summarized by using the words of St. Thomas Aquinas who described the basic elements of a eucharistic theology in the famous antiphon to the Magnificat which all Dominicans would have known:

O Sacrum Convivium, in quo Christo sumitur:
Recollitur memoria passionis ejus.
Mens impletur gratiæ et futuræ gloriæ
nobis pignus datur.

O Sacred Banquet in which Christ is received! The memory of His Passion is recalled. The soul is filled with grace and a pledge of future glory is given to us.[3]

Both Hildegard and Tauler make use of a full eucharistic theology in which they understand the Mass as the summit of Christian worship. It is a holy event because the presence of God is certain during the celebration. It is a salvific event because it recalls and continues the one salvific event of Christ's sacrificial death in obedience to the Father's will. Further, the Mass is celebrated according to Christ's own command to do this in remembrance of him (Lk 22:19; 1 Cor 11:24). It is a sanctifying event because it brings Christian believers into the presence of the Holy One. The believers feed on the "bread of heaven" and by it are united with Christ and with one another. Both Hildegard and Tauler want to emphasize the importance of the Mass so that the believer will be profoundly changed and grow in faith.

Tauler further explains the importance of the Mass by referring to a contemporary situation: "And this same thing was once seen by one of our sisters up in the country, that an incomprehensible brightness surrounded the priest and the altar, and an appearance of angels and many other lovely things. She saw this with her bodily eyes" ( 311). By including this contemporary event in the sermon, Tauler makes it clear to his listeners that what Hildegard taught through her writings is true and verifiable by contemporary human experience. The importance of the Eucharist and its effect on believers is no past event, but a living reality in the present time. The story of the Dominican nun, the visions of Hildegard, the events of the Paschal Triduum are all linked to the celebration of any Mass. The Dominican nun, the abbess Hildegard, the preacher Tauler, the teachings of the Church, and the Scriptures give faithful testimony to Christ's saving work and to its effect in the world. These living and written testimonials invite the hearer of the sermon to grow deeper in faith. In this case, Tauler uses Hildegard as an authoritative source for a sermon directed most likely to Dominican novices or nuns. He addresses the audience as "Kinder" or "Kint" and speaks of "our sister" in a convent. Tauler uses Hildegard's teaching as a strong affirmation of the many mystical events associated with the Eucharist and experienced by Dominican nuns, just as Henry of Nördlingen uses passages from Mechthild of Magdeburg's *The Flowing Light of the Godhead* to help Margaret Ebner make sense of some of her own mystical experiences.

In the sermon *Ascendit Jhesus in naviculum que erat Symonis* on the miraculous catch of fish in Luke 5, Tauler likewise explicitly mentions Hildegard. When he reaches the point of explaining the significance of the net, he draws an analogy between the net and human nature. Like the net which breaks due to the great quantity of fish, human nature breaks because it is too weak to endure the presence of God within. Such a soul will "never have another healthy day. And it is justly so, as St. Hildegard writes, 'It is not God's custom to dwell in a strong, healthy body'" (175). Tauler connects this passage with the writing of St. Paul, quoting him: "For power is made perfect in weakness," which is part of the lengthier passage from Paul: "'My grace is sufficient for you, for power is made perfect in weakness.' So, I will boast all the more gladly of my weaknesses, so that the power of

Christ may dwell in me" (2 Cor. 12:9). This scriptural reference supports Tauler's preaching on the divine indwelling and the process whereby the believer is remade in the image and likeness of God. Unfortunately, I have not been able to find a text in *Scivias* which matches Tauler's quote. Neither does Hildegard refer to this Pauline passage.

While Tauler's quotation does not have an authentic Hildegardian ring, it may reflect her personal experience. In many places Hildegard writes of her own poor health. Tauler's quote may be a reminiscence of Hildegard's reflections on what Newman termed her "frailty and her openness to the spirit" (*Sister* 106); in another of her visionary works, the *De operatione Dei*, she writes of this as follows:

> Ipsa enim cum inspiratione Spiritus sancti officialis existit, et complexionem de aere habet; ideoque de ipso aere, de pluvia, de vento, et de omni tempestate infirmitas ei ita infixa est, ut nequaquam securitatem carnis in se habere possit, alioquin inspiratio Spiritus sancti in ea habitare non valeret. (*De operatione Dei*, quoted in Newman, *Sister* 106)

> Indeed, she survives only through the offices of the inspiration of the Holy Spirit, and has an airy constitution; and so, because of this air and rain and wind and general storminess, illness is so established within her that the flesh can find no security there. This is why the inspiration of the Holy Spirit desires to live nowhere but in her.

The *Vita* also connects Hildegard's illnesses to visitations by the spirit: *Quo languoris genere non tunc solum laboravit, sed et quotiescunque feminea trepidatione tardasset vel dubitasset supernae voluntatis peragere negotia* [She suffered this kind of illness not only once but whenever she hesitated or doubted to perform the business of the heavenly will through womanly fear] (*Vita* I.2). In the preface to the *Scivias* she hesitates to do what the voice had bidden her to do: "But I, though I saw and heard these things, refused to write for a long time through doubt and bad opinion and the diversity of human words, not with stubbornness but in the exercise of humility, until, laid low by the scourge of God, I fell upon a bed of sickness; then compelled at last by many illnesses, . . . I set my hand to the writing" (60). Sabina Flanagan rightly calls Hildegard's illnesses "potent infirmities," pointing to the beneficial results of Hildegard's sickness (205-211). Illness compelled Hildegard to perform her divine mission or task.

In the absence of any discernible Hildegardian passage that matches Tauler's quotation precisely, one can only wonder whether Tauler knew the *Vita*, the *De operatione Dei* or some other text attributed to Hildegard or whether he merely remembered this detail incorrectly or adapted it to his own purposes. Whether or not he is really quoting from Hildegard's writings, however, Tauler is clearly using the same method as in the two sermons discussed above; he effectively uses Hildegard's writing as an authoritative source to supplement his own argument or teaching and to address the experience of his audience. Suffering is also characteristic of the experience of the Dominicans, for whom it had a two-fold function. Illness frequently invited the Dominican to deeper personal conversion, and continued suffering helped her to grow in compassion for the suffering Christ and ultimately for the suffering of any living thing. The Dominican mystic, Margaret Ebner, had such a conversion experience in 1311, beginning with a pain around her heart which led to paralysis (Hindsley 85).[4] Margaret's contemporary, Christina Ebner began her account of her mystic journey by describing herself as if she were in the pangs of childbirth.[5]

A possible explanation for this quotation or misquotation may have to do with Tauler's reading of Vision Four in Book Three of *Scivias*. There Hildegard writes of the various methods by which unwilling humans, she calls them "compelled sheep," are brought closer to God. In the revelation Hildegard is told, "I compel them by many means to come to life and be snatched from death by my Son's blood. Thus 'compelled sheep' are those people who are compelled by me against their will, by many tribulations and sorrows, to leave their iniquities" ( 365). This is further clarified in the next section: "So, when those who belong to Me resist Me by their deeds, I force them as My knowledge of them directs; and so, through the physical and spiritual calamities they suffer, they are compelled to come to Me and be saved" (365).

Tauler's primary ministry was to cloistered Dominican nuns. His care was often to help the nuns make sense of the things they were experiencing, both spiritual and mystical. I believe he used Hildegard's vision as his source but modified it or remembered it selectively with the experience of his audience in mind. Hildegard writes of this revelation with regard to any sort of sinner. Tauler applies that teaching to the specific situation of cloistered nuns. Their experience links sickness with an invitation to conversion, which, in turn, invites the nuns to surrender wholeheartedly to God's will. This conversion leads them to ever deeper insight into the ways of God and subsequently leads numerous nuns to experience mystical life even to union with God. Such is the experience of Margaret Ebner, for example. Although this nun wanted to grow closer to God, she could not. In 1312 she became deathly ill: "In this first year I endured the greatest internal and external suffering because I had not yet given myself over to the will of God completely, for I still wanted to be healthy" (Hindsley 85). She did not enjoy being sick and sought all sorts of human cures. For thirteen years she lay in bed paralyzed. Eventually, she gave up her own will, became well again and set out on an extraordinary spiritual life which culminated in the mystical exchange of hearts with Christ. When Margaret wrote her *Revelations* beginning in 1344, she looked back to these events of her conversion and interpreted them as having happened because of God's paternal faithfulness to her. He would not abandon her in her illness as her friends had done. Neither would He abandon her to her self-will. Other examples could be given of nuns who had similar experiences. While they were at the stage of being "compelled like sheep," it would be consoling to hear that sickness could indeed be an invitation to union with God for, from the experience of Dominican nuns, those who became ill counted themselves as blessed and as specially chosen by God. They believed that a life without imitating the Passion of Christ was unimaginable. Knowing his audience, Tauler could very well have quoted Hildegard as he did hearkening back to her vision, but then applied its message to other "Dominican" circumstances.

It is clear that Hildegard did influence John Tauler. How far her influence extended among the women is less verifiable in their writings. None of the women writers quotes Hildegard explicitly or even mentions her or her books. Yet we do know that they had knowledge of Hildegard, revered her as a saint and took her seriously enough to display copies of her visions in at least one monastery. It is certain that some Dominican writers knew Hildegard's writings from other important sources as well. Writing to Margaret Ebner in Letter LIII (1349), Henry of Nördlingen made direct reference to Hildegard: ". . . as I have already written about the prophecies granted to St. Hildegard. . . ." (Strauch 267). Apparently Henry had already written to the nuns in some detail about St. Hildegard whom he revered as a prophet. That other letter may have helped the Dominican nuns to understand their own mystical experiences better. Unfortunately the letter is not extant. The contact with Henry was very important for Margaret Ebner at the Monastery of Maria Medingen and for Adelheid Langmann and Christina Ebner at the Monastery of Engelthal. Henry introduced these nuns to important writings bearing upon their own mystical experiences. He sent them or asked them to purchase Mechthild of Magdeburg's *The Flowing Light of the Godhead*, Thomas Aquinas' *Summa contra gentes* and the Middle High German translation of the *Summa theologiae*. The influence of these other texts has been studied, especially that of Mechthild. But what of Hildegard?

Her influence on the writing of the nuns is subtle at best. They share the tendency to interpret events, visions or revelations in a symbolic or spiritual way. They delight in the visual accounts of symbolic clothing, crowns, jewels, and shoes. Such similarities only suggest a confluence, but it may be an even wider confluence than Hildegard and the Dominicans, their writings and visions. However far this may extend, what binds Hildegard and these Dominicans together is an unswerving belief that God considers human beings to be of the highest importance—important enough to communicate with them through Son and sacraments, through Church and community, through prophecy and vision and through personal encounters in prayer.

## NOTES

1. This text from Louise Gnädiger and all subsequent translations from Tauler's Middle High German texts into English are mine.
2. The Hofmann translation replaces "Kinder" with "sisters."
3. This is the antiphon to the Magnificat for the Feast of Corpus Christi. Translation mine.
4. Margaret's compassion was especially all encompassing; after witnessing the suffering of servant girls, cattle, other nuns, the emperor and a dying vagrant, she proclaims, "I had compassion for all things and true compassion for everyone whom I saw suffering, no matter what kind of suffering it was" (Hindsley 90).
5. See Christina Ebner, MS Cent. V, App. 99, Nürnberger Stadtbibliothek, 1r.

## WORKS CITED

### Primary Texts

Hildegard of Bingen. *Scivias*. Trans. Mother Columba Hart and Jane Bishop. Mahwah/New York: Paulist Press, 1990.

Tauler, Johannes. *Die Predigten Taulers aus der Engelberger und der Freiburger Handschrift sowie aus Schmidts Abschriften der ehemaligen Strassburger Handschriften*. Ed. Ferdinand Vetter. Berlin: Weidmannsche Buchhandlung, 1910.

### Secondary Texts

Davies, Oliver. *Meister Eckhart: Mystical Theologian*. London: SPCK, 1991.

Flanagan, Sabina. *Hildegard of Bingen: A Visionary Life*. London and New York: Routledge, 1989.

Gnädiger, Louise. *Johannes Tauler: Lebenswelt und mystische Lehre*. München: Verlag C.H. Beck, 1993.

Hindsley, Leonard P., ed. *Margaret Ebner: Major Works*. Mahwah/New York: Paulist Press, 1993.

Hofmann, Georg. *Johannes Tauler: Predigten*. Einsiedeln: Johannes Verlag, 1979.

Lehner, Francis C., O.P., ed. *St. Dominic: Biographical Documents*. Washington, D.C.: The Thomist Press, 1964.

Newman, Barbara. *Sister of Wisdom. St. Hildegard's Theology of the Feminine*. Berkeley and Los Angeles: University of California Press, 1987.

———. "Introduction." *Scivias*. By Hildegard of Bingen. Ed. and trans. Columba Hart and Jane Bishop. Mahwah/New York: Paulist Press, 1990. 9-53.

Strauch, Philipp. *Margaretha Ebner und Heinrich von Nördlingen: Ein Beitrag zur Geschichte der deutschen Mystik*. Freiburg/Tübingen: Akademische Verlagsbuchhandlung von J.C.B. Mohr, 1882; reprint Amerstadam: P. Schippers, 1966.

# The Jewish Mother-in-Law
## Synagoga and the *Man of Law's Tale*
*Christine M. Rose*

*After this, I saw the image of a woman, pale from her head to her navel and black from her navel to her feet; her feet were red and around her feet was a cloud of purest whiteness. She had no eyes, and had put her hands in her armpits; she stood next to the altar that is before the eyes of God, but she did not touch it. And in her heart stood Abraham, and in her breast Moses, and in her womb the rest of the prophets, each displaying his symbols and admiring the beauty of the Church. She was of great size, like the tower of a city, and had on her head a circlet like the dawn.* And again I heard the voice from Heaven saying to me: "On the people of the Old Testament God placed the austerity of the Law in enjoining circumcision on Abraham; which He then turned into sweet Grace when He gave His Son to those who believed in the truth of the Gospel, and anointed with the oil of mercy those who had been wounded by the yoke of the Law."

### I The synagogue is the mother of the Incarnation of the Son of God.

Therefore *you see the image of a woman, pale from her head to her navel;* She is the synagogue, which is the mother of the Incarnation of the Son of God. From the time her children began to be born until their full strength she foresaw in the shadows the secrets of God, but did not fully reveal them. For she was not the glowing dawn who speaks openly, but gazed on the latter from afar with great admiration and alluded to her thus in the Song of Songs: ... "Who is this who comes up from the desert, flowing with delights and leaning upon her beloved." [Song of Solomon 3:6, 8:5][1]

Hildegard of Bingen's fifth vision personifies the people of the covenant in the form of a woman, Synagoga, who is the "mother of the Incarnation" and thus the mother-in-law of the Church, Ecclesia. In recounting her vision, Hildegard adopts the terms of biblical exegesis of the Song of Solomon and a traditional medieval iconography in which the two women are rivals: Synagoga, the mother, rejected and blinded because of her unbelief and supplanted in favor of Ecclesia, the Bride (*sponsa*) of Christ, the gentile Church (Newman, Introd. 29). Hildegard's explanation of the vision asserts that Synagoga, deserted by God in favor of Ecclesia, "lies in vice"(134). The parti-colored figure of Synagoga is pale above, but "black from her navel to her feet." Her feet are red (Plate 1). The visionary explains these colors, saying Synagoga is "soiled by deviation from the Law and by transgressions of the heritage of her fathers . . . for she disregarded the divine precepts in many ways and followed the pleasures of the flesh" (*Scivias* 134) and waded in the blood of Christ. But, despite her crimes, the outlook Hildegard's vision foresaw for Synagoga was ultimately a positive one, representative of an early position in the Jewish/Christian polemic: "So too the Synagogue, stirred up by Divine clemency, will before the last day abandon her unbelief and truly attain the knowledge of God." Far from being everlastingly condemned for her unbelief, Synagoga will in the final days be enfolded into the Church of Christ: "Here the old precepts have not passed away but are transformed into better ones" (135). Hildegard's vision of Synagoga "stresses the saving interrelationships" between the Church and the community of the Jews and represents a somewhat dignified, if melancholy, Synagoga, her body enfolding the Old Testament prophets, relinquishing her sway to Ecclesia (Eckert,303). Eckert offers that from this meditation on her vision it is evident that Hildegard recognized "the intrinsic solidarity of Church and Synagogue; she knew of the ultimate gift of salvation for all Israel" and thus reflected, or even surpassed in forbearance, the twelfth-century attitude of relative tolerance for contemporary Jewry (310).[2]

Plate 1: Synagoga. *Scivias* I, 4.

Both Hildegard's vision and its accompanying explanation have their roots in traditional exegetical and typological commentaries on the Song of Solomon, which figure the Church as the Bride of Christ. Such readings were "universally familiar" by the twelfth century.[3] Imagistically, in medieval art the Synagogue's literal belief in the Old Testament and blindness to Christ's truth were often equated to darkness and the moon's half-light, while the Church corresponded to the light of the fulfillment of the prophecies and the sun's radiance.[4] I want to suggest here that Hildegard's twelfth-century allegorical representation of Synagoga, as blind, vicious, as the murderer of Christ, yet simultaneously the genesis and pre-figuration of the new Church, in fact the agent of its transformation, might profitably be seen as part of the complex code underlying two episodes in Chaucer's late-fourteenth-century *Man of Law's Tale*. There, two wicked and non-Christian mothers-in-law of the heroine, Custance, attempt to banish her from their realms and bar her from marriage to their sons, and more particularly, try to prevent her from procreating and thus usurping their dominion and the dominion of their religions. Chaucer's depictions of the mothers-in-law evoke Hildegard's vision of the supplanted rule of the Old Law by the Christian Church, the Bride of her Son.

What I will attempt to set forth here, using Hildegard's vision as my touchstone but travelling far away from her to late-medieval England, is some notion of the cultural matrix into which we might place Chaucer's rendition of this tale and our reading of it. The tale of the Man of Law, when coupled with some exploration of its sources, both the immediate literary ones, Nicholas Trevet's fourteenth-century Anglo-Norman universal history *Les Cronicles* and John Gower's *Confessio Amantis*, and its more remote folktale ancestors which have been identified as inhering in the tale, such as analogues to the early fourteenth-century English romance *The King of Tars*,[5] and when read against Hildegard's visionary theology as a representative of the *mentalité* of the Jewish/Christian *disputatio*, gestures towards the identification of the evil pagan mothers-in-law with Jewry and the allegorical figure of Synagoga. Further, I would also argue that the method by which Chaucer composes his tale and selects his source material, with some touches he adds not present in his immediate sources, highlights the association of the repudiated and vicious mothers-in-law with the feminized, marginalized Synagoga of both Hildegard's vision and an entire medieval iconographic and intellectual tradition of opposition between Synagoga and Ecclesia. Thus, what has generally been recognized by critics of the tale as Custance's poetic opposition to the vaguely pagan and demonized feminine Eastern/Muslim Other should be extended to include her opposition to that equally threatening Other, the Synagogue.[6]

In the space of this essay, I can only undertake to sketch out the contours of that complex matrix against which to read this tale, the matrix that conjoins the allegorical opposition between Ecclesia and Synagoga to the tale. The topics which must be attended to in such a study are: a) the tradition of biblical exegesis of the Song of Solomon to which I have alluded; b) medieval artistic representations of the Ecclesia/Synagoga *altercatio*; c) literary and theological depictions of this *altercatio* or *disputatio*, including dramatic interpretations of the exiling of Synagoga; d) the history of the Jews and of anti-semitism in the Middle Ages in Europe. Picking salient bits from scholarship and evidence in each of these categories—while claiming no expertise as a theologian, art historian or historian—I hope to show that Chaucer's two mothers-in-law are not merely Orientalized villains as they have generally been identified but are depicted in Chaucer's poetic imagination in such a way as to render them reminiscent of the Synagogue, with its traditional opposite, Ecclesia, represented by the tale's heroine, Custance. Chaucer's allegorizing, furthermore, is not purely exegetical but informed by historically current constructs. It is my contention that this tradition of *disputatio*, of Jewish/Christian polemic about the place of Synagoga, was central to a medieval visual semiotics, which as literary critics we have ignored. The powerful visual impact of such images which surrounded medieval writers and readers/audiences makes Chaucer's tale work on levels we have hitherto left unexplored.

Moreover, this mother-in-law/daughter-in-law relationship between Synagoga and Ecclesia in Hildegard's description and interpretation of her vision evokes the contours of the tale Chaucer assigns to the lawyer on his Canterbury pilgrimage. At its thematic heart, the tale of the Man of Law is about families and pedigree.[7] Custance, Christian daughter of the Roman Emperor, becomes a mother through her second husband Alla of Northumberland, who has converted to Christianity; her son Maurice returns with his mother to Rome from England and by dynastic right becomes the next Roman Emperor. Carolyn Dinshaw has demonstrated that the narrator Chaucer assigns to the tale, the Man of Law, is an adept at *family* law of: "marriage gift, legitimacy of offspring, rules of descent, the establishment of the household, and succession to property" (90). So it comes as no surprise that family in the tale and the issues of "law"— religion being only one of the inexorable "laws" operating in the tale (others include the inexorable "law" of the rhyme-royal stanza form, the rule of the stars, the domination of male authority, the "law" of Fortune, etc.)—form a locus of anxiety. Dinshaw elegantly argues that the lawyer tells a tale which represses the story of incest and gender asymmetry which the patriarchal code within the tale must not articulate. I would add to Dinshaw's analysis of the familial dynamics that in a large sense the tale demonstrates a kind of Oedipal hostility towards the mother (Synagoga, orientalized as Other) and old ways of matriarchy, turning to embrace the patriarchy which in the tale is aligned with (despite the feminine noun) Ecclesia.[8] It might also be construed as a figure of the repudiation of sinful mother Eve in favor of her redeemed descendant the Virgin Mary.[9] And the mothers-in-law do in fact become poetically associated with Eve in the tale, as Custance does with the Virgin. The endogamy which the evil mothers-in-law wish for their sons is replaced by the exogamy of their marriages to Custance, marriages which doom the pedigree of those pagan empires and their religions. Likewise, exhortation to endogamy is a marked feature of many Old Testament books; exogamy and proselytizing a feature of the New. Christianity's descendants as well as its ancestors are depicted in the families at the center of the *Man of Law's Tale*. I want to propose that in small (at the level of individual poetic detail) and in large ways, Chaucer's poem, when read through the matrix of late-medieval culture which I suggest, can be seen to allude to, but not overtly name, the overriding and central Mother-in-law/Daughter-in-law conflict perceived by the Middle Ages: that between Synagoga and Ecclesia.

In both medieval law and imagination, the Jew and the Muslim "were inextricably linked together in the consciousness of Christians."[10] The two idolatrous creeds were conflated in the object of the Crusades—the retrival of the Holy Land—and the xenophobia of the Crusaders was directed at the undifferentiated infidel who hindered that quest. But if we attempt a cultural reading of the *Man of Law's Tale*, especially one which considers art historical monuments, taking care to contextualize "the relations between images and people in history,"[11] the Jewish Other irrupts from its classification as pagan and defies the strategies of containment in the tale. It is repressed within the text yet seemingly abundantly available in the medieval context of art, history or theological debates. This repression is symptomatic of the Jew as the essential Other to the medieval Christian West despite the presence of pagans and Muslims in the tale.

What kind of cultural work such a tale might perform and why Chaucer's tale identifies the pagan women with Synagoga more specifically than his immediate source in Trevet are topics worth pondering. In her work on anti-semitism in the *Prioress's Tale,* Louise O. Fradenburg sees representations of the Other as revealing an important perspective on Western Christian self-representations. As Fradenburg maintains, the *Prioress's Tale* is shaped by the fear of being cut off from language and community (82).[12] Such concerns permeate *The Man of Law's Tale* as well, where the mothers-in-law, who fear for their communities, are silenced. Custance, bereft of her community early on and sent off by her parents to appease political exigencies, journeys through the tale, generally silent except to pray, at several points (ll. 525ff, 981-982), even refusing to speak to reveal her own identity. The voice of the text—the Man of Law—dominates (and obviates) as the victorious Christian voice, refusing to validate the sentience of those who are outside the community. As both Fradenburg and Susan Schibanoff contend, this silencing of the evil Other serves to strengthen social structures against a common enemy. Sheila Delany, noting the Orientalism in Chaucer's *Legend of Good Women,* poses that anxiety about Ottoman expansion in the fourteenth century, fueled by threats and actual confrontations in the 1390s, could have been of real concern to an English diplomat like Chaucer, and thus Delany sees nothing unusual in the pervasive use of the essentialized Oriental Other in Chaucer's work.[13] Still, no one has yet recognized the conventional anti-semitic elements in the *Man of Law's Tale,* veiled and muddled as they are with the generalized pagan and Saracen threat. It is conceivably that anxiety of the recurrent Muslim threat admixed with the age-old yet vacillating Jewish one which the *Man of Law's Tale* encodes. Chaucer here appropriates from his sources a tale about appropriation, making what he takes "new," like the New Law which Custance propagates and which reigns at the end of the tale.

## MEDIEVAL IMAGES OF SYNAGOGA

I turn now to the images which accompany this essay in order to contextualize in terms of visual semiotics the pervasive images of Synagoga in both the *Man of Law's Tale* and Hildegard's allegorical vision of the Synagogue, the reading of which first alerted me to the potent strand of contrast between Synagoga and Ecclesia implicit in Chaucer's tale. Traditional medieval iconographic representations of the Synagogue reflect the notions which inform Hildegard's vision: the Synagogue is blind to the event of the Incarnation, therefore pictorial or sculptural representations of her often show her veiled, blindfolded, eyes downcast, averted, or in some position in which she cannot see what is manifestly there. But she is not demonized, as she will appear in later images. Blindness is a constant theme in the tale of the Man of Law, too: the mothers-in-law are "blind" to the truth of the God Custance follows; Custance cures a blind Briton in Northumberland, and this miracle causes the constable of the realm to be converted (ll. 572-574). Some medieval art depicts Synagoga's eyes covered by a serpent wound about her head. Hildegard allows that her Synagoga "had no eyes," yet, interestingly, the image in the now lost manuscript of her *Scivias* has the eyes painted as closed. The notable discrepancy between written vision and painted image renders Synagoga able to see but refusing to in the latter, whereas Hildegard's words imply that she could not see, even if she tried, since she has not the capacity to do so, a conundrum which might lead one to believe that the artist did not comprehend exactly the delicacy of Hildegard's forgiveness of Synagoga's lack of recognition of her errors.

Synagoga as the personification of the old Church was superceded in its rule when the veil which hid the Holy of Holies in the Temple at Jerusalem tore as Christ died: "And, behold, the veil of the temple was rent in twain from the top to the bottom; and the earth did quake and the rocks rent" (Matt. 27:51).[14] Traditional exegesis of this event decodes it as the end of the rule of the Synagogue and the illumination, through the death of Christ, of a law that had been hitherto hidden in darkness (Schiller 110-112). Light came to a previously dark area, the prophesies of a messiah, yet the Temple itself remained benighted in its continued unbelief. From the time of the early medieval Church, this triumph of light over darkness, of Ecclesia over Synagoga has been interpreted iconographically in a variety of images, most notably Crucifixion images. Synagoga traditionally occupies the position on the crucified Christ's left hand, with Ecclesia on his right; the one turning away, the other facing and welcomed by the figure on the cross. Often, Synagoga is depicted as falling or off balance. Such images carry out the theme of the replacement of the Old Law by the New, of the Old Synagoga/mother, by the New Ecclesia/Bride of Christ and daughter-in-law. Synagoga represents both the murderer and the murdered, the rejector and the rejected (Camille 179). The pictorial opposition of Synagoga / Ecclesia became an important part of Crucifixion images, and Gertrude Schiller traces in such medieval artistic productions a growing hostility between the figures of Ecclesia and Synagoga. Seiferth describes an illustration from the Sacramentary of Bishop Drogo (ca. 850, Metz), which represents "the first ascertainable portrait of Ecclesia at the foot of the cross" (1).[15] In the Crucifixion scene within the historiated initial "O" in this early medieval prayer book, a haloed female Ecclesia stands at the foot of the cross, carrying a banner, holding aloft a chalice to receive the blood from the wound of Christ: "The Christian Church receives her mission and authority from Christ at the hour of his death" (1). Opposite Ecclesia, and apart from the cross, sits a white-haired male figure who raises his right hand to the cross, seemingly grasping a symbol of his authority in his left. Probably, as Seiferth and Schiller agree, the artist meant this figure to represent the Old Covenant of the Jews. This early mise-en-page arrangement of the three figures formed a powerful iconic statement which for centuries of artists both connected the Old and New Law through the cross and separated them by it. Over time and varying from location to location, this theme became transformed, becoming less temperate and more virulent. In place of the old man stands a female allegorical figure "Hierusalem," then "Synagoga" (Seiferth, 3). The allegorical opposition between these two female figures of Ecclesia and Synagoga, like that of Eve and the Virgin to which I have alluded previously, becomes a fixture of medieval representation in varied mediums and over many centuries throughout Western Europe. From the twelfth century onwards, Ecclesia and Synagoga appear regularly in Crucifixion images (Schiller 112).

What seems, then, to begin as the representation of a partnership between Synagoga and Ecclesia in birthing the New Law (depicted in such an image as appears in the Sacramentary of Bishop Drogo) changes to an adversarial position beneath the cross, contention between the Christian Church and the hostile Jews. Hildegard, too, seems to partake of this early tolerant image of Synagoga in transition and not as terminally evil: Synagoga "gazed on the latter [Ecclesia] from afar with great admiration. . ." (*Scivias*, 133). Nevertheless, as Schiller demonstrates, stern scenes of the "deposition of Synagoga" became increasingly common iconographic motifs (110). In such scenes, Ecclesia demands of Synagoga that she surrender the symbols of her sovreignty: the lance (*basta*) or sceptre (*baculus*) to which a three-tongued standard (*flammula*) is attached, the globe (*tympanum*), and the crown.[16] Schiller explains that such an image typifies a growing attitude demonizing the Jews in the ninth century and later. This demonization, as Seiferth indicates, fluctuated during the Middle Ages, with the era's political vicissitudes, Jews being more and less reviled according to the economic and political tenor of the times and how optimistic the corporate Church was at any given moment about their imminent conversion and about their kinship to the New Testament Law.[17]

Scenes of the deposition of the Synagogue in early medieval art display Ecclesia appropriating the insignia of power from Synagoga and have been read exegetically to mean that Christ has given the Church power that had, until his death, belonged to Synagoga and the people of the Old Covenant. Tellingly, in Crucifixion scenes and other images, Synagoga acquires new attributes which emphasize her defeat and that of Jewry, stressing the contrast between the Jewish cult of sacrifice and Christ's sacrificial death: the veiled, defeated Synagoga droops, grasping a broken staff or lance with a banner, sometimes displaying a scorpion on it; the tablets of the Law slip from her hands; a crown falls from her head; a blindfold/veil may display her failure to recognize the Messiah and his New Law—a much harsher picture than the one Hildegard's vision provides. On some depictions, the Lamentations of Jeremiah are put into the mouth of Synagoga, or alluded to: "The Crown is fallen from our head: Woe unto us, that we have sinned! For this our heart is faint; for these things our eyes are dim" (Lamentations 5:16-17). The plates included here (as well as those in Seiferth, Mellinkoff and Schiller) represent images from diverse eras and locales, yet the artists share an unmistakable devolving and pejorative iconographic tradition. Synagoga embodies the blind and proud Jews who did not perceive the Messiah in their midst and must therefore be punished. In such artistic representations, she might wear the symbols of Christ's sufferings as the mark of her sins: the crown of thorns, the rod with the sponge attached, the lance. A he-goat may accompany her, as a symbol of the Old Testament sacrifice, but also a symbol of lust and demonization (Seiferth figs.29, 40). She occasionally rides upon an ass which may be shown collapsing on its knees before the cross, and she may hold the knife of the circumcision, figuring the Old Testament baptism but also calling to mind the medieval legendary association of the Jews with ritual murder and blood libel. She may be shown being driven away by an angel, like Adam and Eve from the Garden of Eden. She may be leading the Jews into hell, a serpent wrapped about her head or be shown with a devil shooting into her eyes. Synagoga is even on occasion a masculine figure, or a man costumed womanishly, figuring the Jew as of ambiguous gender, debased by association with feminization and gender reversal and the *virago*.[18]

Images showing the fall of Synagoga and generally associated with Crucifixion scenes, persist into the fifteenth century, providing an important source of iconic notions of Ecclesia and Synagoga and their relationship, at times familial, at times hostile. I would argue that Chaucer could not have helped coming into contact with such an image contrasting Synagoga and Ecclesia in his reading, in the art and drama around him, or in his travels. In fact, at Canterbury Cathedral, perhaps the locale in England most associated with Chaucer, the stained glass contains the figures of Synagoga and Ecclesia facing each other across the northeast/southeast transept. The rose window in the northeast transept (late twelfth century, contemporary with Hildegard but available to Chaucer) features Moses and Synagoga of the Old Law sitting at the center surrounded by prophets. They face the Blessed Virgin and Ecclesia (in a reconstructed window) in the southeast transept, representing the New Law, allowing the viewer to contemplate "themes of light and dark, old and new" (Brown 13). The growing hostility to the Jews in England, of course, resulted in their expulsion in 1290. The denigration of the tone of the artistic images of Synagoga becomes a part of this general antagonism to the Jews in England and in the rest of Europe. Iconographic depictions grow more reprehensible during the later Middle Ages; Synagoga is no longer passing the torch as an ancestor or even a sad bystander but is envisioned as the enemy of Ecclesia, standing in league with sin and death and damnation. She may be shown wearing a Jew's pointed hat, generally a negative attribute. A color such as yellow, which Mellinkoff demonstrates as iconographically associated with the unpleasant (treachery, heresy, greed, jealousy, spittle and urine) often amplifies the negative connotations of her figure (*Outcasts* 35-36). While the artists' choices about her attributes vary, common to all the later portraits of Synagoga is the "resounding note of her defeat" (Mellinkoff, *Outcasts* 49). Mellinkoff designates c. 1100 as the point after which Synagoga is rarely represented as the fulfillment of the Old Testament by the New, who will ultimately embrace the New Law of

Christ, the Synagogue which will ultimately *become* the Church. Instead, Synagoga is rendered symbolic of contemporary Jewry in each era's portraiture, despised for denying Christ and rejecting Christianity. The fierce opposition between Ecclesia and Synagoga evinced in some images represents the allegorical struggle between Life and Death, Good and Evil, Dark and Light. Like Cain, whose Jew's hat she sometimes wears, Synagoga may be figured as a murderer of kin. And here lies another obvious likeness with the Sultaness in the *Man of Law's Tale,* to which I will soon turn: she has murdered her child, the Sultan, on his wedding day. The marriage of the Old Law and the New has not been consummated. Interestingly, though, neither mother-in-law kills Custance outright, reflecting perhaps some awareness that they cannot conquer her and her "Law" but may, for a time, elide the inevitable consequences which the New Law will bring.

Latin replaces Hebrew as the official sacred language of the Law, as the Church replaces the Synagogue. Further artistic evidence of the Ecclesia / Synagoga opposition is orientalized pseudo-Hebrew lettering often found on Synagoga's clothing or on something she carries. This lettering figures the typological argument that Moses' writing of the Torah in Hebrew *conceals* the mysteries of God until the world was ready to receive them (Mellinkoff, *Moses* 97). [19] (Plate 2) The diptych of the tablets of the Law which Synagoga often carries as one of her attributes or is about to drop recalls her blind obedience to the letter of the Law, and not its significance. She is iconographically associated with Satan, who may also be pictured holding a scroll on which pseudo-Hebrew writing appears. I might note here that the mother-in-law Donegild of Chaucer's tale also has this duplicitous connection with writing and Satan (see the lines quoted below, ll. 778-784). In an illustration in the Psalter of Amesbury Abbey (c. 1250-55), Christ has Latin on his scroll; Satan, Hebrew.[20] This tradition thus depicts the Jews and Satan united in a common language (Mellinkoff, *Outcasts* 104).

By far the most distressing iconography of the opposition between Ecclesia and Synagoga are the late medieval group of images of the "Living Cross," which Schiller describes (158-162). (Plate 3) While these images are, strictly speaking, contemporary to neither Hildegard nor Chaucer, they are important to my study in that they embody the lengths to which the Synagoga/Ecclesia bifurcation was taken in the late Middle Ages and depicted in powerful icons of popular theology. Only when read through Hildegard's early explanation of Synagoga's fallen—yet redeemable—state do we see the vituperative fulfillment in these later images of the demonization of the Jewish law of the kind reflected in Chaucer's work. In these images of the "Living Cross," the cross's extremities terminate in hands that do not belong to the figure of Christ, and, as Schiller notes, "the antithesis between Ecclesia and Synagoga gains a new actuality during the fifteenth century in this pictorial type and is always linked with this cross" (158). Synagoga, represented as riding on an ass, is actually killed with a sword held in the left hand of the cross. Rather than being merely driven off, or averting her blinded eyes, the murdered Synagoga is judged far more harshly here than in earlier images. The Tree of Life becomes the Tree of Death to the infidel Synagoga. In such an image, as in all Crucifixion portrayals, the scene is divided in four, with Ecclesia and Synagoga separated by the shaft of the cross and by the body of Christ, whose face turns towards Ecclesia, as the cross stabs Synagoga. One is of course reminded of the two who were crucified with Christ: one thief damned, one saved.

Some medieval iconography of the Synagoga / Ecclesia opposition which Chaucer himself may have seen or known of (in addition to the Canterbury windows) are found in Seiferth's plates: Chartres (fig. 20); St. Denis in Paris (fig. 31); possibly the work of the Limbourg brothers, c. 1402-16 (figs. 52 and 54), Paris; and a late twelfth-century medallion from the cross at Bury St. Edmunds (fig. 65), now at the Metropolitan (Cloisters) Museum of Art. All these represent fairly typical renditions of the relationship between Synagoga and Ecclesia which I have outlined above. The main portal of Notre-Dame de Paris, where a devil in the form of a serpent coils itself around Synagoga's head covering her eyes, built during the twelfth-century reign of Philip Augustus who drove the Jews out of France in 1182, was in place for Chaucer to have seen it on his diplomatic missions, and later readers of his tale would no doubt have experienced the continued currency of this iconographic representation in such a public site (Seiferth 99).[21]

Medieval dramatic records, scanty as they unfortunately are, do contain scenes of Synagoga and Ecclesia approximating those representations we see in medieval art. For example, the *Play of Antichrist,* an ambitious twelfth-century Latin drama about the end of the world (c.1150), roughly contemporary in time and proximate in geography to Hildegard, probably composed in Kloster Tegersee in Bavaria, portrays the Jews and the Synagogue, together on the stage with Ecclesia; this play evokes some sympathy and respect for the Old

Plate 2: Panel from the Altarpiece of the Mirror of Salvation by Conrad Witz, c. 1435. Basel, Öffentliche Kunstsammlung Basel, Kunstmuseum.

Law and some optimism for the conversion of the Jews, as Hildegard's vision does.[22] When the Jews fall to Antichrist, since they are powerless against evil without God's help, the Prophets Enoch and Elijah arrive and reveal the word of God to the Jews, who are instantly converted and denounce Antichrist: "Our error shames us, but now our faith is sure / Despite all persecution we shall endure" (Wright 59; ll. 399-400, p. 97). In contrast, the staging directions for a fourteenth-century presentation play of Phillip de Mezieres (c.1372) calls for "a most beautiful woman, aged about twenty, who shall be called *Ecclesia* and who shall represent the Church. Then there shall be a woman of advanced age who shall be called *Synagoga*, and who shall represent the law of Moses and the Old Testament" (Meredith and Tailby 208). Records from this play also describe Synagoga's costume: she has a veil, a broken banner, stone tablets with writing "like Hebrew" tilted downwards, and her demeanor is to have her "face inclined to the left" "as if sorrowful" (219). She weeps and complains, and is driven out of the playing space to the west by angels. Here surely the scene was construed as comedic, since the stage directions prescribe that "the instruments shall play for a short while and until the people have quietened their laughter at the expulsion of Synagoga" (220). The tablets of the Law are destroyed by hostile actors in the play. The Lucerne play costuming directions have the serpent veiled with a crown on its head, in an interesting (albeit late, 1583) connection with the figuring of Synagoga (130).

Typological interest in the *Concordia veteris et novi testamenti* occupied theologians who wrote about Jewish matters in the early Middle Ages. One testament "figuring" the Other was a dominant theme and is as well a dominant compositional principle in art (Seiferth 16). Hildegard's vision, at once theology and art (since she had her visions painted), certainly partakes of this tradition. Writings of Paul, Augustine, Prudentius, even Dante, articulate the new as obviating the old while arising out of it.[23] Two influential early works both attributed to Augustine although unlikely to be his, *Altercatio Ecclesiae et Synagogae* and *Sermo contra judeos, paganos et arianos, de symbolo,* exacerbate the conflict between the two rules, denying the memory of *concordia* (according to which the New Law is the fulfillment of the Old Law) and instead teeming with accusations against the Jews who must surrender to Ecclesia (Seiferth 33-37). The dialogue and confrontational nature of the *Altercatio* mark the Synagogue's "transformation into a living and suffering creature [in art]" and

Plate 3: Codex Monachensis 23041 f.3v (late fifteenth century). Note the position of Eve, on Synagoga's side of the Cross. Staatsbibliothek Munich.

"coincided with the growing conflict between Christian society and the Jewish minorities." Synagoga is thus "subjected to the fate of medieval Jewry" (41).

Some of Chaucer's contemporaries wrote more overtly about Christian establishment of domination over the infidels and Jews than he did in the *Man of Law's Tale.* Elisa Narin Van Court, in her study of *The Siege of Jerusalem,* a late-fourteenth-century alliterative Middle English poem, argues that despite the banishment of Jews in 1290, late-medieval England evinced a "significant and ongoing interest in Jews and Judaism" (228) and that in the fourteenth-century liturgy, sermons and drama (such as plays of the destruction of Jerusalem) there was a "discourse of displacement and supersession currently in vogue, and directed quite specifically against Jews" (230). Using the *Siege* as her example, Van Court notes the "Jews and their texts superseded in the chronology of the poem by the Christians and *their* texts" (230). She finds fourteenth-century writings evincing at times a kind of "slippage," a "radically ambivalent" interest in the Jews, condemnatory as well as sympathetic. The *Siege* poet reifies the Jews and the Jewish threat (ultimately vanquished) for an English audience who had no or little experience of Jews.

## THE MOTHERS-IN-LAW

Chaucer characterizes the first of the two mothers-in-law in the tale told by the Man of Law as a "Sowdanesse" from "Surrye" (Syria), belonging to a "barbre nacion" (l. 281)[24] and loyal to the "creance" of "Makomete" or "Mahoun," a religion competing with Christianity, obviously linking her to the Islamic East, just as the generic term "Saracen," was used widely in the Middle Ages to classify Eastern non-Christian populations. "Orientalism" and an interest in the exotic generalized "East" as an imaginative locus has been discussed as a feature of many of Chaucer's works including *The Squire's Tale, The Monk's Tale, The Franklin's Tale,* and, as I mentioned, *The Legend of Good Women.*[25] The second mother-in-law, Donegild, whom Custance acquires three years after the murder of her first husband by his Sultaness-mother and her subsequent casting of Custance adrift on a rudderless and oarless boat, is the mother of Alla, king of "Northhumberlond" in England where everyone is pagan (l. 534). Nonetheless, the kingdom seems to have some relic of a Christian past. "A Britoun book, written with Evaungiles" (l. 666), is produced during a murder inquiry, on which a man who accuses Custance of murder is made to swear. This Donegild, from the marginalized north of England (and we might remember that in early English texts, even the Irish and the Flemings are at one time or another "Orientalized") comes to be the genetic link to Christianity, since she is the grandmother of Maurice, the next Holy Roman Emperor, as it turns out in the tale. Both situations, as Chaucer and his source, Trevet's Anglo-Norman *Les Cronicles,* reproduce them, are puzzlingly vague about the religions of the mothers-in-law—although the first is considered a Mohammedan—but both pagan women are tarred with the same brush of violence and jealousy towards Custance, who as a kind of Crusader coming to reclaim the Holy Land, has managed to convert their sons and entourage. Her conversion of the spirit is opposed to the matriarchal Jewesses and the flesh they represent, which is repudiated by both sons as they embrace the new Word.

What Chaucer says about both evil women demonstrates in his language and his narrator's tone an affiliation between these women and the figure of Synagoga, whose representation in art, as I hope to show, reinforces this point. Both mothers-in-law are portrayed as desirous of political power, challenging the patriarchy represented by their sons and his wife whom they fear will bear Christian heirs to usurp them. The first mother-in-law,

> This olde Sowdanesse, cursed krone,
> Hath with hir freendes doon this cursed dede,
> For she hirself wolde al the contree lede. (432-434)

Later, Donegild is similarly depicted:

> But who was woful, if I shal not lye,
> Of this weddyng but Donegild, and namo,
> The kynges mooder, ful of tirannye?
> Hir thoughte hir cursed herte brast atwo.
> She wolde noght hir sone had do so;
> Hir thoughte a despit that he sholde take
> So strange a creature unto his make. (694-700)

The Sultaness does, indeed, worry about the abandonment of the "olde sacrifices" (l. 325)—an inherently Jewish/Old Testament term—by her son and declares her intent to remain faithful to her "Law" no matter whether her people are forced to convert or not. In discussing

with her council Custance's upcoming marriage to the Sultan, who has
converted in order to marry her, the Sultaness fumes:

> "Lordes," quod she, "ye knowen everichon,
> How that my sone in point is for to lete
> The hooly lawes of our Alkaron,
> Yeven by Goddes message Makomete.
> But oon avow to grete God I heete,
> The lyfe shal rather out of my body sterte
> Or Makometes lawe out of myn herte!
>
> What sholde us tyden of this newe lawe
> But thraldom to oure bodies and penance,
> And afterward in helle to be drawe,
> For we reneyed Mahoun our creance? . . ." (l.330-340)[26]

She plots with her retinue to convert, as a ruse, to take Baptism and
its "coold water" and trade it for the "rede" of Christian blood. It is
hard not to find this clever and blasphemous speech humorous: [27]

> We shul first feyne us cristendom to take—
> Coold water shal nat greve us but a lite!—"
> And I shal swich a feeste and revel make
> That, as I trowe, I shal the Sowdan quite.
> For thogh his wyf be cristned never so white,
> She shal have nede to wasshe awey the rede,
> Thogh she a font-ful water with her lede. (351-357)

At this point, in a tirade of invective, Chaucer's Man of Law
accuses the Sultaness, worried about her kingdom's and her religion's
future and concerned for her own disempowerment, of being in league
with Satan who has confounded Eve and now is making the Sultaness
serve him too:

> O Sowdanesse, roote of iniquitee!
> Virago, thou Semyrame the secounde!
> O serpent under femynymytee,
> Lik to the serpent depe in helle ybounde!
> O feyned womman, al that may confounde
> Vertu and innocence, thurgh thy malice,

Is bred in thee, as nest of every vice!

O Sathan, envious syn thilke day
That thou were chaced from our heritage,
Wel knowestow to wommen the olde way!
Thou madest Eva brynge us in servage;
Thou wolt fordoon this Cristen mariage.
Thyn instrument so—weylawey the while!—
Makestow of wommen, whan thou wolt bigile. (358-371)

But perhaps the most telling invective the Man of Law hurls upon
the Sultaness is just before she throws a marriage feast for the
newlyweds (a kind of anti-Cana and slaughter of the Innocents
combined) at which she has Alla and his newly converted retinue
killed:

But this scorpioun, this wikked goost,
The Sowdanesse, for al hire flaterynge,
Caste under this ful mortally to stynge. (404-406)

The scorpion, a detail not found in Chaucer's sources, is
iconographically associated with the figure of Synagoga from the early
times of her allegorical depiction and can be seen in many extant
medieval artistic representations of Synagoga and Jews which Chaucer
himself might have also experienced.[28] So, this believer in "Mahoun's"
law comes to be in Chaucer's poem a kind of hybrid, conflated threat to
medieval Christendom—"feyned womman," serpent like, a
"scorpioun," and, most importantly, coupled with Satan and Synagoga.
After killing all the new Christians in her empire, the Sultaness casts
out Custance in a kind of reverse Exodus, to wander the seas in a
rudderless boat. But Custance's God takes care of her just as the Jewish
God cared for the Jews in their desert wanderings.[29] As V.A. Kolve
suggests, the boat as an emblem of the Church has a long history.[30]
Significantly, in the tale the rudderless boat (*naves* = ship; the church
building's central space is called a "nave" following this allegorical
mind-set of the ship as the Church, and a cathedral's triangular sections
of its ceiling bisected by ribbed vaulting are called *veles*, sails) is
launched by the Synagoga-figure of the wrong headed and wicked
mother-in-law. God, however, is the navigator and propeller ("He that
is lord of Fortune be thy steere!" [l. 448]). At this mythic level it is the

Old Testamant figure of Synagoga who unwittingly launches the ship of the Church, carrying Ecclesia/Custance away from the East to proselytize and convert the Western world, where she finds more fertile ground but also more travails as she marries yet another pagan king-convert.

One sinister mother-in-law is rapidly traded for another. Donegild, the second mother-in-law, when confronted with the reality of Custance's having given birth to her Christian grandchild, waylays the messenger who bears the news to Alla, warring on the Scottish front, and herself forges a substitute message accusing queen Custance of having borne a "feendly creature," a monster child:

> And stolen were his lettres pryvely
> Out of his box, whil he sleep as a swyn;
> And countrefeted was ful subtilly
> Another lettre, wroght ful synfully,
> Unto the kyng direct of this mateere
> Fro his constable, as ye shal after heere.

> The lettre spak the queene delivered was
> Of so horrible a feendly creature
> That in the castel noon so hardy was
> That any while dorste ther endure. (745-753)

Interestingly, the monster-child motif is also encountered in many of the folktale analogues of Custance's story, with its most salient representation in the various versions of the early-fourteenth-century Middle English romance the *King of Tars* (Hornstein, "A Folklore Theme").[31] The malformed child transformed to beauty upon his baptism or that of his parents is often represented as a child half-black/half-white, who thence changes entirely to white after baptism. Hornstein notes, "It was also generally believed that the union of a white with a Moor (a Christian with a heathen) would produce offspring partly black and white," such as Feirfis, Parzival's half-brother (85). The "miracle" enacted by the child becoming entirely white was symbolic evidence of the "complete spiritual acceptance of the true faith" (87). This black-and-white child, part Christian, part "Moor" is relevant to consider in the context of the tale of Custance because of the parti-colored picture of Synagoga Hildegard has provided, incompletely accepting spiritual truth, "pale from her head to

her navel and black from her navel to her feet." Absent or repressed in
Chaucer's version (and in his immediate source) is the piebald nature of
the monster-child, but when read against its analogue, the
pagan/Christian child Maurice is indeed reminiscent of the medieval
religious symbolism of the black and white Synagoga which Hildegard
explicates, and here again the tale and its cultural context asks us to
consider the Jewishness of the mothers-in-law as well as the struggle
for the acceptance of the Christian faith that the tale inscribes.

Upon the return of the messenger with Alla's admonition to "keepe
this child, al be it foul or feir / And eek my wyf, unto myn hoom-
comynge" (774-775), Donegild again befuddles the messenger with
drink and writes a missive to the court purporting to be from Alla that
Custance and her son are once more to be exiled in the rudderless boat.
The wicked mother-in-law Donegild hideously usurps male hegemony
in her jealous political and religious (and suggestively incestuous)
desire for power in her kingdom. Chaucer, who omits from his tale
Trevet's painstaking description of his Constaunce as an educated
woman, one who receives letters in her own right and was known for
her scholarship, elaborately describes the viciousness of Donegild (as
well as that of the Sultaness) probably to polarize the two kinds of
women, evil and good, writing and non-writing, duplicitous and honest,
Christian and infidel, in the tale. Donegild's reading and rewriting of
the missives between the court and her son show her to be as clever as
the Sultaness—after all, she is literate—and her letters display a
disruptive and evil intent. The narrator of the *Man of Law's Tale* takes
pains to tell us that Donegild's counterfeiting of the two letters to Alla
informing him that his wife had been delivered of a monster-child was
a perversion of nature: "ful subtilly" "wroght full synfully" and that
Donegild was, in fact, an "elf, by aventure / Ycomen, by charmes or by
sorcerie, / And every wight hateth hir compaignye" (ll. 754-56). Like
the Synagogue who cannot correctly interpret the prophecies and
thereby misuses the letter of the Law, Donegild uses words corruptly.
The narrator berates her in another venemous passage but demurs that
he has:

> . . . noon Englissh digne
> Unto thy malice and thy tirannye!
> And therfore to the feend I thee resigne;
> Lat him endited of thy traitorie!
> Fy, mannysh, fy!—o nay, by God, I lye—

Fy, feendlych spirit, for I dar wel telle,
Thogh thou heere walke, thy spirit is in helle! (ll. 778-784)

Her "mannysh" "feendlych" nature, is poetically akin to that of the Sultaness—"Virago, thou Semyrame the secounde"—and grossly opposed to the pure, passive and Christian Custance. Alla, upon his return, kills his mother for her duplicity and wickedness (an act for which he later repents and is confessed of at Rome, a move which neatly brings him to a reunion with his wife, who has found her way there in her boat). Meanwhile, the Sultaness and her "Surryens" have all been slaughtered by Custance's father, the Emperor of Rome, when he gets wind of the massacre at the wedding feast. Thus the two female Oriental threats are quashed by the Christian male rulers in the tale. Accordingly, Chaucer tells his tale to conform to his own poetic agenda which includes a discussion of gendered power and the necessity of the passive "feminine" virtues of humility for the truly Christian. Significantly, both the orientalized Other and the agency of Custance are annihilated at the end of the tale: the mothers-in-law are marginalized and defanged by the triumph of the Church and especially by the example of the good woman, Custance, whose faith in the Law of her God is the force for conversion and change in this tale. But at the tale's conclusion Custance herself returns to her father's house and his "governance" and "thraldom" from which she had earlier been sent out as a kind of treaty-gift to the Muslim king—her first husband—in order to secure certain rights for the Christian empire and to guarantee the conversion of that Muslim empire. Her famous line on setting out for that first marriage—"Wommen are born to thraldom and penance / And to been under mannes governance" (ll. 286-7)—becomes eerily fulfilled from first to last.

So, one of the available readings of the tale of the Man of Law is an allegorical one in which Custance represents Ecclesia, triumphant over pagan vice and converting nations to Christianity in opposition to the Jewish and Saracen threats. This reading can be enriched by the prevalent iconographic and traditional view, typified by Hildegard's vision, of Ecclesia as the daughter-in-law of the vicious and envious black-and-white Synagoga, whose progeny—in the tale, Custance's son Maurice—is transformed into the Holy Roman Emperor, leader of the newly Christian world. Maurice unites both religion and the state, Old and New, in himself and eclipses his mother in the realm of history, the tale suggests, if not actually in the tale Chaucer tells. Custance, in

Chaucer's tale and in Trevet's, is the agent for Christianizing much of
the known world, represented in the tale as the blind and Orientalized
East ("Surrye") and the remote and equally blind and Orientalized
North of England. She is as well the object of jealousy and hatred by
her two successive heathen mothers-in-law who do their best to be rid
of her and her influence but to no avail. Like the representations of the
veiled, fallen, and misguided Synagoga, the mothers-in-law are
mistresses of the Old Law and old ways, the letter but not the spirit, and
no match for the usurping force of Western Christian progress.

Kathryn Lynch, arguing about the connection between gender and
Orientalism in Chaucer's tales of the Squire and the Franklin, uses
Edward Said's conceptualization of Orientalism as

> the expression of Western power over the space outside its cultural
> perimeter, space that bears only an oblique relationship to its real
> geographical counterpart. Indeed, the transactions that constitute
> Orientalism are primarily, as Said insists, textual ones, participating
> in a tradition of discourse about power and images of the Orient that
> themselves enact the Orientalist's will to power. ( 532)

Lynch also notes Chaucer's connection of the exotic East to "an
excess of female sexual power" in both tales (530) and probes medieval
Orientalism's "complex relationship to gender":

> If the East is geographically and culturally the Other to the West, it is
> also made sexually strange, especially acting as the site where gender
> distinctions are blurred, the threat of the feminine more explicitly
> acknowledged, and the relationship between the sexes subtly but
> fundamentally redefined. (532)

I would extend Lynch's insight to argue that the Orientalism of the
*Man of Law's Tale* also concerns Western power and the feminine
threat to that power which the tale represents and necessarily conflates
as Muslim *and* Jewish.[32] That there are *two* mothers-in-law in the tale
presents problems for any strict reading of them as representing the
Synagogue (the power of the repetition of the pattern may have more to
do with the conventions of the romance mode which the tale partakes
of); but perhaps seeing them as a conflation of the Islamic/Jewish
hegemony rejected by the tale and its teller—and always a threat in the
real world of the fourteenth century—in favor of the New Law of

Christianity and the Holy Roman Empire accounts for the undeniable presence in the tale of both Others as feminine, Eastern and Muslim and the traces of imagery and iconographic influence which suggest that the feminine Other is also Jewish. They are two threats; they are the same threat.[33] Steven F. Kruger suggests that

> Indeed, perhaps it is *because* Islam is more distant than local Jewish communities, evoking a different sort of anxiety than these more proximate "others," that it can be described more fully. With the distinction between the Christian and the Muslim secured by geographic distance, an obscure, unfamiliar Islam can be brought into clear focus to represent what is to be ruled out of communal Western European identity. (194)

In the same vein, Susan Schibanoff's fine recent piece on the *Man of Law's Tale* recognizes the discourse of Orientalism in the tale as issuing "a clarion call for unity—not among the general *communitas* of the faithful, but specifically among Christian men of his [the lawyer's] audience." [34] This unity of the men on the pilgrimage, says Schibanoff, is achieved at the expense of dehumanizing and reducing women and the East as they appear in the tale: "And what this tale-teller most fears—similitude—he exploits to realize this objective" (63). To Schibanoff's explication of the tale I would add that not only Orientalism and anti-feminism but concern for cancelling the specifically Jewish and carnal threat are evident in the tale Chaucer borrowed and retells through his Man of Law. By highlighting the pervasiveness of the traditional Christian image of Synagoga as mother-in-law, as Hildegard explained it, and as it may well have been known to Chaucer, his source-texts and his readers, I want to propose that the mothers-in-law can be read in the terms which Hildegard sets out in the explication of her vision. That is, they can be understood as incorporating the traditional features of Synagoga as outcast, but an outcast familially related—and thus showing forth the repudiation of its own origins—to the dominant and triumphant ideology of the tale, male Western Christendom. This overcoming, repudiation, punishment and ultimate conversion of the Jews is suggestively laid out in the tale. The deep connection with Judaism which Christianity acknowledged to a greater and lesser extent in different periods of the Middle Ages is typified by the genetic connection between Custance and her son Maurice, the mother-in-law's/Synagogue's grandchild, the future

Roman Emperor. While imagery Chaucer has employed in the *Man of Law's Tale* clearly suggests identification of the malevolent mothers-in-law with the medieval iconography of Synagoga that Hildegard has manifested in her *Scivias*, it would be wrong to allege any *intent* on the part of Chaucer in the tale to figure Synagoga in the representations of the mothers-in-law. Rather, this attitude was in the air. We might seek to enrich our own context for reading the tale Chaucer presents and the cultural work it performs by considering some of the larger interpretive and iconographic structures within which literary events are produced.[35] What Barbara Newman has called "St Hildegard's theology of the feminine" might be operating here as part of the climate which gave rise to both Trevet's and Chaucer's texts (and Trevet's, of course, was dedicated to a woman, Mary of Woodstock).[36] This image of Synagoga as mother-in-law and Other and outcast was in the store of available medieval images, and the two episodes of mothers-in-law in the story Chaucer retells may represent the different guises of the Jewish threat to Christianity and the inscription of Christianity's triumph as perceived by him in gendered terms. In the tale, the mothers-in-law's attempts at pre-emptive matriarchy are thwarted by male domination and the New Law. Their endeavors to change a woman-hostile world by direct action are quelled. The tale might be seen as a mirror held up to Western male social values. The insistence on the displacement of the Old Law by the New, the matriarchal by the patriarchal, Islam by Christianity, the East by the West, the letter by the spirit, Synagoga by Ecclesia, is embedded in this narrative. The threat of the Jews is reinscribed, transferred and blurred into a version of that essentialized, orientalized female Other, the evil mothers-in-law whose Jewish affiliations pervade the imagery in Chaucer's tale, who are displaced and marginalized, and the antipathy to whom on the part of the Man of Law can hardly be overlooked but whose name as Synagoga he cannot say.

The point I have tried to make along the way in this essay is that Chaucer's perplexing and intricate tale of the Man of Law, while overtly decrying the "Law" of the pagans and "Saracens," represents a veiled evocation of that other threat to Christian hegemony, the Jew. What initially may seem a tenuous connection between the mothers-in-law and the Synagogue, and even between Chaucer and Hildegard, can be revealed to be more securely coupled to a reading of the tale. When one unpacks and destabilizes the unified Eastern Other, which at first demarcates the mothers-in-law, one allows for that figure of the mother-in-law, related yet different from Custance, to suggest the ubiquitous medieval icon of the blind, reviled and deposed Synagogue to Custance's triumphant Ecclesia, the image which Hildegard's mystical theology reaffirms as crucial to the apprehension of Christianity. Chaucer's reinscription—conscious or not—of this central and paradoxical allegorical image for Christianity allows us to perceive within the poem a recognition of both the kinship and the necessity of repudiation of the origins of Western Christianity in the Synagogue and demonstrates the continued potency of the vexed dyad of Ecclesia / Synagoga for the Western imagination.[37]

## NOTES

1. Hildegard of Bingen, *Scivias*, trans. Mother Columba Hart and Jane Bishop, introd. by Barbara Newman; preface by Caroline Walker Bynum (New York: Paulist Press, 1990), p. 133. See plate 1.
2. See Eckert for Hildegard's vision of Judaism and its contemporary context. Eckert does allow that from her reading of her vision and despite her respect for the Jewish faith, Hildegard probably did not have a Jewish mentor with whom to discuss her conception of Synagoga because of some misunderstandings of Jewish law she conveys in *Scivias* (306, 310).
3. Schiller, vol. 1, 24. Schiller notes that such commentaries were by Rupert von Deutz, Honorius Augustoduniensis, Anselm of Canterbury and others. Gradually, the place of Ecclesia/Sponsa is taken over by the Virgin in allegorical and iconographic interpretations of the scene, says Schiller.
4. See, for example, Hassell's commentary to *The Holkum Bible Picture Book*, pp. 66, 79, 135, where Synagogue is associated with Cain, the owl who prefers darkness to light, and the moon as opposed to the sun in Crucifixion portrayals.
5. The section of Trevet's *Les Cronicles* pertaining to the tale of the woman he names "Constaunce," is found in British Library MS Arundel 56, edited by Edmund Brock and printed in *Originals and Analogues of Some of Chaucer's Canterbury Tales,* eds. F.J. Furnivall, Edmund Brock and W.A.Clouston (1872; rpt. London: Trubner, 1887): 1-53. The Constaunce selection from Oxford Magdalen 45, edited by Margaret Schlauch, is printed in *Sources and Analogues of Chaucer's Canterbury Tales*, eds. W.F. Bryan and Germaine Dempster (1941; rpt. New York: Humanities Press, 1958): 165-81. This work also identifies numerous other works related to the MLT. See also Margaret Schlauch, *Chaucer's Constance and Accused Queens* (1927; rpt. New York: Gordian Press, 1969) for the folktale background. Ruth J. Dean's studies of Trevet's work and milieu is invaluable; see especially her "Nicholas Trevet,

Historian," in *Medieval Learning and Literature:Essays Presented to R.W. Hunt,* eds. J.J.G.Alexander and M.T. Gibson (Oxford, 1976):339-46 and "The Manuscripts of Nicholas Trevet's Anglo-Norman Cronicles," *Medievalia et Humanistica* 14 (1962): 95-105. Robert Correale is currently preparing an edition of Trevet's French *Les Cronicles,* based on a study of all nine extant Anglo-Norman manuscripts, for the *Chaucer Library* project. His "Chaucer's Manuscripts of Nicholas Trevet's *Les Cronicles,*" *Chaucer Review* 25, no. 3 (1991): 238-265, previews some of his findings about Chaucer's source manuscript and concludes it was probably one related to Paris, Bibliothèque Nationale, franç. 9687, fols. 1va-114va (c.1340-50). For Gower's work, see John Gower, *Confessio Amantis* in *The English Works of John Gower,* ed. G.C. Macaulay, EETS o.s. 81-2 (1900; rpt. 1957), 2:587-1598. There is a lengthy debate among scholars over whose version of the Constance story was earlier, Gower's or Chaucer's, which poet's work may therefore be dependent upon the other, and to what extent either used Trevet's chronicle. The current consensus is that Gower's version was first and that Chaucer may have borrowed from or been influenced by Gower's treatment of the tale. Peter Nicholson in "*The Man of Law's Tale*: What Chaucer Really Owed to Gower," *Chaucer Review* 26 no.2 (1991): 293-308 makes an eloquent case for Gower's version being Chaucer's most immediate source, suggesting "that Gower's version rather than Trevet's might be a more appropriate point of comparison in assessing Chaucer's achievement in the tale," and arguing "it was Gower's tale rather than Trevet's that Chaucer chose to retell" (171). My sense is that Chaucer worked from both Gower and Trevet, responding to and redacting both versions, although he may have been more keen to answer directly the sharply focused and pointed work of Gower with a problematic and slippery tale of his own. But Trevet's chronicle as the source of both works is what I rely on. It is outside the scope of this essay to probe Gower's rendition of the tale or to remark extensively on what changes Chaucer made to Trevet's rendition. The most interesting work on *The King of Tars* and its connection to the tale of Custance, for my purposes, is by Lillian Herlands Hornstein.

6. See Susan Schibanoff's insightful essay on Orientalism and the Muslim East in the *Man of Law's Tale* as the best and most recent example of such a study of the Muslim Other.

7. There will, of course, be those Chaucerians who disagree with this assertion, and surely it does not account for all the richness of the tale. But, the idea of family history cannot have been far from Trevet's mind as he composed his chronicle including the tale of Constaunce, connecting the family of Edward II with the establishment of Christianity in England and with the history of the world. A genealogical diagram of Edward's lineage appears as the sole

illustration in some of the extant manuscripts of Trevet's Anglo-Norman chronicle. In the last few years there has been a steady stream of publications about *The Man of Law's Tale* to which I am indebted for wise material on this problematic tale. To name those (aside from those pieces cited in this essay and in these notes) most useful in my own reading of the tale: David Raybin, "Constance and History: Woman as Outsider in Chaucer's *Man of Law's Tale,*" *SAC* 12 (1990): 65-84; Sheila Delany, "Womanliness in the *Man of Law's Tale,*" *Chaucer Review* 9 (1974): 63-71; Winthrop Wetherbee, "Constance and the World in Chaucer and Gower," in *John Gower: Recent Readings*, ed. R. F. Yeager (Kalamazoo: Medieval Institute Publications, 1989): 65-93; Ann Astell, "Apostrophe, Prayer and the Structure of Satire in the *Man of Law's Tale,*" *SAC* 13(1991): 81-97; and R. A. Shoaf, "'Unwemmed Custance': Circulation, Property, and Incest in the *Man of Law's Tale,*" *Exemplaria* 2.1 (1990): 287-302. While Elaine Tuttle Hansen's *Chaucer and the Fictions of Gender* (Berkeley: Univ. of California Press, 1992) does not engage the *Man of Law's Tale* extensively, her ideas on the feminized male in some of Chaucer's other works have refined my own vision of that aspect of the tale. She provides a provocative and nuanced discussion of Chaucer's engagement with the late-medieval debate about "the nature and meaning of sexual difference, 'men' versus 'women'. . ." (93); her work is a valuable feminist scholarly resource and pertinent to the male/female opposition which obtains in the reading I propose about East/West, Synagoga/Ecclesia and their antithetical positions in the tale.

8. I am not, of course, arguing here for Judaism as essentially matriarchal but for its conceptualization in the tale and in representational art as generally feminine, despite its occasional portrayal in both late-medieval art, drama and in the tale as transgendered or mannish. Synagoga, the allegorical figure, like all proper nouns describing abstract concepts in Latin (Fortuna, Ecclesia), is feminine in gender, and this feminization is carried out in iconographic and sculptural programs as well.

9. In this vein, Hildegard herself wrote several antiphons exalting the Virgin as triumphant over the sinful Eve similar to the triumph of Ecclesia over Synagoga (nos. 5, 6, 7, 11). For example:

> Because the malice that flowed from one woman,
> This woman has wiped away hereafter;
> She has established the sweetest odor of virtues,
> And she has honored and adorned heaven
> Far more than she earlier disordered the earth.
> Petroff, Antiphon 11, p. 158; trans. Barbara L. Grant

Chaucer certainly suggests the identification of his Custance with the Virgin when she prays to Mary for delivery from her travails and her prayers are answered (MLT, ll. 841-854; 920-924; 977-978).

10. Camille, 164. He notes that Canon 69 of the Fourth Lateran Council prevented both Muslims and Jews from holding office; Innocent III's dress codes and "badge of shame" were laws against both Muslims and Jews at once.

11. Freedberg, xvii. Denise L. Despres offers an important cautionary word to those critics who would "read" symbols without anchoring them in their contexts of ritual spirituality, art history or the political/historical milieu in order to see "a larger pattern of meaning." See "Cultural Mystification." I try here to provide enough relevant context to make the reading I suggest tenable. See also Régis Debray, "A Plague without Fleabites," *TLS* (July 4, 1997): 14-15, who argues against Dan Sperber's "epidemic" model to explain cultural milieu and problematizes the terms "representation," "culture," and "belief," inquiring about how one *does* discuss the survival of certain diffuse cultural notions.

12. See also Despres's "Cultic Anti-Judaism" for further insight into medieval anti-semitism as it is encoded in the tale of Chaucer's Prioress.

13. Delany argues that Orientalism, identified against the Ottoman empire and Muslim incursions into fourteenth-century Europe, might have affected the courtier/diplomat Chaucer, and that "Orientalism becomes a rhetorical device enabling Chaucer to do two things: to create a moral structure in the poem and to offer a veiled commentary on some aspects of English foreign policy" (173).

14. *Holy Bible*, King James version.

15. Bibl. Nat. Paris MS Latinus 9428. Seiferth's Plate I, p. 171.

16. Schiller explains that the scenes in early medieval art showing such a deposition of the Synagogue are likely based on the work by Pseudo-Isidore, *De altercatione ecclesiae et synagoga dialogus*, of the mid-ninth century. See *Patrologia Latina*, ed J. Migne (Paris, 1878-90), vol. 42, col. 1131ff. But Schiller also clarifies that "the theme is older, particularly in Syrian tradition" (111).

17. It is not the sphere of this essay to chart the history of the Jews or of anti-semitism in medieval Europe, but merely to indicate the kinship between literary and artistic representation and the general climate of increasing enmity towards the Jews during the Middle Ages, which scholars have demonstrated. See the work of Cohen, Despres, Trachtenberg, Stacey, and Seiferth (Chaps. 5-7) for excellent background on this topic. Kruger's essays also document antagonistic representations of Jewish bodies in medieval literary texts.

18. Kruger in "The Bodies of the Jews" demonstrates the pervasiveness in the late Middle Ages of the notion of the Jews as having disgusting bodies: "Jews

were often seen as the possessors of diseased and debased bodies." Jewish bodies were likened to the bodies of women, traditionally repudiated as contaminated and foul. Myth had it that Jewish men menstruated as a symbol of their foulness and gender ambiguity, and therefore a symbol of their evilness (303).

19. See also Irven M. Resnick, "Lingua Dei, Lingua Hominis: Sacred Language and Medieval Texts," *Viator* 21 (1990): 51-74.

20. This book (c. 1250-55) might have been seen by Nicholas Trevet or his patroness, a nun at Amesbury. It is now in Oxford All Souls College Library MS 6; the scene is on fol. 64v (Mellinkoff, 104). Camille includes a plate of fol. 5r of this MS., a Crucifixion scene which has the traditional veiled, falling deposed Synagoga, the triumphant Ecclesia, the sun (right hand of Christ-figure) and moon (left hand) (177).

21. See the *Riverside Chaucer*, xv-xxvi, "Chaucer's Life," by Martin M. Crowe and Virginia E. Leland, for some of the salient details of Chaucer's diplomatic career and travels on the continent.

22. Munich MS 19411. See the English edition by Wright, who accounts for the sympathetic portrait of Jews with reference to the twelfth century being "generally regarded as a relatively peaceful and tolerant period in Jewish-Christian relations" (57). The protective attitude of monarchs towards Jewry was "expedient" and "paternal" (58) at best, claims Wright, and the official position of the Church as of Pope Calixtus II's *Sicut Iudeis non* (c. 1120) was "physical toleration coupled with doctrinal opposition" (57).

23. Seiferth's Chaps. 2 and 3 detail much of this discussion of the intellectual history of the images of *concordia* and *altercatio* between the Church and Synagogue, as does Schlauch, "Allegory".

24. References to Chaucer are to the *Riverside Chaucer*, ed. Benson, and are noted parenthetically in the text.

25. See, for example, the work of Delany, Lynch, Schibanoff, and Fyler, on what Lynch calls the "exotic alterity" and "insistent Orientalism" of some of Chaucer's works. Delany, Lynch, and Schibanoff are overtly dependent in their analyses on the concept of "imaginative" Orientalism which Edward Said distinguishes as structuring an oppositional relationship, separating Orient from Occident, as well as his concept of the kind of Orientalism which is a "Western style for dominating, restructuring, and having authority over the Orient." See Delany, 165; Said, 2-3.

26. Trevet's version of this scene is worth noting:

> And yet at that tyme was Kyng Alles moder alyfe a lady in fayre
> poynt And a full feerse and cruell in corage. And the whyche hated

dedly Constaunce the Quene, ffor she had full grete disdeyne and scorne that her son the kyng Alle shulde take a woman of a straunge londe. And morou*er* that her linage and byrthe was nat knowen to her. And also the kyng her son shulde forsake hys furst lawe, the whyche all hys Auncestirs had full entierly kept and holden. And on the oo party she had full grete enuy and sore hit hurte her at her herte that Constaunce was so wele beloued w*ith* all pepull riche and poore w*ith*oute eny comparison of her. And more worshypped and made of for her goodnesse and for her hoolynesse and her m*er*ueylous beaute." [f.55v &56r]

(Trevet goes on to say that Domild was further annoyed that her own worship was diminished by that given to Constaunce, and that it angered her terribly that the maidens sang carols of praise for Constaunce.) The passage quoted from Trevet is from my edition of the c. 1440 Middle English version of Trevet's Anglo-Norman chronicle, *Trevet's Englished Chronicle:Houghton Library Harvard University fMS Eng 938* (forthcoming). Scribal breviographs have been expanded. The Middle English chronicle appears on fols. 9ra -91rb of this interesting miscellany of English provenance. The Middle English translator follows the Anglo-Norman fairly closely in the section which contains the tale of Constaunce. See also Christine M. Rose, "The Provenance of the Trevet Chronicle (fMS Eng 938)" *Harvard Library Bulletin* 3 no. 4 (New Series, Winter 1992/93): 38-55. The Middle English chronicle is a copy of an earlier exemplar, perhaps made during Chaucer's lifetime. The Furnivall volume *Originals and Analogues* (see n. 5) prints the Constaunce extract from the Acland-Hood manuscript (now Harvard Houghton fMS Eng 938) pp. 223-50, although that extract from the Middle English chronicle, prepared by Edmund Brock and Alfred J. Horwood contains a number of transcription errors. William V. Whitehead also edited the Trevet section of this codex as his 1961 Harvard University dissertation, unpublished.

27. See Robert Stacey on the Jews and conversion in thirteenth-century England, and how some Jews surely pretended to be converted in order to stay and conduct their business.

28. See the plates in Mellinkoff, Schiller, Seiferth, and the figures which accompany this essay. Although the plates are not always large enough adequately to identify the scorpions, they *are* there on some of the banners Synagoga holds. Crucifixion scenes often have Roman / Jewish soldiers carrying banners decorated with scorpions.

29. Van Court calls this motion a kind of "reading of displacement" (228).

30. Kolve, in his wonderful and classic *Chaucer and the Imagery of Narrative: The First Five Canterbury Tales*, approaches the tale of the Man of Law iconographically through the use of the images of the rudderless boat and the sea, which I am perfectly convinced by his reading is a dominant image in the poem, as part of a larger pattern of imagery in the first Fragment of the *Canterbury Tales*. I would only add that traces of other iconographic, allegorical motifs such as that of the blind and outcast Synagoga reinforce Kolve's reading of the Christian imagery in the tale while suggesting political and gender issues not overtly focused on by the tale or Kolve's reading of it. I wish there were more space in this essay to attempt a fuller discussion about the issue of gender in the tale, as I think it is inextricably linked to the repudiation of the carnal/literal mothers (Sultaness and Donegild/Synagoga) for the spiritual mothers (Custance/Ecclesia).

31. See Schlauch,*Chaucer's Constance and Accused Queens* for further material on folk motifs in the tale.

32. Lynch also maintains that the "shift of focus from West to East, also registered as a shift from masculine to feminine," "gives the *Squire's Tale* its peculiar chiasmatic shape." Further, "complicating this shift is the association of the masculine Cambyuskan with the feminine East and of the feminine Canacee with the masculine West"(542). I would add to this that it is not only in the *Squire's Tale* where such displacement and "shifts" occur, but Chaucer also composes/retells his story in the *Man of Law's Tale* to evoke such gender and power displacements, where the feminine reigns on the margins ("Surrye" and "Northumberlond") but is defeated and controlled by and at the center (Rome); where Alla is "feminized" by his acceptance of Christianity, and Custance portrays the religious and political imperialism of the masculinized Roman empire.

33. See Kruger's "Medieval Christian (Dis)identification" where he discusses the conflation of Muslim and Jewish and the destabilization of the differences between the two in medieval Christian thinking. He shows them "liable to be demonized in an especially anxious and hostile manner" because of their close links to Christian spiritual understanding (187).

34. Schibanoff goes on to explain the tale's focus on reductive thinking, which dehumanizes and essentializes the woman and the East to foster the Man of Law's own agenda: "to preserve and enhance such difference—between women and men, East and West, Islam and Christianity, ultimately between western patriarchal culture and the Other" (63).

35. Paul Strohm in *Hochon's Arrow: The Social Imagination of Fourteenth-Century Texts* (Princeton, 1992) contends, that "'historical readings' do not have to consist of "good literary detective work, leading to the identification of

discrete events or occasions to which a work refers" (p. 117), but rather, may indicate "a broadly available environment of ideas," gesturing towards a way of interpreting the witness under consideration and assembling the evidence.
36. See Dean's "Nicholas Trevet, Historian," and "The Manuscripts of Nicholas Trevet's Anglo-Norman Cronicles," which describe the manuscript witnesses and their dedicatory phrases to Princess Mary, plus the attribution of the work to Trevet. Princess Mary was born in 1279 and seems to have led a rather unascetic convent life, with rumors of gaming debts and lovers tainting her biography. See M. A. Green, *Lives of the Princesses of England,* ii (London, 1849): 404-422; Eileen Power, *Medieval English Nunneries* (Cambridge, 1922): 346-60.
37. Especial thanks to Prof. Denise L. Despres for reading a draft of this essay and offering valuable suggestions, for reminding me of the usefulness of Mellinkoff's work for this study, for allowing me to read her unpublished work on anti-semitism in English manuscripts, and for the benefits her friendship and stimulating conversations about medieval literature have brought to me.

## WORKS CITED

### Primary Texts

Chaucer, Geoffrey. *The Riverside Chaucer.* ed. Larry D. Benson. Boston: Houghton Mifflin, 1987.
Hildegard of Bingen. *Scivias.* trans. Mother Columba Hart and Jane Bishop. Introd. by Barbara Newman; preface by Caroline Walker Bynum. New York: Paulist Press, 1990.

### Secondary Texts

Avril, François. Manuscript Painting at the Court of France: The Fourteenth Century. New York: Braziller, 1978.
Brown, Sarah. *Stained Glass of Canterbury Cathedral.* Cathedral Gifts, Ltd., 1991.
Camille, Michael. *The Gothic Idol: Ideology and Image-Making in Medieval Art.* Cambridge: Cambridge University Press, 1989, esp. "The Idols of the Saracens" and "The Idols of the Jews," 129-196.
Cohen, Jeremy. *The Friars and the Jews: The Evolution of Medieval Anti-Judaism.* Ithaca, NY: Cornell University Press, 1982.
Delany, Sheila. *The Naked Text: Chaucer's Legend of Good Women.* Berkeley: University of California Press, 1994, esp. "Geographies of Desire: Orientalism in the *Legend*," 164-186.

Despres, Denise L. "Cultic Anti-Judaism and Chaucer's Litel Clergeon," *Modern Philology* Vol. 9, No.4 (1994): 413-427.

————. "Cultural Mystification: Seeing the Jews in the Carew Poyntz Hours." *Jewish History*, forthcoming.

————. "Mary of the Eucharist: Cultic Anti-Judaism in Some Fourteenth-Century English Devotional Manuscripts." In *From Witness to Witchcraft: Jews and Judaism in Medieval Christian Thought.* Ed. Jeremy Cohen. Wolfenbuttel in Mittlealter-Studien. Wiesbaden: Harassowitz, 1996: 375-401.

Dinshaw, Carolyn. "The Law of Man and Its 'Abhomynacions.'" Chap. 3 of *Chaucer's Sexual Poetics.* Madison: University of Wisconsin Press, 1989: 88-112.

Eckert, Willehad Paul, O.P. "The Vision of Synagoga in the *Scivias* of Hildegard of Bingen" trans. from the German by N.L Quigley and L.Frizzell. *Standing Before God: Studies on Prayer in Scriptures and in Tradition with Essays.* Eds. Asher Finkel and Lawrence Frizzell. New York: KTAV Publ., Inc., 1981: 301-311.

Fradenburg, Louise O. "Criticism, Anti-Semitism, and *The Prioress's Tale.*" *Exemplaria* I.1 (March 1989): 69-115.

Freedberg, David. *The Power of Images: Studies in the History and Theory of Response.* Chicago: University of Chicago Press, 1989.

Fyler, John. "Domesticating the Exotic in the *Squire's Tale.*" *ELH* 55 (1989): 1-26.

Hassell, W.O. and M. A. Hassell "Introduction" and "Commentary" to *The Holkam Bible Picture Book.* London: The Dropmore Press, 1954.

Hornstein, Lillian Herlands. "A Folklore Theme in *The King of Tars.*" *Philological Quarterly* 20 (1941): 82-87.

————."The Historical Background of *The King of Tars.*" *Speculum* 16 (1941): 404-414.

————. "Trevet's Constance and *The King of Tars.*" *Modern Language Notes* 55 (May, 1940): 354-357.

Kolve, V.A. *Chaucer and the Imagery of Narrative: The First Five Canterbury Tales.* Stanford University Press, 1984. Chap. VII "The Man of Law's Tale: The Rudderless Ship and the Sea": 297-358.

Kruger, Steven F. "The Bodies of the Jews in the Late Middle Ages." in *The Idea of Medieval Literature*, eds. James Dean and Christian Zacher. Newark: University of Delaware Press, 1992: 301-323.

————. "Medieval Christian (Dis)identification: Muslims and Jews in Guibert of Nogent." *New Literary History* 28, No. 2 (Spring 1997): 185-203.

Lynch, Kathryn L. "East Meets West in Chaucer's Squire's and Franklin's Tales." *Speculum* vol. 70, No. 3 (July 1995): 530-551.

Mellinkoff, Ruth. *The Horned Moses in Medieval Art and Thought*. Berkeley: University of California Press, 1970.

————.*Outcasts: Signs of Otherness in Northern European Art of the Late Middle Ages*. Berkeley: University of California Press, 1993. 2 vols.

Meredith, Peter and John E. Tailby, eds. *The Staging of Religious Drama in Europe in the Later Middle Ages: Texts and Documents in English Translation*. Medieval Institute Publications, 1983. Early Drama, Art and Music Monograph Series, 4.

Newman, Barbara. Introduction to *Scivias*, op. cit. 9-53.

————.*Sister of Wisdom: St. Hildegard's Theology of the Feminine*. Berkeley: University of California Press, 1987.

Petroff, Elizabeth Avilda, ed. *Medieval Women's Visionary Literature*. Oxford: Oxford University Press, 1986.

Said, Edward. *Orientalism*. New York: Pantheon, 1978.

Schibanoff, Susan. "Worlds Apart: Orientalism, Antifeminism and Heresy in Chaucer's *Man of Law's Tale*." *Exemplaria* VIII No. 1 (Spring 1996): 59-96.

Schiller, Gertrude. *Iconography of Christian Art*. Trans. Janet Seligman. 2 vols. Greenwich, Conn: New York Graphic Society, 1971-72.

Schlauch, Margaret. "The Allegory of Church and Synagogue." *Speculum* 14 (1939): 448-464.

————. *Chaucer's Constance and Accused Queens*. New York: Gordian Press, 1927, rpt. 1969.

Seiferth, Wolfgang S. *Synagogue and Church in the Middle Ages: Two Symbols in Art and Literature*. trans. Lee Chadeayne and Paul Gottwald. New York: Frederick Ungar, 1970.

Stacey, Robert C. "The Conversion of Jews to Christianity in Thirteenth-Century England." *Speculum* 67 (1992): 263-83.

Trachtenberg, Joshua. *The Devil and the Jews: The Medieval Conception of the Jew and Its Relation to Modern Anti-Semitism*. Philadelphia: The Jewish Publication Soc. of America, 1983.

Van Court, Elisa Narin. "*The Siege of Jerusalem* and Augustinian Historians: Writing About Jews in Fourteenth-Century England." *Chaucer Review* 29, No. 3 (1995): 227-248.

Wright, J., trans. and introd. *The Play of Anti-Christ*. Toronto: Pontifical Institute of Medieval Studies, 1967.

# Two "Sisters in Wisdom"
## Hildegard of Bingen, Christina Rossetti, and Feminist Theology

*Frederick S. Roden*

> "O feminine form, Sister of Wisdom, Great is your glory!"
>
> Hildegard of Bingen, *Symphonia*
>
> "And well may she glory, inasmuch as one of the tenderest of Divine promises takes (so to say) the feminine form: 'As one whom His mother comforteth, so will I comfort you'"
>
> Christina Rossetti, *Seek and Find*

Hildegard of Bingen and Christina Rossetti may seem an unlikely pairing. The twelfth-century abbess who resolutely recorded her Divine revelations and spoke in her political arena, while simultaneously writing scientific works and spiritual songs, is a figure whom feminist historians, literary scholars, and theologians have in recent years recovered. Hildegard has also been the subject of—and jumping-off point for—many interperiodic "studies" of varying degrees of academic rigor, most of them of interest and relevance to students of contemporary mysticism in praxis.[1] While Hildegard's theology has perhaps been read out of context at times, Rossetti's works have not fared much better. The Victorian poet's theology, while immensely popular in her age, has largely been forgotten. As has happened with Hildegard in the past decade, within a twenty-year period, a mythic

Rossetti has evolved. Having given up the image of the unhappy spinster who, unlucky in love, renounced the world, scholars are now most familiar with the Rossetti of *Goblin Market*, the creator of a utopian world of female relationships.

In recent years, feminist theology has sought to reclaim women's voices in speaking of—and from—the Divine. Historical theologians and literary scholars have looked to the works of medieval women mystics to understand the ways which, within a hegemonic, patriarchal culture, women have striven and succeeded in finding a voice to speak with authority on matters of the spiritual life. Concurrent with these projects have been inquiries as to the place and space of what might be called the "feminine" aspect of the Divine. Several theologians in the past decade have looked to Biblical Wisdom (Sophia) and sapiential tradition through late antiquity to trace the development, perhaps arrested development, of this phenomenon.[2] Such theological inquiries have indeed altered the ways in which the body—both spiritual and corporeal—is viewed.[3]

In the past fifteen years, Hildegard has gained her rightful acclaim as a female theologian. Her unique place, as at once existing within her tradition—an inordinately male and orthodox one—and somehow speaking from outside of it, makes her work striking to a twentieth-century reader. Her *Vita* demonstrates her determination and adherence to her purpose. In our own transitional age, on the cusp of a new millennium, we find in the apocalyptic theologian an extraordinary expression of strength.

Within the religious discourse of the Victorian period, many women such as Christina Rossetti found voices offering the potential for self-realization well beyond those available in secular culture. It is my argument that the power to be found for women in religion during this period is intrinsically linked with what might be called the "return of the body" in English culture and church of the nineteenth century. With the revival of interest in incarnational theology through the Oxford Movement, the relationship between religion and sexuality, spirituality and gender, began to be re-examined. In glorifying the beautiful body of Christ in the Real Presence, religious discourse took on a more body-centered voice. In some ways, in a far different time and place (pre-Reformation Western Christianity) the relationship between body and spirit, sexuality and spirituality, was also spoken in a similarly religious voice. Hildegard's world, while different from Christina Rossetti's, nevertheless allowed within its patriarchal matrix a unique place for woman to speak from her body when giving voice to God. Whether in the turbulence of the German states and ecclesiastical hierarchy of the twelfth century or the Tractarianism of the English High Church of the nineteenth, some women seem to have enjoyed a window of opportunity to speak, write and be taken seriously by their culture when claiming the voice of prophecy.

The argument which I attempt to put forth here is a statement that we may be authorized, indeed justified, in practicing comparative work between two religious women writers from distinct time periods. The suggestions I make perhaps point us in a direction of an essentialist "feminine" theologizing mind. It is not my intention to ignore the substantial work on the social construction of gender that has richly shaped feminist studies in the past quarter of a century. I do not wish to slight the many culturally-specific variables which inflect the development of gender identity any more than I intend to disregard contemporary historicist concerns in scholarship. I nevertheless must acknowledge the work in feminist theology which has contributed to and permitted the development of the type of comparative analysis I practice here. Intuitively, to posit a "feminine aspect" of the Divine necessarily postulates some gendered essence. Whether we are prepared to claim this "essence" as "essential" and locate the gendered "feminine" as existing in a one-to-one correspondence with the biologically "female" is quite another matter. It is secondary, I would argue, to an examination of the theology practiced by those who self-identify as "female" or even "feminine" in a given society. To seek to analyze the ways by which women in different historical periods, sharing similar Biblical Christian paradigms, might find comparable answers to equally pressing theological questions does not negate the numerous factors which contribute to "gender" as we know it. Rather, the many similarities between the theologies of two culturally and chronologically separate women, as I aim to demonstrate here, instead problematize the determinacy of those very culturally-specific variables which scholars have claimed as stable entities in the calculus of gender construction. Further, similarities between individuals of two disparate periods, locations and societal matrices serve historicist studies—indeed, "cultural studies"—in the search to better analyze, understand and indeed quantify those determinants that inflect and produce "culture."

During the later years of her life, that is, from the 1870s through the 1890s, Christina Rossetti published six volumes of what might be termed devotional prose.[4] The works vary from books of daily prayers to exegetical commentaries designed for reflection. The volumes were primarily aimed at a female audience, whose role in the religious sphere was in transition during this period. Beginning in Rossetti's youth, English women once again could claim a space which had been denied them since the Reformation, as the sisterhoods were re-established in the Church of England during the 1840s. It is clear that the revival of monasticism in England during the nineteenth century relied strongly on earlier models. While looking to contemporary Roman orders for guidance, the religious of the English Church seem to have been particularly interested in the simplicity of Benedictine monasticism of another age, as they imagined that time to have been.[5] A few women countered their procreative, patriarchal, cultural matrix by asserting themselves in becoming abbesses and founding convents. Like Hildegard's well-born Benedictines, these sisters were most often from fairly affluent families. They found in the religious life a vocation apart from marriage and their biological ties. Victorian professions to the sisterhoods received considerable criticism. Although nineteenth-century nuns were most often portrayed in the literature and art of the period as embracing the contemplative life, in reality most found an active life of service to be their preferred calling. Such a career was an opportunity and a license to move about the world in a manner that their secular sisters could not.[6]

Largely due to the Oxford Movement, the English nineteenth century was by no means ignorant of the early and medieval church. The revival of interest in church history led to the reprinting of works of the Greek and Latin fathers in addition to those of later religious writers. Numerous translations became available. Christina Rossetti was greatly influenced by Tractarianism. One of her prose volumes, *Time Flies*, is a reading diary for the minor feasts of the Church year. Rossetti cites *The Golden Legend* and S. Baring-Gould's seventeen-volume *Lives of the Saints* as sources for this essentially hagiographic text.

Rossetti wrote several works concerning the religious life. Her first is *Maude*, a novella composed during her teen years and not published until after her death. In this story, a devout young poet, very conscious of both her pride and her religious devotion, is discouraged from becoming a nun. In contrast with a close friend who takes the veil, Maude instead is mortally wounded in an accident. She writes her best poetry on her deathbed. In addition to several shorter poems about nuns, Rossetti also published the lengthy "Convent Threshold" in 1862. Here a female speaker begs her earthly beloved to shun the world and seek God, as she has done, so that they might be together in paradise.[7] Francesca Maria Steele, author of *The Convents of Great Britain*, like Rossetti, published works in the 1880s and 1890s which concern the religious life. After the turn of the century, Steele authored the first-known modern English translation of Hildegard, eventually published in 1914. Hildegard was also published in Migne's *Patrologia Latina* in 1855. A number of translations of the abbess's works, particularly the *Scivias*, appeared in French and German throughout the nineteenth century. Christina Rossetti's sister, Maria, joined an Anglican religious order and studied, if not translated, early Church material. In this essay, while I do not argue that Christina Rossetti necessarily had access to Hildegard's works, I do not find that hypothesis to be an impossibility. Given the poet-theologian's cultural and intellectual milieux, a translation of Hildegard could have passed through her hands. Whether or not Rossetti was directly familiar with Hildegard's works, the way in which two religious women from different times and places reached strikingly comparable conclusions on similar questions about the Divine and their place as women within God's creation is sufficiently noteworthy to place them in textual dialogue in this essay.

Theoretically, it is my goal to locate the spiritual lives of both medieval and nineteenth-century women with respect to hegemonic patriarchal religious frameworks. I am interested in the ways in which religious discourse may function as an alternative avenue to power for those who might otherwise be disenfranchised: namely, women in both medieval and Victorian culture (by virtue of their gender) and men of same-sex desire, whose identity was named at the last *fin-de-siècle*. One may argue that during both the medieval and Victorian periods, religious literature served to empower those who did not identify as "male" or "heterosexual" in their relationships to a Divine, fostering the creation of religiosities which simultaneously satisfied the spiritual needs of individuals and offered voices from which to speak with authority.[8] The flesh of medieval woman—empowered through her humility, her likeness to Christ—commanded her to "cry out and write" in Hildegard's words (*Scivias*, "Protestificatio" 97-8).[9] A non-dominant position has the potential to call forth reconciling perspectives for the lost physical body in spirit-centered Christian theology.

Rossetti establishes her authority to speak in a religious voice by associating her humanity and humility with Christ's, as her medieval foremothers did. She forcefully likens woman to God Incarnate throughout her prose. Rossetti writes in *Seek and Find*: "And well may she glory, inasmuch as one of the tenderest of divine promises takes (so to say) the feminine form: 'As one whom his mother comforteth, so will I comfort you'" (31). The writer looks to Christ's maternal behavior. One of Hildegard's sacred songs may be compared to this passage: *O feminea forma, soror Sapientie, quam gloriosa es* [O feminine form, sister of Wisdom, how glorious you are] (*Symphonia* 264). Aside from the similarity of language used by these two women writing theology, there is also similarity in their content. Hildegard's song is entitled "O magna res" [O greatness]. The work praises Divinity within all material creation: "O greatness that lay hidden in nothing created, so that it was neither made nor created by anyone but abides in itself" (*Symphonia* 265). The song laments that through the female death came into the world. However, Woman is finally exalted as the form that gave shape to eternal Life, providing God with human flesh. *Seek and Find* comments on the Benedicite, the exaltations of God's works. Rossetti's incarnationalism is rooted in a creation-centered, Divine embodiment. On the organic and inorganic worlds, she states: "One thing however is absolutely clear: they are entrusted to man's sovereignty for use, not for abuse" (*SF* 115). This "ecologically friendly" statement is in line with contemporary eco-feminists who lay claim to Hildegard's celebration of creation's greening.[10]

Like Hildegard, Rossetti inflects gender in natural theology. For the Victorian, Christ serves as pattern. Although her cosmology is flawed, Rossetti's interpretation of the male-female relationships in the natural world may similarly be compared to Hildegard's complex cosmogony and natural science inquiries. In *Called to Be Saints*, Rossetti assigns a plant and gemstone for each of the major saints' days. Their designations, in many cases, have little precedent. In this project, Rossetti recalls Hildegard's interest in botany and geology. She speaks of the sun-moon, that is, "male-female," dichotomy in *Seek and Find*. Rather than the moon being a mirror to the sun, "careful observation leads toward the observation that she also may exhibit inherent luminosity" (*SF* 31). "Subordinate as she seems, yet is she the very foundation on which all stands; her characteristic instability reappears transmuted into a characteristic stability" (*SF* 190-1). The balance of male and female essences in the cosmos which Rossetti depicts is reminiscent of the twelfth-century abbess, whose cosmology maintained a sense of complementarity in all aspects of creation.

The nineteenth-century theologian's *Letter and Spirit* seeks to place men and women as equal before God. On the commandment against coveting another's wife, Rossetti writes that one should not covet another's husband either. Her commodification of husbands as well as wives draws attention to the bodies of both as property. Women's bodies, are, however, located in a revered place, as Hildegard likewise suggested before her:

> [Woman] appears to stand as the connecting link, akin to both, between what the man is and what he has; even as Christ's sacred humanity, bridging over the severing gulf, unites the Godhead to the Church (193).

Woman's body is associated with Christ's body by Rossetti. The holy place accorded to the female body by Hildegard in the continuum of creation is demonstrated by her countless sanctified figures of woman in her theological works. It is useful to consider the doctrine of the Real Presence at the Eucharist when contemplating Hildegard's and Rossetti's theologies of the female body. C. W. Bynum has observed the medieval association of female bodies with Christ. Rossetti's exegesis recalls the illustration from the manuscript of Hildegard's *Scivias* depicting the female figure of Ecclesia, the Church, in two poses (II.6.1). She simultaneously catches Christ's blood in a chalice, while He hangs on the cross, and awaits Him at the altar, bearing a cup. Woman's eating of Christ, her participation in his eucharistic Incarnation, serves to recapitulate both her role in his first carnal birth in the world through Mary and matter's reception of the original breath of Divine Wisdom which created humanity. In *Letter and Spirit*, Rossetti established that

> God in Christ reconciles the world unto Himself. . . not that she should thenceforth abide afar off as a trembling slave. . . but that as a beloved bride she should sit down with Him in His Throne (308).

Bride/Bridegroom nuptial theology is at the heart of Rossetti's view of the Divine. While at first glance this male figure seems to substitute for an earthly husband, such a paradigm also affirms a Hildegardian sense of complementarity. Given this carnal matrix, the spiritual is clearly sensual and the material world holy for these two theologians.

Literally tangible bodies serve to bridge the gap between the material and the spiritual. During the nineteenth century, the English Church returned to greater license for prayers to particular saints. Such supplication directly points to the place of the physical body in the act of devotion. The veneration of the body of a saint through prayer draws attention to the body of the supplicant. This point is especially important to keep in mind when considering the devotional lives of women, whose bodies were gendered by medical and psychosexual discourse of this period. In *Time Flies*, published in 1886, Rossetti seizes upon particular holy bodies for devotion. From these *picturae*, we find traits which the theologian has prized in her earlier prose works. Rossetti's models and lessons teach of souls who discover a special, particularly sensual, relationship with the Divine. Their connections to God empower the saints, in some way enabling them to live more fully in their worlds.

In her entry for January 13 of *Time Flies*, the Feast of St. Hilary (d. 368), Rossetti writes of the saint's daughter, Apra. She "devoted herself. . . to the exclusive love of Christ" ( 11). The theologian observes,

> Now of St. Hilary's wife I read nothing further, beyond such a hint of her career as is involved in that of her husband; wherefore of her I am free to think as of one "unknown and yet well known": on earth of less dignified name than her husband and daughter, in Paradise it may well be of equal account. For many are they of whom the world is both "not worthy and ignorant."
>
> Moreover, it is written: "Many that are first shall be last; and the last shall be first" (11-2).

This commentary indicates the place of those who are set apart, specially chosen to be brides of Christ. Rossetti continues this theme with St. Agnes, a virgin martyr (d. 304):

> By the name "chaste" (Greek) and "a lamb" (Latin), this loveliest girl of thirteen, noble and wealthy, was sought in marriage by a youth of distinguished birth. But she, for spouse, would have none save the Lamb of God: Who keeping her pure alike in body and soul, accepted her as His whole burnt offering. Nevertheless the lighted pyre on which she prayed died out of itself: and unscathed by that death, and

unshackled by man, she won her victory by submitting to the sword in the persecution under Diocletian. . . .

And we may rejoice with St. Agnes, who along with the greater, may also these fifteen hundred years have inherited the lesser love "in spirit and in truth," in that land where "they neither marry nor are given in marriage" (17-8).

The stress upon virginal purity is strong in the diary. On the Vigil of the Purification, Rossetti writes that the feast "bids us watch and keep guard: for purity is soon sullied and not easily restored" (25). Two significant female martyrs follow the Purification. The first is St. Agatha (d. 251), a virgin who was tortured and imprisoned because she would not accept "base love" (27). Rossetti declares, "The love of Christ, like a touchstone, has tested much human affection, and over and over again has proved it dross" (27). Further, the Feast of St. Perpetua celebrates a married woman who endures brutal death for her faith. Her strong bond to another woman, a slave, is evidenced in the latter's willingness to die with her. The strong bond of sisterhood, shared femaleness, is reminiscent of that emphasis in the poet's *Goblin Market*. All of these female saints clearly defy the strictures of a culture based on biological reproduction. Like Ursula's 11,000 virgins, these women long for the Lamb. However much their spiritual spouses may be configured as male (and Christ is a rather ambiguously gendered "man," associated as he is with much that is deemed "feminine"), these women's earthly companions are almost exclusively female. Same-sex bonds seem to have been equally significant in Hildegard. The abbess's strongly sensual depiction of Saint Ursula, in addition to the many other songs in the *Symphonia* addressed to virgins, seems to imply a devotional homoerotic. Virginity is fetishized in Hildegard's songs. One may imagine an all-female religious community harmonizing in adoration of virginal female bodies.[11] Virginal purity, in devotion to the ambigendered body of Christ, hence may be read as a profoundly queer choice for religious.[12]

Male same-sex alliances are demonstrated by Rossetti in the dual Feast of Sts. Philip and James on May 1:

On their Feast Day they stand before us as it were hand in hand: "Behold, how good and joyful a thing it is, brethren, to dwell together in unity."

Whatever remains uncertain about them, of two facts we rest
assured: they loved God, and therefore cannot but have loved one
another (*TF* 83).

Hildegard's "feminization" of male saints, such as Rupert,
Disibod, and John the Evangelist, is apparent in the way in which they
are allied with female virgins in the *Symphonia*. Set apart from other
mortals by their love for/from God, these men are set on a par with
female virgins. Rossetti writes extensively in her devotional prose of
the special love Christ had for John.[13] The mystic's sensual spirituality
clearly defies biological gender. In classic Bernardian biological
gender-crossing through the Song of Songs, the Bridegroom embraces
His Bride, the soul, regardless of the gender of the body which contains
her.

*Time Flies* includes important saints of the Church calendar that
demonstrate Rossetti's awareness of the heritage of monasticism and
the "Fathers." She praises the monkish love of poverty of Pope Gregory
the Great (d. 604). The abbot St. Benedict is rightly called the
"Patriarch of Western Monasticism" (56). St. Augustine is described as
bishop and "Doctor of the Church" (166). Ironically, Augustine, known
for his lascivious early life, is indirectly feminized in his chastity:
"Thence forward, allowing for human frailty, he retained of the serpent
only its wisdom, and put on harmlessness as a dove: yet not, alas,
without putting it off under provocation" (166). In his conversion,
Augustine somehow had to become "womanly"; the description is
almost castrating. Rossetti extends the Biblical symbol of the harmless
dove to woman later in *Face of the Deep*. Taking on chastity, as it
were, for these men, involved putting aside "masculinity." In the
*Scivias,* Hildegard repeatedly makes use of clothing imagery when
speaking of gender, as if that distinction were a garment which could be
changed at will.[14] In the entry for St. Jerome, "Priest, Doctor, and
Ascetic," Rossetti writes,

> Of strong natural passions and still stronger will, he strained that
> strong will to the uttermost to overcome the natural man; and the
> desert he sometimes inhabited witnessed his life and death struggle
> with evil, his occasional ecstasy, his hard-won triumph (*TF* 189).

The conversion experience in some way necessitates that one
become like the "weak maid" that was St. Faith (*TF* 194) rather than

remain a "natural man." Hildegard's exaltations of male virgins as well as female acknowledge all who would put off the active material passion in favor of an inner spiritual passion for the source of the Living Light. Inverting her own association of female with (holy) flesh, it is the "active" male who is more carnal than the transcendent female.

In addition to looking to the Church of late antiquity, Rossetti also studies medieval saints in *Time Flies*. She is particularly interested in saints of England and the Teutonic peoples. Bede's feast is celebrated, in addition to that of St. Etheldreda (d. 679), "Virgin Queen an Abbess" (200). The study of the latter saint gives insight into Rossetti's notions of medieval religious communities. Etheldreda's first husband, in compliance with her will, forbore enforcing his marital rights. She separated from her second husband and built a monastery for men and women on the Isle of Ely. Etheldreda's death scene is depicted by Rossetti: surrounded by tearful brothers and sisters of the community, she implored them "never to let their hearts rest on the earth, but to taste beforehand and, by their earnest desires, that joy in the love of Christ which it would not be given to them to know perfectly here below" (200).

The Victorian theologian's religious writings demonstrate her concern with earlier powerful women of religion. The conclusion of Etheldreda's *vita* turns to anti-materialistic questioning. Rossetti's theology, while grounded in the physical body, is ultimately transcendent, as is Hildegard's. The kiss of the soul which crosses the [mystical] bar between body and spirit as well as life and death is the vehicle of such movement of the soul. Both theologians balance an utter grounding in creation's substantive nature while affirming the holier universe of forms from which materiality is inseparable. A spiritual embrace, as demonstrated in all of Hildegard's works, is accomplished in Rossetti's *Face of the Deep*, first published in 1892, two years before the theologian's death. The text is "apocalyptic" on many levels. A lengthy devotional commentary on the biblical Book of Revelation, *Face of the Deep* also draws on other apocalyptic scripture. The fact that Rossetti wrote this work during the *fin-de-siècle* should not be ignored. The genre of prophetic writing recalls Hildegard: a sense of an imminent ending is pervasive in both theologians' works. It does not seem coincidental that Rossetti chose this book of the Bible to analyze. By the 1890s, she was not well. Her sister Maria and her mother had both died, while her own health was deteriorating. Finally, cancer ended her life in 1894. Rossetti wrote expectantly in *Face of the*

*Deep:* "Bitter it is to long for life and die; more bitter to long for death and it cometh not" (387-8). The bliss of death and entry into Paradise had been the subject of her poetry and prose since teen years. In *Face of the Deep*, she prepares for the joys enjoyed by those "gone before."[15] A sense of an imminent ending, mirroring the turbulence of one's political world, is as pervasive in the twelfth century as at the end of the Victorians' age. The final movement from substance to celestial form is enacted in this text, as in every work by Hildegard, as it is ritually in each act of transubstantiation of the Eucharist at mass.

Near the conclusion of *Face of the Deep*, Rossetti issues her retraction. "If I have been overbold in attempting such a work as this, I beg pardon" (551). Earlier in the same work, Rossetti had claimed authority in weakness:

> Far be it from me to think to unfold mysteries or interpret prophecies. But I trust that to gaze in whatever ignorance on what God reveals, is so far to do His will. If ignorance breed humility, it will not debar from wisdom. If ignorance betake itself to prayer, it will lay hold on grace (146).

Looking to the natural world to understand the workings of the Divine, Rossetti finds her own space to speak within God's creation:

> But God has not bidden us to be mighty as eagles, but be harmless as doves. I suppose a dove may be no more fit than myself to look steadily at the sun: we both might be blinded by what would enlighten the stronger bird. The dove brings not much of her own to the sun, yet the sun caresses and beautifies her silver wings and her feathers like gold: it would be a sore mistake on the dove's part were she to say, Because I am not the eagle I am not a sun bird, and so were to cut off from the sun's gracious aspect (146).

The dove and the eagle are contrasted as weak/strong, hence representing female/male. Further interpretations can, however, be drawn from Rossetti's example. In *Face of the Deep*, the writer also waxes eloquent on the special love Christ has for John. Traditionally, each of the four evangelists is associated with a particular animal. John's is the eagle. Hence, to compare oneself as dove to John's eagle is to compare the love Christ had for his Beloved to the love He has for oneself. Furthermore, in contrast to the humility the speaker claims, to associate oneself with the dove rather than the eagle is to be more implicitly identified with Jesus Himself than with His "mirrors" on earth. The dove has significance as a symbol of the Holy Spirit. Rossetti states that ignorance will not debar from wisdom. The position of dove, while not participating in certain approaches to God, will not prevent one from receiving his grace through the Paraclete, revealed Wisdom. Wisdom is the cornerstone of *Face of the Deep*:

> To expound prophecy lies of course beyond my power, and not within my wish. But the symbolic forms of prophecy being set before all eyes, must be so set for some purpose: to investigate them may not make us wise as serpents; yet ought by promoting faith, fear, hope, love, to aid in making us harmless as doves (195).

Christ is referred to as "Wisdom" throughout this work. It/She is clearly a feminine strategy to claim authority to speak on spiritual matters. Barbara Newman has established Hildegard's place as a sapiential theologian. Rossetti may join her foremother in this rank. In her visionary works, Hildegard created many "figures of Woman" representing various aspects of material and immaterial creation. Wisdom is among these:

> You see standing at the summit of the same level, as it were, the most beautiful apparition: it is as if this virtue has been in the highest Father before all created thing, setting in order for each by counsel the embellishments of the creatures, who are made in heaven and on earth; this same figure is a great ornament shining in God and the broadest stairway of stairways of other virtues, existing in the very sweetest embrace, joined together in a dance of ardent love. She looks out at people in the world: truly she always guides those who choose to come under her roof, and, conscientious, she intently keeps watch over those who stand firm in her. For this very image represents the wisdom of God: because through her all things are created and guided by God. Her head shines like lightning with such a brightness that you may not be able to look at it head-on: for indeed the Divinity, who is at once terrifying and seductive to all creatures, sees and contemplates all things, just as the human eye declares what happens to be placed before it; however, it has power to be led to heights in the depth of its mystery by nothing human (*Scivias* III.9.25).

In *Time Flies*, Rossetti includes an entry on Wisdom, quoting a Latin hymn. "'O Wisdom, Who comest out of the mouth of the Most High, reaching from one end to another mightily, and sweetly ordering all things, come and teach us the way of understanding'"(241). Rossetti explains: "'O Sapientia'—'O Wisdom:' that is, 'Christ. . . the Wisdom of God.' Whom we adore not only as the Word of God, but also as 'Christ Jesus, Who of God is made unto us Wisdom" (242). The femininity of Biblical Wisdom and Her connection to Incarnate Divinity is central to the sapiential theology of *Face of the Deep*. Christ is described as "O Lord the Word, Wisdom, Truth" (494).

Christ as man cannot exist rigidly fixed within the male gender. The Wisdom of God, as connected with the feminine aspect of the Divine, becomes in Christic theology another type of the Virgin Mother. In the multiplicity of female figures of the universe as seen by Hildegard, Sapientia doubles as Ecclesia and Virginitas, the Bride of Christ who is also the Mother of Christ. She is also Christ Her/Himself, as in the New Testament Christ is called the Wisdom of God. This Wisdom, however, is tangible. As material, it is female. In Hildegard's realization, the ultimate source for the embodiment of God—who existed as Wisdom in the mind of God—is as female as the female essence breathed into her.

The fourteenth-century English mystic Julian of Norwich also specified the nature of God's "femininity":

> I saw and vnderstode that the hygh myght of the trynyte is oure fader, and the depe wysdome of the trynyte is oure moder, and the grete loue of the trynyte is oure lorde; and alle these haue we in kynde and in oure substanncyall makyng (XIV.58.34-7).[16]

Julian places Wisdom within material creation infused by the Spirit:

> And oure substannce is in oure fader god almyghty, and oure substannce is in oure moder god all wysdom, and oure substannce is in oure lorde god the holy gost all goodnesse, for oure substannce is hole in ech person of the trynyte, whych is one god (XIV.58.59-63).

For Julian, spiritual Wisdom cannot be separated from earthly creation:

Thus Jhesu Crist, that doth good agaynst evyll, is oure very moder; we haue oure beyng of hym, where the ground of moderhed begynnyth, with alle the swete kepyng of loue that endlesly folowyth (XIV.59.9-11).

Christ tells Julian, "'I it am, the wysdom and the kyndnes of moderhode'" (XIV.59.14-5). In an extraordinarily bold gesture, Julian names motherhood as the trope of both creation, the "grounde of oure kynde makyng," and Incarnation, the "takyng of oure kynde." In giving flesh to spiritual Wisdom, all bodies are reclaimed from their fallen state:

> I vnderstode thre manner of beholdynges of motherhed in god. The furst is grounde of oure kynde makyng, the second is takying of oure kynde, and ther begynnyth the moderhed of grace, the thurde is moderhed in werking. And therein is a forth spredyng by the same grace of lengt and brede, of hygh and of depnesse without ende; and alle is one loue (XIV.59.43-8).

Julian's reflections on motherhood are complementary with Rossetti's development of Wisdom Incarnate in *Face of the Deep,* where Christ as Wisdom serves as the embodiment, specifically, the motherhood, of God. They represent a manifestation of sapiential theology in the work of another female religious writer. Wisdom takes on many inflections as a virtue besides existing as a personification. The virtue of wisdom gives women such as Rossetti, Julian and Hildegard a claim to the right to speak in religious discourse. It/She defies categories of gender and privilege, as revelation does not depend on (male) schooled intellects. The quality of wisdom is feminized in both Jewish and Christian scripture, like the gender of the body who personifies the virtue. Learned religious women throughout history have seized upon sapiential theology as a means of empowerment in speech. In claiming to be only scribes for the voice of prophecy, denied teaching authority because of their sex, such women are exonerated from blame. They are only lowly vessels of Divine inspiration, hence free to speak.

Rossetti asserts the power of wisdom as opposed to knowledge. "Whoso learns humility learns wisdom if not knowledge: and wisdom being better than knowledge, 'the word' even in this occult instance will thus become by no means unfruitful" (*FD* 262). As "Word" of

God, woman and Revealed Wisdom are truly Christ. Rossetti's earlier association of humility with Christ and femininity strengthens this link:

> For the special purpose in question, he "that hath understanding" excludes, I should surmise, most men, and very likely all women. For the masses Wisdom resides elsewhere, is an immediately practical grace, and is far more readily accessible (349).

The writer follows this quote with more than a dozen Biblical references which praise wisdom. She concludes, "Whoever by loving submission turns intellectual poverty into voluntary spiritual poverty, has discovered a super-excellent philosopher's stone, apt to transmute ignorance into wisdom" (350). Rossetti adopts the anti-intellectualism, specifically, the anti-Scholasticism, of the mystic, preferring other forms of contemplative knowledge that are more accessible to the greater number:

> Far from being necessarily an insurmountable disadvantage, I think that ignorance of the historical drift of prophecy may on occasion turn to a humble but genuine profit. Such ignorance entails (or wisely utilized might entail) that a general lesson, a fundamental principle, essence not accident, will be elicited from the abstruse text. Further:—instead of attention being directed to the ends of the earth, our eye must be turned within (396).

The "eye . . . turned within" describes Rossetti as woman poet. It also describes the individual who pursues the contemplative life. Far from being ignorant, like Hildegard in her self-abnegation, Rossetti utilized not only "wisdom" but obviously "learning" as well. Written at the end of her career, *Face of the Deep* serves to validate all of the Rossetti corpus. In this *magnum opus*, the theologian reconciles her place as devotional writer with her identity as a poet. In *Time Flies*, Rossetti praised the "inflexible virtue" of St. Catherine of Alexandria (225). Her "wisdom proved victorious in an argumentative contest she had with fifty philosophers" (225). Both the author and the saint are reminiscent of Hildegard's audacity in engaging and critiquing male prelates and secular authorities.

Significantly, Rossetti makes final preparations to become the exalted, powerful woman in the afterlife whom she has glorified for decades. In a sweeping turn uniting Biblical personification with practical virtue, Rossetti at once grafts herself upon and becomes Holy Wisdom:

> So teach us to number our days that we may apply our hearts unto wisdom; that we may receive the instruction of wisdom, justice, and judgement and equity. O Lord, Who givest Wisdom, Who layest up sound wisdom for the righteous; teach us in the way of wisdom, lead us in right paths. Furnish our lips with wisdom. Grant us wisdom with the just, the lowly, the well advised; that with the prudent we may understand our way, and ceasing from our own wisdom may learn of Thee, Lord Jesus Christ our Wisdom. Amen.
>
> The virtuous woman whose price is far above rubies "openeth her mouth with wisdom; and in her tongue is the law of kindness." Wisdom, then, associates with kindness: to cultivate kindness is to frequent the society of wisdom. A clue especially vouchsafed to us women (*FD* 405).

As in her Benedictine foremother, the nineteenth-century writer critically re-examines and reclaims sinless/sinful woman as God's link to our humanity. Appropriate to a theology which affirms the material embodiment of God's Holy Spirit in a vessel like Herself, Rossetti plays devil's advocate for the mother of material creation in *Letter and Spirit:*

> Eve, equally with Adam, was created sinless: each had a specially vulnerable point, but apparently not the same point. It is in no degree at variance with the Sacred Record to picture to ourselves Eve, that first and typical woman, as indulging quite innocently sundry refined tastes and aspirations, a castle-building spirit (if so it may be called), a feminine boldness and directness of aim combined with a no less feminine guessiness as to means. Her very virtues may have opened the door to temptation. By birthright gracious and accessible, she lends an ear to all petitions from all petitioners. She desires to instruct ignorance, to rectify misapprehension: "unto the pure, all things are pure," and she never suspects even the serpent. Possibly a trace of blameless infirmity transpires in the wording of her answer "*lest* ye die," for God had said to the man ". . . in the day that thou eatest thereof thou *shalt surely* die": but such tenderness of spirit seems even lovely in the great first mother of mankind; or it may be that Adam had modified the form, if it devolved on him to declare the

tremendous fact to his second self. Adam and Eve reached their goal,
the Fall, by different routes. With Eve the serpent discussed a
question of conduct, and talked her over to his own side: . . . Eve may
not have argued at all: she offered Adam a share of her own good
fortune (17-8).

The dignity of woman is an issue which Rossetti considers very
seriously in *Face of the Deep*. As an apocalyptic theologian like
Hildegard, Rossetti locates the figure of woman in a cosmic context
from creation through the end of the world. Her description of Eve's
"kindness"—simultaneously her compassion and her place in revealed
history—could as easily be used in speaking of the Virgin Mary. This
similarity is not inappropriate in a theologian who reads cosmic
continua into the bodies of women. In *Seek and Find*, Rossetti writes
that "Pharaoh's daughter adopting Moses in her womanly compassion,
was exalted unawares to be the nursing mother of the Church" (129). In
Hildegard's theology of the body, all women are mother Eves: not
hopelessly fallen, but Christ-like and Sapiential in incarnating and
containing God. Significantly, Rossetti validates non-biologically-
procreative women, the Brides of Christ, in her interpretation of
Scripture.

Eve, the representative woman, received as part of her sentence
"desire": the assigned object of her desire being such that satisfaction
must depend not on herself but on one stronger than she, who might
grant or might deny. Many women attain their heart's desire: many
attain it not. Yet are these latter no losers if they exchange desire for
aspiration, the corruptible for the incorruptible: "Thou shalt no more be
termed Forsaken; neither shall thy land any more be termed Desolate:
but thou shalt be called Hephzibah, and thy land Beulah: for the Lord
delighteth in thee, and thy land shall be married." "The desolate hath
many more children than she which hath a husband." "'Give me
children or else I die,' was a foolish speech: the childless who make
themselves nursing mothers of Christ's little ones are true mothers in
Israel" (*FD* 312).

After exalting earthly virginity, Rossetti turns to the Heavenly
Woman of the Apocalypse: the type and model of all souls who
renounce physical passion in favor of spiritual longing. She is the
ultimate figure of the feminine, comparable to Hildegard's figure of
Wisdom. Once again, "she" can be the model of the female or the male:
whoever may choose God and become Christ-like and womanly:

"A woman clothed with the sun, and the moon under her feet, and upon her head a crown of twelve stars."—Whatever else may here be hidden, there stands revealed that "great wonder," weakness made strong and shame swallowed up in celestial glory. For thus the figure is set before our eyes. Through Eve's lapse, weakness and shame devolved on woman as her characteristics, in a manner special to herself and unlike the corresponding heritage of man. . . .

She will be made equal with men and angels . . . arrayed in all human virtues, and decked with all communicable Divine graces: whilst the moon under her feet portends that her sometime infirmity of purpose and changeableness of mood have, by preventing, assisting, final grace, become immutable; she has done all and stands; from the lowest place she has gone up higher. As love of his Lord enabled St. Peter to tread the sea, so love of the same Lord sets weak woman immovable on the waves of this troublesome world, triumphantly erect, despite her own frailty, made not "like unto a wheel," amid all the changes and chances of this mortal life (*FD* 309-10).

Hildegard's figures of celestial Virginitas and Ecclesia are forms of the woman of splendor of Revelation. Maternal Virginitas, like her other spiritual figures of women, is compared to the heavenly Jerusalem:

This is innocent Virginity. . . she is the noblest shoot in celestial Jerusalem, namely the glory and honor of those who have shed their blood for the sake of the love of virginity, and who in humility's brilliance, guarding their virginity for Christ, have slept in the sweetness of peace; for she was betrothed to the Son of all-powerful God, the king of all, and brought forth the noblest race, that is, the most refined choir of virgins when she was strengthened, advancing the peace of the Church (*Scivias* II.5.6).

In the works of both Hildegard and Rossetti, the material and immaterial nature of the embodied Divine / Divine bodies is inseparable:

Now because "righteousness is immortal" and the memorial of virtue immortal, this august Woman, if we may regard her as a figure of Mother Church, is immortal and blessed. Yet even thus there remains

a mortal side to the members who make up her immortal personality
(*FD* 328).

The mortal side to the members who make up the Church in
Heaven is the humanity which connects them to the first incarnation of
Holy Wisdom, elevated in the later Incarnation of Christ in Mary.
Rossetti reclaims fallen humanity, fallen woman, through the fallen
mother, Eve, and the trope of mothering. All mortals, whether or not
they biologically procreate, are blessed with the Divine creative ability
to "mother." Such people—the Church, by necessity feminine—are
simultaneously Bride of Christ / Mother of God: "Because the Church
is moulded after Thy likeness, her least and last member is thus
moulded" (*FD* 278). Motherhood and maternal qualities are the
likeness of God. This assertion elevates all biological mothers, a point
Rossetti does not hesitate to underscore:

> And yet, even as at the foot of the Cross, St. Mary Magdalene, out of
> whom went seven devils, stood beside the "lily among thorns," the
> Mother of sorrows: so (I humbly hope and trust) amongst all saints of
> all time will stand before the Throne, Eve the beloved first Mother of
> us all. Who that has loved and revered her own immediate dear
> mother, will not echo the hope? (*FD* 311).

Nevertheless, the cosmic fecundity of the virgin transcends her
lack of children on earth. Further, in awaiting Christ as Bridegroom, the
Bride may procreate plentifully in singing God's praise in devotion.
When the moment arrives, Rossetti gives a lengthy commentary, which
can only be described as Hildegardian, on New Jerusalem coming
down from God out of heaven, prepared as a bride adorned for her
husband:

> New Jerusalem comes down "from God out of heaven," not as
> leaving God, but inasmuch as His Presence goeth with her. As when
> of old that Adorable Presence led the elder Israel in the stages of the
> Exodus, so now that Same Adorable Inalienable Presence leads her
> out and brings her in, is beneath her for stability, over her for
> benediction, around her for acceptance. As a chaste virgin espoused
> she comes down, longed for, toiled for, Self-sacrificed for, bought
> with a great price by Him Who gave His whole Substance for love.

She has received all and now she gives back all. She is "adorned for her Husband," for her Beloved Who is indeed more than another beloved. He loved her first, and now she returns His love. He is the sun, and now as His moon-mirror she appears clear as the sun. He is the Life, and now she has received life from Him and lives to Him. She is His lily, no longer among thorns because He once wore those thorns so that He might take them out of her way. He is All-Holy: and now, her heart purified by His Blood and sanctified by His Spirit, she sees Him Whom to see beatifies. His graces shed on her form the ornament to her head and the chains about her neck. Beautiful are her feet shod with the preparation of the gospel of His peace. Behold her in tenderness His dove, in likeness His sister, in union His spouse.

Behold her! yea, also, and behold thyself, O thou called to be a saint. Her perfections are thy birthright; thou are what she was, what she is thou mayest become. That Goodness which is her fountain of good overflows to thee likewise. Covet earnestly gifts such as hers, practise self-adornment for love of Him who loveth thee. Reserve gems and pearls for immortality when thou shalt be flawless as they. Adorn thyself meanwhile with flower-like graces: humility the violet, innocence the snowdrop, purity the lily; with sweetness for a honeysuckle, with penitence for a fruitful thorn. To-day put on the garments of salvation prepared for thee, that tomorrow thou mayest be promoted to wear the garments of praise (*FD* 480-1).

Both "sisters of Wisdom," Hildegard of Bingen and Christina Rossetti, offer us enlightening perspectives for the future of feminist theology. In their spiritual visions, humanity—particularly female humanity—is redeemed and made holy. Woman's relation to transcendent Wisdom negates her limitations in material creation. Stylizing oneself as a Bride of Christ, a flower of the tones bejewelled to receive Him in the communion feast, was one highly effective means of attaining a voice within Rossetti's culture. The same may be said for Hildegard's. Religious life offered women in both the twelfth and nineteenth centuries greater opportunity for speech. Medieval spiritual writing cannot be read outside of its context, any more than we may impose our own *fin-de-siècle's* paradigms upon nineteenth-century English culture. Nevertheless, for these women, liberation was found through renunciation. Their many body-affirming, indeed life-affirming, gestures in speech recapitulate the ultimate Christian paradox of life through death.

It has been my goal in this essay to seek a better understanding of those categories which we employ in our periodization which make terms such as "comparative" necessary. I have sought to develop an argument and provide evidence for similarities, under the rubrics of "gender" and "culture," between two distinct sites of analysis. In the context of Hildegard studies, I have attempted to contribute to the development of what might be termed a "Hildegardian" reading of later texts: an effort to employ the twelfth-century theologian as a means of hermeneutical exegesis of other works. In using Hildegard in this manner, I wish to suggest the abundance of modes by which such an approach can be applied. In my method, I have endeavored to suggest both subtle and direct subversions of the boundaries of categories—such as period and gender—whose construction I have simultaneously participated in by my critical practice here. In this effort at articulation yet manipulation of "essences," I can only hope that I have been sufficiently and truly Hildegardian.

## NOTES

1. See Barbara Newman's *Sister of Wisdom: St. Hildegard's Theology of the Feminine* for a scholarly study of the abbess. There are numerous New Age interpretations of Hildegard received with considerable skepticism in the academy. Matthew Fox's *Illuminations of Hildegard of Bingen* provides some interesting translations which work within the creation-centered paradigm in contemporary mysticism.

2. An early readable work on this subject is Cady et al., *Sophia: The Future of Feminist Spirituality.* Numerous feminist theologians have written on Sophia. A recent work is Schussler Fiorenza, *Jesus: Miriam's Child, Sophia's Prophet: Critical Issues in Feminist Christology.*

3. By the late 1980s, theologians such as Carter Heyward and James Nelson were developing practical "body theologies," attempting to reconcile the many scholarly projects on gender and sexuality with contemporary social issues. See Heyward's *Touching Our Strength;* see also Nelson, *Body Theology* and (ed. with Sandra P. Longfellow) *Sexuality and the Sacred: Sources for Theological Reflection.*

4. Recent studies of the prose are few: Westerholm, "'I Magnify Mine Office': Christina Rossetti's Authoritative Voice in Her Devotional Prose"; Hobbs, "A View from 'The Lowest Place': Christina Rossetti's Devotional Prose"; D'Amico, "Eve, Mary, and Mary Magdalene: Christina Rossetti's Feminine Triptych"; and Stanwood's "Christina Rossetti's Devotional Prose." Most

book-length studies treat Rossetti's prose only in passing. Jan Marsh's recent biography is an exception.

5. On Benedictine influence and interest in monastic revival, see Kollar, "The Oxford Movement and the Heritage of Benedictine Monasticism"; Anson, *Building Up the Waste Places.*

6. Regarding Victorian reception of the sisterhoods, see, for instance, Casteras, "Virgin Vows." See also Hill, *The Religious Order* and Vicinus, *Independent Women* for two different perspectives on the sisterhoods in Victorian England; as well as Anson, *The Call of the Cloister;* Heeney, *The Women's Movement in the Church of England ;* and Reed, "'A Female Movement.'"

7. For a consideration of Rossetti and the religious orders, see D'Amico, "'Choose the Stairs That Mount Above'".

8. On this subject, see, for instance, Dronke, *Women Writers* ; Beer, *Women and Mystical Experience*; Nolan, *Cry Out and Write*; and Petroff, *Medieval Women's Visionary Literature,* for medieval references. Krueger's *The Reader's Repentance* demonstrates this phenomenon during the Victorian period. Recall the Methodist preacher Dinah in George Eliot's *Adam Bede* for a consideration of the place of woman within the nineteenth-century religious milieu outside of the High Church. The place of the emergent male homosexual in the Victorian High Church is detailed in Hilliard, "'Unenglish and Unmanly'".

9. All translations of Hildegard in this essay are mine, in consultation with those in Barbara Newman's edition for the *Symphonia,* and, for the *Scivias,* in consultation with the translation of Columba Hart and Jane Bishop.

10. On Marian celebrations of fecund nature, see "O frondens virga" and "O viridissima virga" in *Symphonia* (120,126).

11. See, for instance, "Favus distillans": "A dripping honeycomb / was Ursula the virgin" (*Symphonia* 234), as well as Hildegard's other ecstatic songs. On the subject of homoeroticism in Hildegard's music, see Holsinger, "The Flesh of the Voice." In this context, it is also interesting to consider Hildegard's relationship with her nun, Richardis. Although their bond can be read as that of a strong, possessive mother expressing her desire for her daughter's dependence, Hildegard's attachment to Richardis underscores the unique relationship of body and spirit which exists between members of a religious community. Erotic passion unites these lovers of God whose earthly bodies sing celestial harmony. Physical consummation of this love need not manifest in order to attest to the depth of the emotional-spiritual attachments of the cloister. Scholars of gender have argued for the presence of "romantic," if genitally unconsummated, same-sex friendships between women in the

nineteenth century. Perhaps the monastic life can be considered as a site of similar intellectual unions during the Middle Ages.

12. This point is especially significant in considering "Brides of Christ." Wed to the Wisdom of God, as the Incarnate is called, the gender of the "Body of Christ" may be inflected in multiple manifestations, since Divine Wisdom is assigned a "feminine form."

13. In particular, her *Called to Be Saints* and *The Face of the Deep*. In these works, the theologian invokes the love between David and Jonathan as prefiguring the great love of the New Testament, that of Christ and the Beloved. In "O speculum columbe," an antiphon for St. John the Evangelist, Hildegard addresses the Beloved as "mirror of the dove / of most chaste beauty, / who looked upon the mystical largesse / in the purest fountain" (*Symphonia* 166). She celebrates the virginal male body's "flowering" like the female's, calling John the "Lamb's special son / in the chosen friendship of a new generation" (*Symphonia* 166). Rupert is associated with "flowering" in "O beatissime Ruperte," and is sung as an ideal virgin without stain in "O Ierusalem" (*Symphonia* 190, 192-8). Clearly, in a Hildegardian model, virginal femininity does not require a genitally female physical body. In the *Scivias*, where chaste virgins are called "sweetest flowers" (I.2.24), Christ is the "flower of virginity" and John the "beloved virgin" (II.5.7).

14. See, for instance, *Scivias* II.6.77: "A man should never put on feminine dress or a woman use male attire, so that their roles might remain distinct." It is possible to consider this revealed proclamation in the context of anxieties over cross-dressing and "female"/"male" roles in the Church. However, the association of "roles" with gender performance in sexuality is expressed further in a passage which follows. "A woman who takes up devilish ways and plays a male role in coupling with another woman is most vile in [God's] sight, and so is she who subjects herself to such a one in this evil deed" (*Scivias* II.6.78). Lest we judge Hildegard as particularly harsh on homosexual relations, we must remember that any genital practice—including procreative, heterosexual copulation between married couples—is described by the abbess as vile, inferior to her ideal of virginity. Dress is significant elsewhere in the *Scivias*, as in the extensive representational explications of the female Virtues' clothing in III.3, 6, and 10.

15. For a study of the culture surrounding death in the nineteenth century and Victorian ideas about the life beyond the grave, see Wheeler's *Death and the Future Life* .

16. All quotations are taken from the Long Text. In these passages it is important to recall the meaning of the Middle English "kynde," which refers to

nature and what is "natural" in material creation. Likewise, "substanncyall makyng" may be translated as "material creation."

## WORKS CITED

### Primary Texts

Hildegard of Bingen. *Scivias*. Eds. Adelgundis Fuhrkotter and Angela Carlevaris. CCCM XLIII. Turnhout: Brepols, 1978.
———. *Scivias*. Trans. Columba Hart and Jane Bishop. New York: Paulist Press, 1990.
———. *Symphonia: A Critical Edition of the* Symphonia armonie celestium revelationum. Trans. Barbara Newman. Ithaca: Cornell University Press, 1988.
Julian of Norwich. *The Book of Showings to the Anchoress Julian of Norwich.* Eds. Edmund Colledge and James Walsh. Toronto: Pontifical Institute of Mediaeval Studies, 1978.
Rossetti, Christina G. *Annus Domini: A Prayer for Each Day of the Year, Founded on a Text of Holy Scripture.* Oxford: James Parker & Co., 1874.
———. *Called to Be Saints: The Minor Festivals Devotionally Studied.* New York: E. & J.B. Young, 1897.
———. *The Face of the Deep: A Devotional Commentary on the Apocalypse.* New York: E. & J.B. Young, 1895.
———. *Letter and Spirit: Notes on the Commandments.* London: SPCK, 1883.
———. *Seek and Find: A Double Series of Short Studies of the Benedicite.* New York: Pott, Young, & Co., n.d.
———. *Time Flies: A Reading Diary.* New York: E. & J.B. Young, 1902.

### Secondary Texts

Anson, Peter. *Building Up the Waste Places: The Revival of Monasticism on Medieval Lines in the Post-Reformation Church of England.* Leighton Buzzard: Faith Press, 1973.
———. *The Call of the Cloister: Religious Communities and Kindred Bodies in the Anglican Communion.* London: SPCK, 1955.
Beer, Frances. *Women and Mystical Experience in the Middle Ages.* Woodbridge, Suffolk: Boydell Press, 1992.
Bynum, Caroline Walker. *Holy Feast, Holy Fast: The Religious Significance of Food to Medieval Women.* Berkeley: University of California Press, 1987.
Cady, Susan, Marian Ronan, and Hal Taussig. *Sophia: The Future of Feminist Spirituality.* San Francisco: Harper & Row, 1986.

Casteras, Susan. "Virgin Vows: The Early Victorian Artists' Portrayal of Nuns and Novices." *Victorian Studies* 23(1981): 157-83.

D'Amico, Diane. "'Choose the Stairs That Mount Above': Christina Rossetti and the Anglican Sisterhoods." *Essays in Literature* 17(1990): 204-21.

———. "Eve, Mary, and Mary Magdalene: Christina Rossetti's Feminine Triptych." *The Achievement of Christina Rossetti.* Ed. David A. Kent. Ithaca: Cornell University Press, 1987: 175-91.

Dronke, Peter. *Women Writers of the Middle Ages: A Critical Study from Perpetua (d. 203) to Marguerite Poirete (d. 1310).* Cambridge: Cambridge University Press, 1984.

Fox, Matthew. *The Illuminations of Hildegard of Bingen.* Santa Fe: Bear, 1985.

Heeney, Brian. *The Women's Movement in the Church of England 1850-1930.* Oxford: Clarendon Press, 1988.

Heyward, Carter. *Touching Our Strength: The Erotic As Power and the Love of God.* New York: HarperCollins, 1989.

Hill, Michael. *The Religious Order.* London: Heinemann, 1973.

Hilliard, David. "Unenglish and Unmanly: Anglo-Catholicism and Homosexuality." *Victorian Studies* 25(1982): 181-210.

Hobbs, Colleen. "A View from 'The Lowest Place': Christina Rossetti's Devotional Prose." *Victorian Poetry* 32(1994): 407-28.

Holsinger, Bruce Wood. "The Flesh of the Voice: Embodiment and the Homoerotics of Devotion in the Music of Hildegard of Bingen (1098-1179)." *Signs* 19(1993): 92-125.

Kollar, Rene. "The Oxford Movement and the Heritage of Benedictine Monasticism." *Downside Review* 101(1983): 281-90.

Krueger, Christine L. *The Reader's Repentance: Women Preachers, Women Writers and Nineteenth Century Social Discourse.* Chicago: University of Chicago Press, 1992.

Marsh, Jan. *Christina Rossetti: A Writer's Life.* New York: Viking, 1994.

Nelson, James P. *Body Theology.* Louisville: John Knox Press, 1992.

———— and Sandra P. Longfellow, eds. *Sexuality and the Sacred:Sources for Theological Reflection.* Louisville: John Knox Press, 1994.

Newman, Barbara. *Sister of Wisdom: St. Hildegard's Theology of the Feminine.* Berkeley: University of California Press, 1987.

Nolan, Edward. *Cry Out and Write: A Feminine Poetics of Revelation.* New York: Continuum, 1994.

Petroff, Elizabeth. *Medieval Women's Visionary Literature.* New York: Oxford University Press, 1986.

Reed, John Shelton. "'A Female Movement': The Feminization of Nineteenth Century Anglo-Catholicism." *Anglican & Episcopal History* 57(1988): 199-238.

Schussler Fiorenza, Elisabeth. *Jesus: Miriam's Child, Sophia's Prophet: Critical Issues in Feminist Christology.* New York: Continuum, 1995.

Stanwood, P. G. "Christina Rossetti's Devotional Prose." *The Achievement of Christina Rossetti.* Ed. David A. Kent. Ithaca: Cornell University Press, 1987. 231-49.

Steele, Francesca Maria. *The Convents of Great Britain.* St. Louis: B. Herder, 1902.

————. *The Life and Visions of St. Hildegarde.* London: Heath, Cranton, and Ousely, 1914.

Vicinus, Martha. *Independent Women: Work and Community for Single Women, 1850-1920.* Chicago: University of Chicago Press, 1985.

Westerholm, Joel. "'I Magnify Mine Office': Christina Rossetti's Authoritative Voice in Her Devotional Prose." *Victorian Newsletter* 84(1993): 11-7.

Wheeler, Michael. *Death and the Future Life in Victorian Literature and Theology.* New York: Cambridge University Press, 1990.

# Contributors

*Kathryn L. Bumpass* is professor of music at California State University, Fresno. She earned a B.A. in English (Austin College), and an M.A. (Columbia University) and Ph.D. (University of Illinois) in historical musicology. She has published articles on 19th century European and American music; her current research explores aspects of music and religion.

*Marcia Kathleen Chamberlain* is a graduate student at Rice University in Houston, Texas. She officially studies American Literature. However, the many stacks of books and papers in her house and her car trunk suggest that her reading and writing passions are more diverse than her transcript indicates.

*Jan S. Emerson* received her Ph.D. in German from Brown University. She is writing a book entitled *Virtuous Realities: Body and Soul in Hildegard of Bingen's* Scivias *and Brother Marcus's Vision of Tundal* and coediting, with Hugh Feiss, a forthcoming Garland anthology under the title *Imagining Heaven in the Middle Ages: A Book of Essays.* She has been a translator for the international music journal *Sonus* and is writing her first book of poems, *Moving Pictures.*

*Sabina Flanagan* is the author of *Hildegard of Bingen: A Visionary Life*, the standard biography of the saint.

*Rebecca L.R. Garber* is a graduate student at the University of Michigan at Ann Arbor, where she is completing a dissertation entitled "Women Writing Women's Lives: Religious Texts by Medieval

German Women Writers (1100-1450)". She has given numerous conference papers on women writers and their representation of gender ideals. She has been known to describe herself as a feminist new philologist and is presently working on the "sister-books" of the fourteenth-century German Dominican women.

*Leonard P. Hindsley* is professor in the Department of Modern Languages at Providence College. He is the author of several books on the spiritual milieu of medieval Germany.

*Kenneth F. Kitchell, Jr.* is professor and head of Classics at Louisiana State University. He has written numerous articles on such subjects as bees and bee lore, death by bull's blood, and ancient cities forced to relocate because of animal incursions. He is the author (with H. Dundee) of "A Trilogy on the Herpetology of Linnaeus's *Systema Naturae X*," *Smithsonian Herpetological Service* (1994). His collaborations with Irven Resnick include "Albert the Great on the 'Language' of Animals" in the *American Catholic Philosophical Quarterly* (1996) and a translation of Albertus Magnus's *On Animals: A Medieval Summa Zoologica*. He is presently at work on a book on the classics in the American Civil War.

*Maud Burnett McInerney* is visiting assistant professor of English at Haverford College, where she takes great delight in introducing students to Hildegard in the context of courses on gender issues in the Middle Ages. Her research interests range from medieval women's writing to mysticism to Arthurian literature. She has published articles on *Pearl*, Julian of Norwich, Middle English saint's lives, and Chaucer's *Troilus* and is presently at work on a book on the medieval ideal of virginity.

*Beverlee Sian Rapp* is a doctoral student at the Centre for Medieval Studies at the University of Toronto. Her research areas of interest include women's studies, the Florentine Renaissance, and medieval ethnomusicology. She presented a paper on the hidden mass in Dante's *Purgatorio* with a colleague at the 1997 Congress on Medieval Studies at Kalamazoo, Michigan.

*Irven M. Resnick* is professor of Philosophy and Religion at the University of Tennessee at Chattanooga where he holds the Chair of

Excellence in Judaic Studies. He is the author of *Divine Power and Possibility in St. Peter Damian's* De divina omnipotentia (Leiden, 1992) and the translator of Odo of Tournai's *On Original Sin* and *A Disputation with the Jew, Leo, Concerning the Advent of Christ, the Son of God* (Philadelphia 1994). He is a frequent collaborator with Kenneth F. Kitchell, Jr.

*Frederick S. Roden* is completing a Ph.D. in the Department of English at New York University, where he has written a dissertation on gender and spirituality in Victorian medievalism. He has published essays on Christina Rossetti's theology, her fiction, and on religion in Wilde.

*Christine M. Rose* is associate professor of English at Portland State University. Her work on Chaucer, feminism and manuscript studies has appeared in the *Chaucer Yearbook, Exemplaria, Manuscripta,* the *Medieval Feminist Newsletter* and the *Harvard Library Bulletin.* She recently co-edited a volume of essays on rape in medieval and early modern literature.